*David Mamet and Film*

# David Mamet and Film

*Illusion / Disillusion
in a Wounded Land*

*by* GAY BREWER

McFarland & Company, Inc., Publishers
*Jefferson, North Carolina, and London*

British Library Cataloguing-in-Publication data are available


Library of Congress Cataloguing-in-Publication Data

Brewer, Gay, 1965–
    David Mamet and film : illusion/disillusion in a wounded land / by
Gay Brewer.
        p.  cm.
    Filmography: p.
    Includes bibliographical references and index.
    ISBN 0-89950-834-0 (lib. bdg. : 50# alk. paper) ∞
    1. Mamet, David—Criticism and interpretation.   2. Mamet, David—
Motion picture plays.   3. Motion pictures—Production and
direction.   I. Title.
PN1998.3.M344B74   1993
812'.54—dc20                                              92-50951
                                                              CIP

Manufactured in the United States of America

*McFarland & Company, Inc., Publishers*
   *Box 611, Jefferson, North Carolina 28640*

To Claudia Barnett

# Acknowledgments

My sincere appreciation extends to Daniel R. Barnes, Barbara Hill Rigney, and especially Walter A. Davis for their readings, suggestions, and encouragement by example; Harvey and Gail Brewer for a lifetime's support; Michael Ritchie for innumerable newspaper clippings and reviews; Eric Walborn and the staff of Denney 468 for their patience in my illicit use of Ohio State University equipment; and Clein and White Marketing for *Homicide* materials.

# Contents

Acknowledgments    vii

I : *House of Games*    1

II : Recent Plays in Context    29

III : *Things Change*    63

IV : The Screenplays    91

V : *Homicide*    141

VI : Another Furious Season    163

Notes    171

Filmography    197

Bibliography    199

Index    207

# CHAPTER I

# House of Games

## Control, Revenge, and
## the Uninflected Shot

*House of Games,* David Mamet's debut as cinematic director, not only supports and elaborates themes persistently found in his drama, but corroborates what is for Mamet a developing definition of himself as artist, writer, and creator. Mamet's recent book *On Directing Film* restates in a filmic context his concern for society's impending collapse: "it is not the dramatist's task to create confrontation or chaos, but, rather, to create order.... The entropy, the drama, continues until a disordered state has been brought to rest."[1] The director, then, is the godhead who both determines initial disorder and manipulates a situation toward resolution. "Don't let the protagonist tell the story," says Mamet. "*You* tell the story; *you* direct it."[2] The operative word is control, clearly a power Mamet enjoys. "I like to make decisions, and I like to be at the center of things...."[3]

Considering Mamet's remarks in relation to his work, the director's control—and the dramatist's—begins to suggest the ideology of the confidence man, the hustler whose cool head and insider's knowledge elevates him from an unwitting "mark." Filmmaking's central precepts, as Mamet outlines them, are sticking to your plan, keeping it simple, and *"withholding* information."[4] Only barest essentials, minimum necessary facts for drawing an audience deeper into a story should be given. Consider the analogous manipulations of Mamet's salesmen and hustlers: in *House of Games,* head trickster Mike doles out teasing information, "directs" the cuts, scenes, and "movie" of his enterprise. Mamet has frequently contended that the center of interest in a play or film is the desire of the protagonist. "What does he or she do to get

1

it. . . . If you don't have that, you have to trick the audience into paying attention."[5]

While Mamet argues for his respect of audience, a reciprocal admiration, the giving over of oneself to the filmmaker's story, sounds nearly indistinguishable from the mark's gullibility—or from Margaret Ford's enjoyment of the hustlers' demonstrations of applied psychology. Mamet is well aware of the director's power over audience perception and reaction, of his ability to grant, to withhold, to tease, to trick. "It's very easy to manipulate an audience . . . because you've got all the cards,"[6] says Mamet, appropriating a gambling metaphor. Through involvement with story, through acceptance of propelling or explanatory information, an audience effectively casts itself into the film's game. This occurs through the director's careful presentation: "Now we've put the audience in the same position as the protagonist"[7]—note the conspiratorial use of the plural pronoun. The audience, like any set of good marks, perpetrate their own deepening involvement; "it's in the nature of the audience to want to help the story along. . . ."[8]

Analogies between director/con man and audience/mark go deeper in Mamet than any simple metaphoric definition of creator and consumer. Not only are business charlatans, crooks, and shysters rampant in Mamet's plays, several critics have recognized that his cinematic style *per se* suggests a filmmaker's con game. Stanley Kauffmann considers *House of Games* "a series of artifices, like the morality of the world that inhabits it."[9] The deepest thematic deception he finds in the movie, "the illusion of control,"[10] applies to the film as well as to its plot. David Denby calls *House of Games* "especially untrustworthy. It takes us in as it goes along, then reveals that it's been fooling us as a way of gaining our belief"[11]; this latter trick is the central tenet of the hustler creed. Part of the film's manipulative power is, of course, its spiraling intricacies of plot, the story of the professional con man that has always compelled audiences. But Mamet, as director, is culpable in ways beyond plot. "For Mamet," writes Dave Kehr, "the movies are a con game, too— he zeroes in on film's ability to present an apparently unmistakable truth . . . while hiding everything that's most essential."[12] Elements beyond the screen's edge, information withheld, are answers Mamet alone possesses. Peter Travers bluntly observes Mamet's "expertise in sleight-of-hand" that asks us to enjoy our susceptibility at how he "sucked you into the game."[13] Other critics cite an identification with the con man's "constant play with illusion and reality"[14] or suggest the director is actually "bluffing outrageously"[15] in his premiere attempt.

Director David Mamet on the set of *House of Games*. Photo by Lorey Sebastian.

The explanation for such visceral responses by so many critics lies in the cinematic style Mamet has adapted, *à la* Eisenstein. He explains: "You always want to tell the story in cuts. Which is to say, through a juxtaposition of images that are basically uninflected."[16] The effect of this procession of images is a flatness, a calculation both emotionally and intellectually akin to the con game. Mamet's credo of simplicity begins to seem the deceptive ardor of a manipulative agenda. The image on screen must be used to "take charge of and direct"[17] the audience's attention, and the juxtaposition must suggest by implication the proper interpretation and, hence, a "proper" response. The mark observes, thinks, interprets, and yet further implicates himself. "We put the *protagonist* in the same position as the *audience* — through the *cut* — by making the viewer create the idea himself, in his own mind, as Eisenstein told us."[18] The idea conveyed by the cut is persuasive; by Mamet's own confession, audience and susceptible character are interchangeable.

Mamet's perception of actors and effective acting adheres to his method of cool, uninflected suggestion. He scorns the tradition of deep-felt motivational schools of performance. "Instead," he contends, "your best bet is to ask to do his simple physical actions as simply as possible."[19] The results in *House of Games* are performances conspicuously flat, contrived, and opaque. For Canby, the film's style is nearly indistinguishable from the character Mike's insincerity, both of which are "deliberately artificial, which is both comic and scary."[20] The effect is achieved by Joe Mantegna's monotonous, deceptively "simple" delivery — appropriate to the con man, appropriate to the film's style, and carefully intended and overseen by the director. *House of Games'* actors, says Kehr, "don't inhabit their roles as much as they simply present them: They read rather than perform, and there is no attempt to create an illusion of spontaneity."[21] Mamet defines his ideal actor as Stanislavsky's "organic" performer, who realizes that a text calls for action rather than emotion, who comes to the set or stage "prepared to act moment-to-moment, based on what occurs in the peformance...."[22] This recalls the Chicago influence in Mamet's theatrical background. In the overview essay "Chicago Impromptu," Todd London writes: "Viola Spolin wrote the word 'improvisation' and the darkness that was upon the face of Chicago theatre filled up with light."[23] Mamet retains the darkness but applies the principle. Improvising each situation according to other "players," performing with a deceptive surface simplicity grounded in action rather than emotion, his method suggests perfectly the character traits of the rogue, the con man, or, synonymously, the business executive. In inextricable circles of indictment and responsibility reaching far beyond simple analogy, *House of Games* perpetrates a con of plot, of performance, of style, and of direction.

Perhaps the most curious aspect of the emergence of David Mamet the film director is his seeming antithesis to Mamet the dramatist. From nearly the beginning of his career, Mamet was regarded by critics as essentially a "language" playwright; his fame originated from caustic, profane, and idiomatically perfect dialogue. The plays are verbal der-vishes — funny, shocking, fast and stinging as a whip. The transition to a visual medium is surprising. Mamet's language was, most thought, the crux of his power, and this perception shaped critical response: "Mamet's ear . . . is a precision instrument. He recognizes the shaping force of language — how it can be used as a weapon or a shield depend-ing on what a character wishes to convey or conceal."[24] Wit, cunning, and above all verbal facility were crucial to manipulation games enacted by Mamet's salesmen, soothsayers, and men on the make. "All of Mamet's skill at articulating evasion, the half-spoken phrase, the speech that says one thing and means another, are there,"[25] echoes a typical sentiment. Mamet, contended Jack Kroll in 1977, is "that rare bird, an American playwright who's a language playwright. . . . In other words," he puns, Mamet's "language is a shifty business."[26] The consensus was, and remains, that Mamet created a profane and effective poetry out of the rhythms and expletives of his day. This language of elliptical phrasing, insinuation, and suggestion was, moreover, the key to his characters' powers, such as they were. The highlighting of lan-guage provided a thematic consistency to plays continually concerned with storytelling, role-playing, and gaining of objectives. Behind it all lingered a sense of Mamet's controlling intelligence.

As early as his first screenplay attempt — a 1979 adaptation of James M. Cain's *The Postman Always Rings Twice* — Mamet was already articulating the central differences between theatre and film. "In a play . . . the only way you have to convey the action of the plot is through the action of the characters, what they say to each other. With a movie, the action had to be advanced narratively."[27] Throughout the 1980s Mamet the theoretician continued to refine and clarify how he perceived the differences in forms. In a 1984 interview, he contended the play-wright's job to be "to write dialogue, period. A good play should be able to be done on the radio just like that."[28] Two years later he again expressed contrasting ideas of film and stage:

> when you write a movie, you have got to describe pictures, that's what it's for. If a movie were to be *the* excellent movie it would have abso-lutely no dialogue in it. But with a play everything takes place in dialogue, all the action which takes place between two people has to take place right there.[29]

In 1991 Mamet the director offers a similar conception, distilled yet further. "So you should always be striving to make a silent movie."[30] Cinema seems perceived as a vehicle for pure storytelling; it is this aspect he has so enthusiastically embraced, and "the dialogue, if it's good, will make the movie somewhat better; and if it's bad, will make the movie somewhat worse; but you'll be telling the story *with the shots*...."[32] Mamet exposes himself to this theory despite an earlier admission: "The area in which I was most completely ignorant was, unfortunately, the visual."[32] He sets about the task of reducing the *House of Games* screenplay, "a fairly verbal psychological thriller, to a *silent movie*."[33]

Mamet assumed with relish the task of learning a new skill, the visual, as if it were another card in his deck of strategies. This discovery, or rediscovery, of storytelling allowed the author to integrate his established forte, the verbal assault, with a slow, sure, calm procession of suggestive images. His ability to tell an engaging story has widened Mamet's audience, hence his range of control. When one considers the plays from this distance, Mamet's move to film director is, as he suggests of any good resolution, "both surprising and inevitable."[34] The controlled environment of one-on-one interaction so prevalent in his writing is reflected in the peculiarly private communication between director and viewer. "The only reason people speak," argues Mamet, "is to get what they want. In film or on the street, people who describe themselves to you are lying."[35] This comment is conspicuous to anyone who recalls Mamet's relentless writing about his simplicity, his love of directness, his straightforward respect for the audience, where he describes himself and his ideas to us as a salient virtue: "That's my philosophy. I don't know better. If I knew better, I would give it to you."[36] The subject of the preceding comment isn't nearly so important as the tone — guileless, apparently sincere and sharing. Film has given Mamet a much larger playground — in terms of finance, audience, medium, style — in which to let his hucksters roam, and it has more fully implicated Mamet, as director, in manipulations inherent in his method, means, and purpose of control. That for his first film he chose to make explicit the con men who have implicitly crowded nearly every one of his plays is not accident, but teasing. The style suits the subject, the medium fits the idea, and Mamet, entirely in control, enjoys a luxury his created hustlers do not: to tilt his cards into view, to suggest his real speed with the cue stick, and still to win the game. It's his house.

*House of Games* is a fascinating story, well told. The layers of con upon con, the indictment of pop psychology, and Mamet's effective use of traditional *film noir* images all deserve detailed attention. But are there points where Mamet's seemingly incompatible worlds of radio play and silent movie—his extended, idealized definitions of drama and film—intersect? To what extent do *House of Games'* participants conform to these prescriptions? In other words, if one is able to discuss Mamet in terms of stylistic and linguistic confidence games, is it meaningful to consider Margaret Ford and Mike—using Mamet's own specified criteria—as more or less effective "directors" of their *own* scenarios?

Among the most interesting and extensive themes in *House of Games* is the weighing of Ford's clinical psychology against the hustlers' practical street knowledge. One critic described the film as a "revenge movie, a darkly humorous morality play on the dangers of countertransference."[37] "What's more fun than human nature?"[38] Mike asks Ford shortly after introducing her to the short con. For Mike, the big con is hardly less enjoyable—he beds Ford moments later and the games continue. Ironically, the street psychologists, the con men, have both play—cards, pool, games of skill and chance—and playfulness—taking a women to a set-up "stranger's" hotel room, filling a water pistol to purposely "blow the Gaff"—singularly lacking in the arid intellectuality of Ford's professional analyses. The autograph seekers who pursue Ford also suggest a contrast between an exposed, public life and one whose true dealings are entirely *sub*cultural.

Margaret Ford seems particularly unsophisticated as a clinical psychologist. Early in the film, her "breakthrough" of realizing "lurg" inverted is "girl" and her Freudian slips that reveal a deep-seated sexual insecurity and mental instability surely appear to viewers, even out of the film's context, surprisingly juvenile and suggestive of a personally unexamined life; "the urges she's furiously repressing"[39] are lived vicariously through patients. Alfie Kohn, in *Psychology Today,* writes of Ford's professional insensitivity: "She interprets and intellectualizes her patients rather than connecting with them. They are case studies, not people, fodder for her best-selling study of compulsion."[40] Patients are, in other words, marks for her career advancement. This is the very "weakness" Billy Hahn undoubtedly notices during his sessions with the doctor—a lovely inversion of roles—which suggests *her* as a potential mark: ". . . you got your goddamn *book* you wrote . . . it's all a con game, you do nothing. You say you want to help? You want to *help*?"[41] Mamet informs us in *On Directing Film,* in agreement with Aristotle that "character is just habitual action"[42]; here Hahn challenges Ford to a world of participation, of doing something. She is especially vulnerable to the big con because she inhabits not the world of story and imagination and uninflected action—i.e. the world of the con man, the world of film—but rather a static place of books and language. Her intellectual self-confidence is only a façade in the "real world" from which Hahn beckons.

Hahn's "performance" in their first scene is perfectly and simply acted; Mamet's dictates to his actors for direct, uninflected actions work as effectively for the hustler. Just as the *objective of the protagonist . . . keeps us in our seats*,"[43] so too does Hahn's objective compel Ford. "What do you think this is? Some 'dream'? Maan, you're living in the dream, your 'questions,' 'cause there. is. a. real. world."[44] Note the many potent suggestions in Hahn's short accusation. His references to Ford as a man underlines her confused sexuality. The overriding idea is the complex relationship between actual and fabricated worlds; words such as "dream" and "real" and ideas of exemption and responsibility are all reiterated in Ford's meeting with her psychotic murderess. Hahn unknowingly suggests an association between doctor and murderer which will bear out.

The word "dream" is also used significantly in another of Mamet's definitions of film. The dream, like cinema, comprises a series of uninflected images drawing power from juxtaposition. In both cases the purpose is "to answer a question."[45] In effect, Mamet is enjoying a little joke: Ford is indeed living a "dream"—i.e. "film"—and deeper involvement in proper modes of this enterprise—images, juxtaposition, action—will supply the many answers she obsessively seeks. Ford's obsessive behavior, her character of interrogation, mental voyeurism, and neurotic self-denial, renders her excellent prey for the con men, except they underestimate the extent of her personal psychosis.

Later that evening, still compulsively working at her desk and considering Hahn's case, Ford pens a note: *Compulsive succeeds in establishing a situation where he is out of control.*"[46] Ostensibly in reference to Hahn, this comment is of course more applicable to Ford. Recall Mamet's dictate that the dramatist's task is not "to create confrontation or chaos but, rather, to create order."[47] Ford's perception of her confrontation is the opposite of reality: it is her own compulsive behavior that is about to hurl her into a situation uncontrolled and ultimately deadly. Hahn represents all the con men in initiating a small disordering event which will simultaneously result in a restored order and the

protagonist's objective — that is, restoration of a surface world's complacent illusions and economic benefit to the hustlers' successful con. The
con man ethic corresponds remarkably to Mamet's theories of direction
and social entropy; it is no wonder he is compelled — as viewers are in
a more passive, manipulated role — by his subject. Kauffmann, who
contends that deceit is the central theme in Mamet's work and that the
title *House of Games* is analogous to a perception of our world, argues
that the director recognizes deceptive tendencies also in his audience,
"the constant wish in us to maintain surfaces for the advantage of what
is beneath the surface, a wish as common to presidents as to con
men,"[48] and certainly common to both Hahn and Ford in their introductory encounter. Indeed, Kauffmann's analysis of Mamet is a
comment on all of human psychology.

The subsequent scene in Ford's office is significant. *"Ford, alone
at her desk. . . . Smoking. Writing (pause), she sighs. Looks up, takes
off her glasses. Shakes her head from side to side. She picks up off her
desk Billy Hahn's nickeled automatic pistol.*"[49] Note the indecisive
shaking of the head, the contrasting pulls of language/writing and
definitive action/gun. She uncovers an earlier note, another reductive
intellectualization telling more about doctor than patient: *". . . The
character of Mike — the 'Unbeatable Gambler.' Seen as omniscient,
who 'doles out punishment' . . . HOUSE OF GAMES.*"[50] Although Mike
is a "character," it is just that quality of his psychological penetration
Ford perceives during their initial meeting which manifests and exacer-
bates her desire for punishment. Moreover, the roles of clinical and
street psychologists begin to merge, suggesting how one may consume
the other. "She manipulates her clients to discover their best selves;
they manipulate their marks to tap into their worst natures,"[51] offers
Richard Schickel. Which is truly the darker impulse?

Reviewer Tom O'Brien locates Ford's curiosity of confidence rituals
in her recognition of "a profession so paradoxically close to her own, not
in its goals but its subject matter — the simulation of trust, becoming
attuned to the 'feel' of a person or situation, the penetration of masquerade."[52] Anne Dean has noted that not only are the professions of
psychology and confidence trickery interchangeable, but specifically
Ford and head con man Mike are "basically the same under the skin,"[53]
and by the film's end Ford realizes this. Dean further comments that
*House of Games* is told, as Mamet himself has implied, "more through
image and gesture than through words."[54] Both ideas, the kinship of
Ford and Mike and the suggestive visual style of the film, are developed

in Ford's first descent into the House of Games, as a poolroom "the greatest and most determinedly all-male institution in American social life."[55] Mamet, in his nostalgic essay "Pool Halls," laments the death of a locale offering finite, therefore accessible, codes of appropriate action:

> people are supposed to spend their days here in pursuit of skill, cunning, comradeship, and money. No one is supposed to be pompous here, or boring; no one will be held unaccountable for the bets they make, or the way that they comport themselves. . . . The point of the pool hall was the intersection of two American Loves: the Game of Skill and the Short Con.[56]

Such an America, regrets Mamet, has been "supplanted by the Big Con or a life with no excitement in it at all."[57] In this enclosed and perhaps doomed society of male behavior, Ford's first words are significant — an attempted street-tough reticence she imagines proper: "Yeah. I need a match."[58] This answer as to what a man can do for her suggests sexual repression, reintroduces compulsive smoking — in this instance an attempt to integrate her perception of a masculine environment — and ironically foreshadows the movie's finale. Ford will learn, apparently, it is not a man's match she needs, but a woman's lighter.

The doctor continues her hard-boiled clichés to Mike: "Let's talk turkey, pal."[59] Of course, Mike is meanwhile "playing" her, feeding her conceits of perception, and beginning to implicate her with bits of relinquished information. "How come you made me so quick," he asks, "I'm not a hard guy?"[60] He immediately implies his trust in her — and she will soon be taught this as the cardinal rule of confidence trickery — and simultaneously defines himself as a proper Mamet protagonist: "Listen: I want something from you."[61] Not only does con man equal psychologist, but con man equals director. "Mamet is in total control,"[62] says Kroll of the director on his set; change the context, and Mike is the omnipotent being, possessing greater knowledge, leading an audience into deeper involvement and incrimination. In *Glengarry Glen Ross,* Aaronow asks why he is suddenly guilty and vulnerable to consequences. "Because you listened,"[63] is the reply. Mike draws power from a quick mind, seductive speech, and a careful fabrication of uninflected scenes. Ford listens, watches, and by these passive actions plays her role. She hides a coin; each time Mike finds it. This scene moves "their dalliance into a sexual encounter"[64]; that she is naked before him is the "erotic subtext."[65] An alternate title of the film, *The Tell,* suggests the importance of Mike's aggressive perception and the woman's submissiveness.

Ford's attraction to Mike and his world is not surprising. As Kehr contends, the hustler's "quiet power, perfect self-possession and complete freedom from guilt command both her professional interest and her rebellious impulses."[66] She readily accepts his trust, accompanying him into a private chamber of male gambling and communion, more than willing to assist in a short con. She is a natural to the art of roleplaying and deception. When Mike shows her three aces, her "poker face" is that of a consummate professional. The con excites her with a sexual intensity. She waits for the Vegas Man to reveal his tell, the turning of a ring on a finger — not the subtlest of Freudian artifice; when it happens, she moves close to Mike, whispers to him, lights his cigarette off her own. Her arousal is apparent; the evening is, for Ford, uncharacteristically direct engagement. Her excitement will increase as her involvement deepens. As Kroll phrases it, she "finds her own identity disappearing like a card trick"[67]; or perhaps more accurately, her assumed identity will be riven for a truer persona. "The bitch is a born thief,"[68] Mike later exhorts, a tendency in her he easily, utterly awakens. Although Mike is able to articulate his own needs, Ford's remain unclear to her until the end. *House of Games* seems in this regard almost a mystery story. What compels Ford? She is as "driven" as the title of her successful book, but by what? Is the latent conflict something to do with her father, as one slip in speech suggests? As the poker game continues, the camera looks down on a circle of fleshy male hands awaiting cards. One is reminded of croupiers, of magicians, of something vaguely base. Ford is hooked.

Denby cites as central to the hustler that "whatever truth a con artist speaks is only at the service of a lie" and "he gets us to believe in fiction by showing us things that are true. In the end he's a philosophical nihilist. . . ."[69] Artists, he warns, are "the same thing," and Mamet is the master of creating the con man's "sense of self-justification" and celebrating his "warrior pride, his prowess and reach, his delight in the perfect sting."[70] Already briefly considered was a parallel between con man and director; another aspect of the con is theatrical joy of performance. Ford's reaction, once she has "discovered" the poker con, is that of an entertained spectator: "You guys are fantastic."[71] Part of her response may be explained by a professional interest in behavior, but mostly she displays admiration for a play unwittingly attended.

Mike (Joe Mantegna) finds a willing pupil in Dr. Margaret Ford (Lindsay Crouse) in *House of Games*. Photo by Mike Hausman.

The con men share an obvious zeal for their work; they are enthusiastic and facile performers with a familial camaraderie. "Mike's troupe plays to only one spectator at a time, although the exchange is the same: money for entertainment."[72] The illusory elements of performance spill over into the realm of con men as magicians. They are more than willing to impress a captive audience by demonstrating a few tricks of the trade. In the published screenplay, the men perform for Ford a short con called the Tap. "It's like a *kid's* game," says Mike, and Joey adds, like a seasoned character player, "Timing, timing, it's all timing!"[73] In the film, Joey instead shares "a little larceny called the Flue." Partly the scene is to deepen Ford's interest—bait for the "fish"—and partly because they "owe her one," but also because they relish their craft and are childishly prideful of their skills. "Secrets of the pyramids," they call the Flue, and indeed the men demonstrate knowledge and love of the history of a long-standing profession. Unlike the magician, here the rare revealing of technique does not diminish the trick, but rather it highlights the performer's artistry. Such a playful

*Opposite:* Ford (Lindsay Crouse) helps Mike (Joe Mantegna) look for the "Tell" in *House of Games*. Photo by Lorey Sebastian.

account of the con, ergo acting, as an aged human tradition calls to mind Mamet's affectionate *A Life in the Theatre,* a play the writer says is concerned with "how youth and age talk to each other"[74] — which literally transpires between Ford and senior hustler Joey. In the play, a love of craft and the presentation of thespians Robert and John supposedly "off-stage" is analogous to the presumably "off-duty" con men. "You have a job to do," tutors Robert. "You do it by your lights, you bring your expertise to bear, your sense of rightness . . . fellow feelings . . . etiquette . . . professional procedure. . . ."[75] He continues: "Our history goes back as far as Man's. Our aspirations in the Theatre are much the *same* as man's."[76] Neither actor nor con artist is ever off-stage, and both employ Mamet's frequent mentor-student dynamic, which Pascale Hubert-Leibler describes as "first and foremost a power relation."[77] Is the con man a metaphoric broker for this teacher theme, or perhaps, vice versa, is the con man himself central?

The hustlers' behavior here is consistent with the sociological portrait of pool sharks outlined by Ned Polsky in his study *Hustlers, Beats, and Others.* Rather than ostracizing outsiders, the deviant social group will sometimes "rely much more on emphasizing the joys of hustling, talking of its virtues (such as autonomy and heart), rating each other, discussing its technology, telling tales of its heroes and villains, and so on."[78] Of their trade, the hustlers feel "it's exciting, it has a tradition and ideology that can make them feel heroic, it's fun (the game is enjoyable as such). . . ."[79] In short, the con game has all the life-giving energy lacking in clinical psychology. When Ford confesses to her maternal and professional mentor Maria that what they do is "a sham . . . a con game,"[80] the older doctor replies that she needs "joy."[81] Ford admits she enjoyed writing her book—the dry, the intellectual, the safely distant—but Maria counters that the younger woman needs something "in the short term"[82]—note the phrase echoing "short con." There is only one place Ford can derive such comfort; she is compelled, "driven." "You come back to play some pool?" the House of Games proprietor asks her that night. In her reply, "I'm looking for Mike,"[83] the meaning is clear; she has indeed returned to "play pool," both a psychological and sexual commitment.

The self-justification the hustlers elaborate after their frustrated initial swindle is uniquely and centrally Mametic. The response to Ford's discovery, after disappointment and anger, is a childlike penitence. "Ask her is she mad,"[84] whines the Vegas Man, who a moment before was cursing and waving his gun. Mike asks Ford: "You aren't miffed at us, are you, I mean, nothing personal."[85] The innocuous term "miffed," in context of an attempted six thousand dollar larceny, undercuts Ford's anger. Faced with such a peculiar innocence, a sort of inverted honesty that embarrasses her own pretensions, she submits to their charm. This is partly the men's intention, but their apology and fear of reprisal for atrocious actions are reminiscent of *American Buffalo*. "Are you mad at me?"[86] Teach asks Don, sincerely, childishly, pathetically, following a protracted litany of insinuation.

Don's comment on the turbulence of his proposed coin heist closes the first act of *American Buffalo*: "Fuckin' *business*..."[87] Likewise, this is the con men's staple justification. "It was only business," offers Mike; Joey corroborates, "It's the American way."[88] The association of business with crime is a familiar one for Mamet. Paraphrasing Thorstein Veblen, Mamet said in interview that "a lot of business in this country is founded on the idea that if you don't exploit the possible opportunity, not only are you being silly, in many cases you're being negligent, even legally negligent."[89] Polsky comments on this phenomenon in actual field research:

> For example, when a professional criminal describes himself as being "like a businessman" or "just in a different line of business," the criminologist takes this to be merely a rationalization. It is a rationalization all right, but it is by no means merely that, and often it is not even primarily that.[90]

Mamet seems to have centered on a rhetorical justification that indeed points to deep social disease. Throughout Mamet's plays crime equals business (*American Buffalo*) and reciprocally business equals crime (*Glengarry Glen Ross*), but never has the role of confidence games in these relationships been made so explicit as in *House of Games*. Perhaps the addition of cinema's visual suggestiveness to Mamet's career-long exploration of verbal deception made the confidence metaphor irresistibly appropriate for film. Certainly con men may now be added to the list of Mametic synonyms which includes criminal and businessman. Both salesman and con man, says Mamet, "are dangerous, very spontaneous, required to think on their feet, and work under tremendous pressure. The same thing that makes a good con man makes a good salesman — they're able to suspend all feeling of humanity."[91] Mamet draws the comparison between such characters and himself: "I guess some part of me wants to be like the characters I write about. . . . I like pressure situations."[92] And although he claims to be a poor liar, what is effective storytelling, the creation of fictions and manipulation of reaction, but the ancient artifice of the raconteur?

The character of Mike deserves close scrutiny. "Are you a man of your word?"[93] Ford asks at the conclusion of their first evening. Curiously, he *is*, in that he is quite open concerning his deceptions. He gallantly assists her into a taxi and stands in thought as it departs. The simple script directions speak volumes about Mike the manipulator, the magician, the psychologist, the actor whose darker self remains veiled: "*Mike manipulating the coin. A half dollar. He puts the coin in one palm, rubs his hands together, opens one hand at a time, the coin is gone. . . . The cab turning down the street. It is gone.*"[94] As much as he is a performer, Mike is equally an anxious and menacing thief. The camera closes on an inscrutable face looking right, silhouetted in light against an undistinguished blackness. The cab's occupant, as easily manipulated as the coin in his hand, likewise disappears and, he seems to know, will likewise reappear. Just as he has juxtaposed — or directed — those images which will draw her back, so he plays with signs and symbols almost unconsciously, their power suggested in his uninflected façade, in his monotonous and fluid voice. More than merely for money, this is "a larger game of power, in which the stakes are trust and affection."[95] This larger game, in its exploitation of sexual intimacy, will eventually cause his death, if not ideological defeat.

The lighting and cinematography in the previous scene are among many examples of Mamet's use of darkness, a *noir* tone and style of film to complement the shadowed, ambiguous nature of the story. Although filmed in Seattle, the locale is vague and unspecified. Several script references to Chicago were removed. The dark and decayed corners of any city would serve equally well, emphasizing "the banality of place to its particular characters."[96] Schickel suggests the city is lit "like a giant stage set, a succession of false fronts for false behavior."[97] The setting, in other words, supports the themes: haziness, deception, playing of roles. A cogency of mood extends to the film's style: the opening shot, an at first indistinguishable close-up of a grainy surface, pans out across an office complex, lending impressions of colorlessness and texture, of parts of wholes not immediately identifiable. In a later scene, Ford follows Mike and Joey down a stairwell. The camera, steady above, records their spiraling, vertiginous descent; they emerge into featureless corridors both convoluted and restrictive. One has no choice but to continue deeper into the labyrinth of culpability. The effectiveness of

*House of Games qua* film is in its seamless unity of theme and style, image and action. Add to this the corollary of the director's craft to the art of the con, and remarkable levels of interactive complexity emerge, an inextricable convolution of dark implosions both real and unreal.

Ford's meetings with her female patient, the murderess, also elaborate the film's key themes. These clinical, starkly white scenes, more than contrasting the night games of the con men, present an arena where Ford wrestles with her own neurotic demons and foretells her own end.

> WOMAN PATIENT: He said, "I can make any woman a whore in fifteen minutes."
> FORD *(off camera)*: ...and what did you say to that?
> WOMAN PATIENT: I said he couldn't make anybody a whore that was not a whore to start out with.... He said, "I been reading your mail, and you *are* that whore." And... *(pause)* later you see... *(Pause.)* When... then ... then ... 'cause he didn't realize what he had done.
> FORD: And what *had* he done...?[98]

The exchange could easily be Ford's self-interrogation of her relationship with Mike, especially considering its almost immediate proximity to their initial meeting. The con men have called her a "slut" (replacing "crazy bitch" in the script), she has been seen through, and in ways yet beyond her knowledge Mike has "read her mail" — has full professional, and eventually carnal, knowledge of her — and confronted her in such a way that he cannot know the danger. The patient's unarticulated question, the proper response to one's own unforgivable action, is voiced and acted out by Ford. In both cases the crime is the murder of the offending male. The answer to the question: forgive yourself. Ford's confessional slip to confidante Maria further associates her with the murderous and insane: "That poor girl, all her life my father tells her she's a whore. ... *My* father...?"[99]

Ford returns to Mike's night world. That the bartender immediately offers to "help" her is a humorous fusing of social politeness and psychological initiative. As she sits in a booth, waiting for Mike to magically appear (which he does), the script's compulsive smoking is replaced by a primary compulsion of writing, a control method. Ford writes: "The necessity of dark places to transact a dark business." Not only has she granted Mike's enterprise business status but has exposed a truth beyond her conscious intention: the darkness is necessary, yes, but is mostly within, as evidenced in the clinical whiteness of her own professional charade. In fact, Mike begins to teach her his trade—and in essence her own—not in a back alley or smoky lounge, but in a glossy, well-lit Western Union office. "The basic idea is this: it's called a '*confidence*' game. Why? Because you give me your confidence? No. Because I give you *mine*. So what we have, in addition to 'Adventures in Human Misery,' is a short course in psychology."[100] The beautiful irony of Mike's swindle of Ford is that he is indeed a "man of his word." He teases her with his knowledge of the human mind and admits quite clearly and directly, even with "I" and "you" pronouns, his intentions. "I give *you* my confidence." Her professional rigor, a sort of trained myopia, inclines her to interpret definite threat as abstraction; consequently, the more open Mike is, the more he warns, the more Ford as clinician succumbs to proffered trust. She ignores his central principle: "Don't Trust Nobody."[101] Mike's comments remind one of another Mamet character and Mantegna role, Richard Roma in *Glengarry Glen Ross*:

> It's looking forward or it's looking back. And that's our life. That's *it*. Where is the *moment*? *(Pause.)* And what is it that we're afraid of? Loss. What else? . . . I say *this* is how we must act. I do those things which seem correct to me *today*. . . . Listen to what I'm going to tell you now:[102]

Mike, "the natural successor to schemers and opportunists like Teach and . . . Roma,"[103] is like his salesman counterpart a man of his word not only through pop-existential, *carpe diem* directness, but also in linguistic brio and persuasiveness; much of their power is assumed candor, a philosophical ardor which becomes the language of seduction, whether economic, ideological, or in the previous scene from *House of Games*, physical.

Ford's attraction to Mike and his profession, despite her explanations, seems primarily sexual in orientation. Following Mamet's definition of the protagonist, Mike asks her: "Now: what do you get out of this transaction?"[104] Her arousal from the earlier card swindle returns, indeed increases, following her involvement with a successful short con. Mike seems to realize, certainly more clearly than she, that Ford sees in him traditional symbols of male potency—control, calm, penetration, energy, danger—and he engages the expanding rhetoric of the gambler. "Be *real*, babe. Let's up the ante here. . . . Do you want to make love to me . . . ?"[105] Demanding that she be "real" recalls Hahn's argument of a "real world" Ford is missing; Mike must seem to her to constitute that world. That Mike equates intercourse with poker may indicate his own conceit, but also the comparison appropriately refers to a dark, gambling world to which he knows she will respond.

Mike insists that Ford's blushing is another tell; since he has already in effect proven his omniscience to her, she succumbs. Several hints in the hotel sequence suggest Mike — and Mamet — are having fun. Mike's check-in pseudonym in the script is Douglas Johnson; in the film it is the even more obvious pun Richard (i.e. "Dick") White. Of the man's room they borrow, Mike explains his assurance by playing up the con itself: "We would believe he's going out for the evening."[106] In other words, "we," meaning "she," would believe, and in believing be deceived. The script's *"passionate"* kiss is replaced in the film by the obvious gesture of Ford taking the key and 'putting it in' the lock. The lovemaking scene is a crucial one due to Ford's response. The film cuts to afterwards, Ford curled, lazy-eyed, in a slip. Out of context, the sequence is nearly a clichéd recounting of a traditional hotel rendezvous: the man anxious to depart after completed coitus, the woman relaxed, thoughtful, gentle. She's in a mood to coo and romanticize, a mood Mike refuses to indulge. "I'm a con man, I'm a criminal. You don't have to delude yourself. You can call things what they are. You can call yourself what you are." She responds, "What am I?"[107] An answer to her question echoes from the earlier therapy — whore. Instead of this response, however, Mike initiates an evasive yet seemingly earnest lecture, again reminiscent of "Dick" Roma, on "the burden of responsibility" and taking "something from life."[108] His agitation is beyond merely adhering to the con's timetable; he leaves the room, essentially evades her probing, and tries to snap her out of post-coital affection. Mike here is literally and colloquially (in his insensitivity) the Dick he portrays.

Ford looks into the dresser mirror; she combs her hair. Her hand passes over the items there, a virtual testimony to bachelorhood, a man's world: cigars, pocketknife, money, briefcase. She takes the knife, co-opting Mike's advice to assert herself. As the scene shifts to the street meeting outside the hotel, Mike continues in the vein of romantic satire, this variation concerned with the woman being in the way, not cognizant of the subtleties and timing of male business: "This is not 'games,' this is ... Aw, *hell* ... Babe, you're fucken up my timing..."[109] Note the familiar yet impersonal "babe" address. Mike allows Ford to participate in the scene only after a classic male injunction: "You're my *wife*. You follow my cue.... However strange things seem, KEEP YOUR MOUTH SHUT. And the only one you know is me."[110] This is archetypal male fantasy: the silent wife in her place, recognizing no other man. In the ensuing sting, she watches, out of the way, as "businessmen" wax philosophic on the nature and depth of corruption and figure how to split up the money. Ford's poker face remains fixed.

Despite all the psychological similarities of their professions, the schism between Mike and Ford is the ancient one of gender. As effective as he is in separating Ford from her money, he fails to account for wounded female pride. She freely gives him the cash. She has proven herself as gullible to trust as the man in the Western Union office. She watches Mike's cab pull away in a scene paralleling her own initial departure. Now they have parted again, presumably for the last time, and the reversal of roles and fortunes is unmistakable. William F. Van Wert defines the entire con in terms of its economic exchange: "she has gotten adventure, access to a world normally closed to women, sex and role-playing. . . . They have gotten her money."[111]

"The movie is a dream," says Mamet. "The movie should be *like* a dream."[112] Ford agonizes over her supposed murder of the Businessman, a murder that ironically she will not commit until she dedicates herself to doing so: ". . . you've *killed* someone . . . and you say: you say: 'If Only This Was a Dream. . .'"[113] She returns to her office, amid shadows of confusion, admitting to a waiting patient, "I'm very sorry. I'm very sorry. I'm quite ill. I'll have to. . ."[114] Her speech has become increasingly circular, fragmented, and interrogatory. She is indeed in a dream, not only of the filmmaker's design, but of internal layers of deception. The scene of Ford alone in her office is brilliantly executed, a moment to stop conversation and pursuit, to gather one's thoughts, to survey images. Her hand is cut on the broken glass of her diploma. She holds the bloody, stolen pocketknife. *"She looks down; her shirt, inside the jacket, is spattered with blood. She rips off the bloody shirt, throws it in the waste-basket."*[115] Her own blood leads to the larger stain of murder—ironically yet to be committed—and hints at lost virginity. Momentarily she is in only her slip, recalling the hotel tryst. Sexual intercourse is curiously bound, unclearly to her, with the violence it engendered. Luckily the con men make a single error of male bravado that enables her to emerge from the fog of confused dream.

The event that forces the truth upon Margaret Ford, precipitating her act of revenge, is the recognition of Hahn's *"vintage red Cadillac."*[116] Hahn, a novice, doesn't adequately hide the car, and the conceit of the con men to have used it earlier undoes them. The convertible, long, sleek, and shining, is a cruising steel monument to traditional symbols of male potency. Ford stands unmoving by the dumpster, where she would have attempted to discard the evidence of her crime, and by this quiet accident her violation is made apparent. The car also fulfills Mamet's function: *"You've got to be able to recognize it,"*[117] meaning that the audience, with Ford, must remember the car from the earlier scene. This is yet another instance where *House of Games'* external (technical) and internal (narrative) imperatives are difficult to distinguish. In the first of the film's last three scenes, Ford moves through the rain, slips inside the delivery door of Charlie's Tavern, and overhears the men gloating over their "taking" of her as they split the money. Here the movie seems more than ever a film about men and women, sexual exploitation, and the impossibility of nurturing heterosexual relationships. Mike recalls the poker night's water pistol, which "made a puddle big enough to swim in,"[118] suggesting ejaculation. Someone replies, "A taste for the theatrical." They are perfect Mamet businessmen, swindlers going over figures and accounting for expenses, and are meanwhile typical Mamet *men,* gloating, preening, practically snickering about their business acumen—"Some *Dinosaur* con men. Years from now, they'll have to go to a *museum,* see a frame like this,"[119] suggesting their work as both science and art—psychological acuity—"the broad's an *addict*"[120]—and sexual prowess.

> MR. DEAN: Took her money, and screwed her, too.
> MIKE: A small price to pay.
> *Angle—close-up. Ford, recoiling. She leans back against the wall, her back to the booth.*[121]

Significantly, this exchange cuts to Ford's stunned reaction. Van Wert notes: "When she positions herself behind the wooden bars, we have a representation of Foucault's terms of a dialectic of power relations (men bonded together) and confinement (women isolated)."[122] Ford must, with the audience, recognize similarities between herself and her psychotic patient. Mike has "read" her, has made her, in a sense, the whore she felt she was (judging from her reaction to patients, her Freudian slips, her arousal). Watching this scene closely, one senses that sexual violation, more than lost money, even more than wounded professional pride, tortures Ford. Mike is catching a plane for Vegas. He is the gambler he assured Ford he was not. As the men continue flattering

**Director David Mamet arranges a scene with Lindsay Crouse on the set of** *House of Games.* **Photo by Mike Hausman.**

themselves and the scene closes, Ford is eerily divided between dark and light, blackness behind her. The shot recalls Mike's earlier close-up, but the direction has reversed. Ford's impulses, the "good blood, bad blood"[123] Mike taught her of, struggle for which will speak. With shame and certainty come a cold strength deeper than any granted by diplomas and analytical jargon.

On at least one crucial level *House of Games* is about sex. The obsessive lighting and smoking of cigarettes, suggesting flames, fire, impotence, gender transference; the thematic playing with guns ("Help me with this, if you can,"[124] Hahn demands of Ford, waving his pistol); these uses are hardly original to Mamet; indeed, they are stock devices in thrillers—but the director uses them effectively. If the previous scene's reveling in business fraud recalls *American Buffalo* and *Glengarry Glen Ross,* than sexual braggadocio supplies another traditional

Mamet theme, physical exploitation. Several of Mike's comments to his peers show him to be a surprisingly close cousin, in type, to Bernie Litko. "A small price to pay" could be a typical response to the "last night" confessionals of *Sexual Perversity in Chicago*:

> DANNY: And all this time she was nineteen?
> BERNIE: Nineteen, twenty. So down we sit and get to talking. This, that, blah, blah, blah, and "Come up to my room and I'll pay you for the cigarettes."
> DANNY: No.
> BERNIE: Yeah.
> DANNY: You're shitting me.
> BERNIE: I'm telling you.
> DANNY: Was she a pro?
> BERNIE: So at this point, we don't know.[125]

The two bar scenes share a boyish excitement and insensitivity, the same wish for a virgin/whore duality. Dean observes that in *Sexual Perversity in Chicago* "the whole fabric of heterosexual pairing is something of a confidence trick."[126] Another of Mamet's major themes, sexual subordination, is thus exposed in *House of Games* as an additional manifestation of con work, the game of power, privilege, and conquest constituting human life. Mike's cardinal rule that he give his confidence, ostensibly *his* trust, could be readily applied to the disingenuous nature of men and women together. Just as Mamet's plays are populated by men (*Lakeboat*) and operate by male orientations of power (*Speed-the-Plow*), the night world of *House of Games,* its halls and parlors, is of and for men. The clinical daytime world, white, sterile, and joyless, is distaff, especially for Ford's bullish compatriot Dr. Maria Littauer, who advises the younger woman to enjoy herself, forgive herself the unforgivable, and attempts luncheon and dinner dates. Much of Ford's identity problem lies in sexual confusion: her severely short hair, her pants suits, her generally cold, unfeminine behavior. She alone is the woman who infiltrates, or descends into, a male world of trickery, shadows, and play. She fails as one of the boys, and Mike's subsequent betrayal of her sexual awakening provokes an explosion of violence.

The airport scene, the climax of the story's action, could be considered the penultimate act of a female revenge play. Ford's face is cast in shadows, dark now against white, opposed to the close-up in the bar. Her face is, as usual, impassive, but she seems resolved to the dark. She is dressed in white, again suggesting virginity. Has new knowledge granted her purity? Is this irony? Her own role-playing? Primarily, the white argues for a choice made not for the pure, the good, the wholesome, but rather for symbolic solidarity of the "white" day world of women. Significantly, Ford has discarded her pants for a skirt.

> FORD: No. No. No. I'm so frightened. And . . . Mike: Mike: I . . . I took all my money. I took all my money out of the bank. I'm . . . and you'll help us disappear. We'll disappear together. Mike: I've got a quarter of a million dollars. We can live . . . we . . . I can't believe I'm seeing you . . .[127]

Ford plays a nearly perfect part. She uses the female role—frightened, hesitant, repeating her man's name like a mantra—he has imposed upon her, meanwhile manipulating his rapacity as he exploited her sexual indecisiveness. She has learned the confidence game from "King Kong" himself; she offers trust and dependence and even speaks in the con man's suspended colons. Mike, momentarily off-guard, retreats to stock responses—"I think that's wise,"[128] he says feebly, repeating a comment from the poker game. Ford offers, like a fragile revelation, "My real name is Margaret."[129] While similar to Mike's original monosyllabic introduction, the use of the telling word "real" suggests Ford's choice between worlds. She has finally chosen a real world, the world of women and of light, and is calmed and empowered by the alliance. The decision enables her to relax with her given name. In a reversal of the hotel scene, Ford gives Mike the key to the locker containing her bag. She returns, that is, the phallus she no longer desires, which will now open to Mike his own weakness, cash. Ford confesses her sins and absolves herself. In the radical opinion of Van Wert, the entire airport sequence is a fantasy, a psychological exercise, of Ford's: "Her resources as a therapist are what separate her from Darlene, her murderess. Margaret can effect her purge, her murder of Mike, without externalizing—without subjecting herself to legal consequences. And this is her triumph. . . ."[130] From a model constructed on the shibboleths of Lacan, Derrida, and Foucault, Van Wert argues that such a reading shows Mamet successful "in *his* master con, fake dead body and all, with the spectator as mark."[131]

In any case, during his last moments of life Mike resorts to all his verbal facility. He attempts to reassume the mentor role by showing Ford she "cracked out of turn"[132]; he adopts the rhetoric of gambling, with its attendant sexuality—"You're a bad pony. N'I'm not going to *bet* on you"[133]; he attempts disarming candor— "... you asked me what I *did* for a living ... this is it."[134]

> FORD: You took my money.
> MIKE: How naughty of me.
> FORD: You raped me.
> MIKE: Is that what I did...?
> FORD: You took me under false pretenses.
> MIKE: Golly. Margaret. Well, that's just what "happened," then, *isn't* it? *Okay*: Look: You got "Stung," and you're "Hurt." *I* can understand that. You're *stuck* 'n you're steaming...[135]

The horror of Mike's response is in the absolute trivialization of Ford's experience. He reduces her seduction to a string of behavioral clichés and reductive banalities, including the unfortunate reference to Ford being "stuck" by him.

Ford's final denial of the male world is in turning their own gun against them. She shoots Mike with Hahn's pistol, thus returning the rape and closing her involvement with that world. Mike's failure is in not anticipating the depth to which intercourse would impress Ford; perhaps that he sensed some of this in the hotel room accounts for his nervousness in that scene. Mike dies well: that is, consistent with his male code of behavior. He doesn't beg; he retains the poker metaphor in attempting to call the "bluff" of her profession and life, but in vain. Mike is the masculine voice that must be silenced. He invokes the terms "bitch" and "thief" in an escalating frenzy, then coughs out a final cogent speech on the film's themes: "This is what you always wanted. I knew it the first time you came in. You're worthless, you know it. You're a whore. I knew you the first time you came. You came back like a dog to its own vomit. You sought it out."[136] In the bloody context of the moment, he is persuasive that Ford's mission, from the beginning, has been the self-liberating emasculation of the male. He then calls for his own end with stoic, militaristic toughness in the best tough-guy tradition: "'Thank you, sir, may I have another?'"[137] Mike's last address to Ford is masculine, denying her femininity, yet appropriate in her mastering of him, appropriate, ironically, in her embracing of an all-female world where she assumes an aggressive role. Mike's philosophy, representatively male, is, despite its power games, direct and honest in its fashion. The emotional gist of his last lines is simple, accusing, again almost childlike.

Many critics and viewers find the *House of Games'* ending enigmatic and difficult. O'Brien lists the possible deterents to a satisfying interpretation: "...suggesting either morals about psychology, psychotherapists, assertiveness, self-forgiveness, or feminine anger. The strongest subtext supports the last."[138] Kohn discusses the prevalence of the ending to today's psychological dangers: "While the disease has been cured, the person—the moral agent—has died.... As she sips her cocktail, Dr. Ford, perky, relaxed and free of self-blame, would seem to be the product of a successful analysis."[139] Indeed, a persuasive argument for a female revenge reading of the film's ending is that it explains so satisfactorily a scene otherwise obscure. Ford, with the world of confidence men and taverns behind her, is a woman reborn. *"An open greenhousey restaurant. Ford, tanned, dressed lightly, at the bar, holding a drink. She looks around. A man accosts her."*[140] This man, at first suspected by the audience as a police officer, requests only an autograph. Ford, in a flowered blouse and white hoop earrings, displays a self-assurance and femininity eliciting sycophantic responses from men now as well as women (autograph scenes frame the movie). Here in this woman's world of light, plants, china, and tablecloths, a man may be an "accosting" intrusion but poses no threat.

Ford is able to relax at a meal—complete a "date"—with her true mentor, Maria; the latter, who gave Ford sanction to forgive herself for Mike's murder, addresses her by the very familiar diminutive "Maggie."

> MARIA: Oh, darling. I've missed you. How *are* you?
> FORD: I'm fine. Really fine.
> MARIA: Are you?
> FORD: Yes. I absolutely am.[141]

The intimacy in the women's dialogue borders on that of reunited lovers. Newly dedicated to this female world of expensive restaurants and professional therapy, Ford is confident, assertive, and seemingly happy. An elusive yet definite sexuality pervades the final scene. While Maria is gone, Ford sends a peculiar, almost flirting glance to the woman alone at the next table, the "Woman with Lighter." No men are in sight; almost surrealistically, women sit alone at perfectly white tables with spotless settings. The values—buffets, Waldorf salads—are symbolic rather than trivial. *"Ford is left alone at the table. She looks around the restaurant. The woman at the table backing up theirs is lighting a cigarette with a gold lighter. She and Ford nod slightly at each other.*"¹⁴² This is collusion. The woman lights her own cigarette; she "backs up" Ford's position. These simple juxtaposed gestures are charged with sexuality, with support for female dominance, with balance, self-sufficiency, reserve, a charade carried on in full daylight more menacing and deadly than anything perpetrated by the comparatively childlike antics of the con men. Ford does not so much steal the woman's gold lighter as the torch is passed to her. *"Ford's hands under the table, holding the lighter. . . . Angle. Ford at the table, her hands come up with the lighter, she lights a cigarette, and then holds the lighter covered in her hands. She smiles."*¹⁴³ Recall the fleshy, hairy hands awaiting poker cards; compare this to the menace of Ford's long fingers caressing the lighter, "playing" under the table with her discovered source of heat, another woman's mechanical lighter, not a man's matchstick.

Much has been written on Mamet's predominantly male spheres of action. He has periodically been labeled a sexist. Actor Colin Stinton is among those who argue that Mamet's persistently critical portrayals of men as emotionally arrested thieves make the writer rather a sort of feminist. He depicts men, Stinton argues, "to show up their fragile egos, to show them struggling to find out who they are. He tries to provide some insight into how their minds work."¹⁴⁴ In *House of Games* insight seems equally, if not greater, into the minds of women: one who murders, and another, her companion, who facilitates forgiveness. The movie is finally not a feminist argument but a terrifying sexual revenge story where the last fantasy enacted is the female's. Mamet inverts the popular genre ending, as for example the hard-boiled detective tradition where the murderer is frequently a murderess either brought to justice despite personal feelings of the detective or gleefully killed in a male myth of vindicated orgiastic depravity. The classic ending of Mickey Spillane's *I, The Jury* is typical: "How c-could you?" gasps the bloody and bullet-torn blonde. Mike Hammer just has time to "get it in" before she expires: "It was easy."¹⁴⁵ In *House of Games* there is no retribution for the woman's crime, and this Mike dies by his own boy's gun. One senses that part of the satisfaction in the movie's last scene is Mamet's own, at subverting a popular ending into a tale rather of exacted female revenge, stressing even more the male paranoia of emasculation. What begins as male fantasy ends as the worst of male nightmares. If for a woman to find her identity she must destroy the male, the ending is indeed horrible and bleak. One female reviewer writes of "something almost perverse in denying Ford the satisfying release that 'acting out' one's buried hostilities is supposed to bring. Mamet may have exorcised his demons, but he has not created a believable heroine. . . ."¹⁴⁶ Mamet's ending *is* perverse; he *is* assuaging demons — but perhaps a chic women's magazine must necessarily deny the unsettling catharsis, the dark light, suggested by *House of Games'* closing severity.

# CHAPTER II

# Recent Plays in Context

## *The Shawl,* Selected Shorts, *Speed-the-Plow*

During the 1980s Mamet's involvement with film steadily increased, while his theatrical production declined. Since 1984 the division of energies appears even more radical. A recent bibliography on Mamet[1] lists only one original full-length play since *Glengarry Glen Ross,* yet the writer produced no fewer than ten screenplays in that period. The shorter stage pieces Mamet has written are more than matched by his several unproduced teleplays. He cites as a prime reason for this shift the ability, indeed willingness, of Hollywood to accommodate prolific output:

> I wrote three movies last year—I can get them put on, and that's fine. If I wrote three plays, as I used to do, I would get lambasted because nobody in the critical establishment or in the community wants to see three plays by one person in one year.[2]

This comment, despite its implied resentment of theatre's restrictions, is only partly satisfying as an explanation of Mamet's increased cinematic activity. If the American stage won't tolerate three plays a year from a single playwright, it would certainly sustain, and welcome, more product from Mamet than it's received for several seasons. A tempting speculation is that *Glengarry Glen Ross,* its attendant praise culminating in the Pulitzer Prize, achieved a plateau of acclaim and artistry not easily matched. Mamet's next play, *The Shawl,* was brief, exquisite, and quietly lyrical, conspicuously distant from its predecessor in tone and sensibility.

A shift to film offered not only an outlet for increased production,

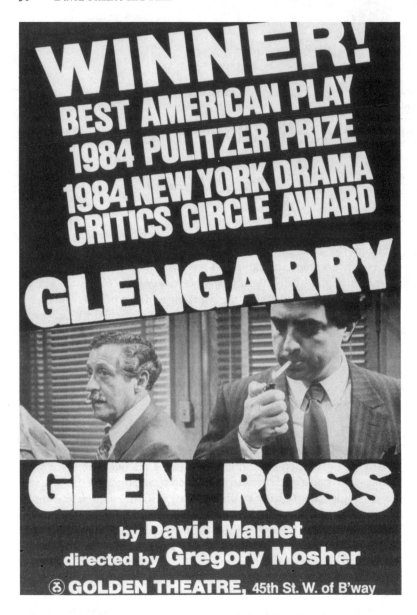

*Glengarry Glen Ross* celebrates its success during the original Broadway production (1984) with Mike Nussbaum (as George Aaronow) and Joe Mantegna
(as Richard Roma).

but another medium to explore. Mamet has always appeared ambitious for new challenges and forms; in the preface to *Writing in Restaurants* he describes his early years as a "happy student"[3] in pursuit of answers to both technical and philosophical problems of theatre. Mamet periodically casts himself in such a role, citing various mentor/authorities in acting (Stanislavsky, Meisner), classical unity (Aristotle), film (Eisenstein), and sociology (Veblen). Often the student role will overlap with a perception of self as teacher, for example in the Socratic dialogues constituting much of *On Directing Film* or the warning of potential "dogmatism"[4] introducing a first collection of essays. The point here is cinema offered not only an alternative to theatre, but an alternative Mamet seemed to embrace almost concurrently with his acknowledged mastery — the winning of its highest award — of theatrical form. Simply put, film offered Mamet new challenges and a vastly larger audience. *House of Games* exposes inherent differences between screen and stage and the great degree of control enjoyed by the film director. That after directing only two films Mamet both taught a course and compiled a book on directing technique and theory evinces his fascination with this newer arena of storytelling, an interest far deeper than merely being able to get more writing produced.

Moreover, those plays Mamet *has* recently offered bear a close relationship with film, further arguing a theoretical attachment. *Speed-the-Plow*, Mamet's only full-length play since *Glengarry Glen Ross*, deals with unscrupulous movie producers. That is, his only "big" play since the shift to Hollywood *concerns* Hollywood. Further, Mamet's involvement with transferring *Edmond* and *Glengarry Glen Ross* to film raises questions concerning the author's commitment to any notion of "pure" theatre, or, to use his own extreme definitions, any significant advantage of "radio play" over "silent movie." Film adaptations of popular plays are certainly nothing new, but that Mamet, theoretician, should be involved in such endeavors is curious and could easily be interpreted as the triumph of support for one medium, film, over another. How Mamet will reconcile play to film, forms he has persistently defined as inherently antithetical, remains to be seen. Although *Edmond's* rapid scenes are suggestively cinematic, the static, linguistic dramatics of *Glengarry Glen Ross* seem resistant to notions of uninflected shot and visual progression.

Much of Mamet's recent theatrical output has been adaptations of Chekhov, productions of "Mamet's" *The Cherry Orchard, Uncle Vanya,* and *The Three Sisters.* Clearly the reason for these is a perceived affinity with the earlier playwright and his concerns. *The Cherry Orchard's* plot, for example, clarified according to its adaptor, resembles a number of Mamet's own scenes: "And we subconsciously perceive and enjoy the reiterated action of this reiterated scene: two people at odds—each trying to fulfill his or her frustrated sexuality."[5] C. W. E. Bigsby adds that both writers seem "to create a world in which time and causality are suspended. Characters talk, apparently idly, but behind the reassuring chatter there is a quiet desperation."[6] Not only does Mamet see his characters paralleled in Chekhov's plays, but also in nineteenth century Russia a corrupt, doomed, gasping society significantly analogous to our own. He offers of *Uncle Vanya*: "It's the absolute end of an era, when the dreams of the play's characters have come to naught, and that's interesting to me."[7] Such comments are nearly indistinguishable from Mamet's own ideas of character—"the action in the play means the progress of a character toward a goal..."[8]—or culture— "... it is the sign of a very decayed and decadent society that we no longer apply ourselves to the old norms to renew ourselves, but have to find new ones."[9] But another, equally important reason Mamet has offered himself as the voice to bring Chekhov to contemporary audiences is that this work has kept him active in theatre. The adaptations have enabled Mamet to remain involved with major stage productions and served as vehicles for issues which concern him, while not demanding original ideas or the premium attention necessary for original work. Moreover, he notches another success in his professional belt— the role of translator/adaptor—and performs a socio-literary service, meanwhile reserving the majority of his energies for the screen. In a peculiar, cyclical fashion, Chekhov's plays are so eerily appropriate for Mamet that they become rediscovered or recycled "Mamet" plays, offering a powerful and continuing concern for social entropy heightened by historical context. The appearance of theatrical priorities has been maintained, the film career solidified.

Besides *Speed-the-Plow*, Mamet's recent original plays have tended to be short and concentrated—works that would not serve as effective film vehicles. Neither do they seem heavily influenced by filmic technique. Indeed, many earlier plays (*Sexual Perversity in Chicago, Lakeboat*...) are comprised of rapid, juxtaposed scenes more cinematic in texture than recent work. Aside from the documented influence on Mamet of Chicago's Second City, perhaps tendencies from the beginning indicate the attraction of film; naturally, as Mamet realized an actual movie career, he was free to abandon the "blackout" technique on

Original Broadway production of *Speed-the-Plow* (1988), second cast.

the stage. Yet recent efforts, most notably *The Shawl,* and the accompanying shorts *The Spanish Prisoner* and *Prairie du Chien*—the latter refashioned from an earlier radio play—inform the film work in significant ways.

## *The Shawl*

*The Shawl,* produced in 1985, was Mamet's last major theatrical offering before *House of Games'* release two years later. The film and play form a fascinating reciprocal relationship of influence and interpretation, connected not only by Mamet and chronology, but by performers and theme. *The Shawl* is archetypal Mamet, concerned with exploitation, teaching, the potency of speech, storytelling and roleplaying. Like *House of Games,* its plot concerns a con artist (fortuneteller John) and a "deeply repressed woman"[10] (Miss A) who comes to him for guidance. The similarity of the two scenarios is striking. And since Mamet's writing offers few women's roles, the consecutive creation of perhaps his two most compelling female characters in itself begs comparisons.

Mamet's habit of recasting actors causes an obscure effect, peripheral yet definite. Joe Mantegna is the primary example, and his recurring presence—as Mike, Richard Roma, Jerry in *Things Change* or Bobby Gould in *Speed-the-Plow*—throws a further connective shadow between roles. As Mamet's troupe becomes stars, the reverberating effect between roles transcends any enclosed theatrical experience. An audience attending original productions of *The Shawl* enjoyed Miss A (Lindsay Crouse) in her vulnerability to the con games and seeming prescience of John (Mike Nussbaum), then undoubtedly recalled these performances when they watched on the screen later Joey (Nussbaum) teach Ford (Crouse) his antiquated swindle the Flue. Farther reaching recognition may occur in reverse; cast lists are invariably printed in published plays, often alongside production stills. Any future reader of a particular play—and publication enables many more readers than viewers—will find the experience altered by the association, before even beginning, of recognized Mamet "players"—Mantegna, Nussbaum, J. J. Johnston, Robert Prosky and others—with particular roles.

This association effect has been greatly increased by the use of the actors in widely distributed films. Bob Daily writes of Mamet's preference:

They are his fellow workers, his Old Cronies, his poker partners. "The Mamet family," they sometimes call themselves.

Few filmmakers or playwrights are so devoted to the ensemble approach. Coming from a broken home, Mamet seems bent on creating the family he never had....

Fun they have had. But, as Mamet scales the heights of Broadway and now Hollywood, there are more tangible benefits. They are getting famous together. From obscurity to the big time, he is taking his "family" with him.[11]

Mamet must be well aware the impact such an ensemble method has on his work. He has, so to speak, set the stage before a film even begins, simply by the presence of his actors. Inversely, as long as cast lists are published, readers will create an immediate "screen" perception against which to encounter the plays. All this serves to highlight the theatricality, artifice, and role-playing themes in Mamet's work. Something of the "character" of Joe Mantegna lingers, whether the actor is portraying con man or mobster, not in the sense that a John Wayne or Humphrey Bogart might simply submerge a part in his persona, but in such a manner that Mamet's œuvre is tightened, pattern and unity are implied. Mantegna and Nussbaum never quite let one forget he is watching a Mamet project, yet their abilities paradoxically heighten awareness and susceptibility to confided trust. Each character, rather than narrowed, is extended, and the familiar hustlers, pitching, scheming, talking, assure both the audience's entertainment and involvement.

Lindsay Crouse speaks of *The Shawl,* and Mamet's intentions, in incriminating terms: "So he set out to exercise plot-writing as a craft. And I think it came out beautifully. Everybody gets fooled at least once in the play."[12] This emphasis on plot demonstrates the influence of screenwriting; yet by "everybody" does Crouse mean every character, or indeed a trick perpetrated on every audience member? The situation recalls the layered, interrelated deceptions of *House of Games.* Crouse continues on playing a peculiar role effectively: "If the audience is told you're a king and you carry yourself like a king, the audience will believe it."[13] The willing gift of trust, then, renders an audience susceptible to any manipulative games of author, director, actor, or character.

Critics' responses to *The Shawl* are also evocative of *House of Games.* Henry I. Schvey, who argues for the play's ending as discovery of a high ideal, nonetheless sees the subject as "a small-time mystic who is out to con a bereaved woman" by "intuiting and accommodating himself to the emotional needs of his prey."[14] Philip C. Kolin writes that in the play "rogues revel in divulging trade secrets to brother or sister crooks. . . . It is a significant postmodern attack on the place illusion occupies in our inner and external reality."[15] According to Bigsby, "Mamet, too, is a trickster. The emotions his play provokes, the imaginations it stirs, are the product of calculation and professional skill."[16] Like his counterparts in *House of Games,* John practices his craft with expertise and pride. Much of *The Shawl* concerns revealing the tricks of a highly theatrical trade. Note also the linguistic similarity between a "psychic . . . merely someone who sees more clearly than others,"[17] and the *psycho*logists of *House of Games.* The human psyche remains the area of specialty and focus.

John compares tellingly to other Mamet characters, such as Roma. Like his predecessor, John's words open and close his first appearance; the deliveries begin with ellipses and "end" with colons, marking a circularity which associates Roma's verbal assault with John's gentler insinuations. Scene three of *Glengarry Glen Ross* shares much with *The Shawl's* first act: both are elaborate sales pitches, the products being self and trust; the language is comparably compelling, dramatic, even hypnotic; the marks' hesitant answers further involve them. Even the salesmen's existential interrogations are reminiscent. Roma intones: "There's an absolute morality? May*be*. And *then* what? If you *think* there is, then *be* that thing. Bad people go to hell? I don't *think* so. If you think that, act that way."[18] And John's argument: "For the question is: WHAT POWERS EXIST? And what powers DO exist? And what looks over us? And . . . do you see? This is a rational concern. *Is* there an order in the world. . . . *Can* things be known."[19] If John's explanation tends to be more hopeful, it is also more obscure, both tendencies perhaps accountable to Miss A's voluntary approach. "You've come to see me," says John. "You wish me to resolve your 'problem.'"[20] Roma, however, is cast as the aggressor, who must more or less create a dilemma before he can solve it with real estate — "I'm glad to meet you, James. . . . I want to show you something. . . . It might mean *nothing* to you . . . and it might not. I don't know."[21]

Rather than share Roma's affected indecision, John must present himself as a confident authority. Whereas Roma's comments work to sympathetically bond him with his mark — two similarly lost and suffering members of the male congregation — John's are designed to suggest wisdom, arcane knowledge of matters Miss A must resolve within herself. In short, John presents himself as teacher and physician. His character's ability is in the gradual revelation of information; such a technique of suspense is discussed by Mamet and credited in himself to "writing for movies. Writing for movies is really all about revealing information: when and how you reveal information."[22] Consequently, not only is *The Shawl's* emphasis on plot influenced by film, and the story itself strikingly like *House of Games,* but the very role of fortune-teller, of soothsayer, is a variation of both con artist and filmmaker. As Crouse implies, audience is culpable comparably to the mark within the play, just as a viewer is susceptible to *House of Games'* convolutions. According to Kolin, *The Shawl* manipulates the willingness to believe:

> danger confronting the third and intermittently skeptical party — the audience. The more John protests that it is all a trick or stresses his limitations, the more we want and look for a magical explanation. Mamet's point is that, like Charles or Miss A, we risk falling into the explanation for the truth when we search for illusions everywhere.[23]

Humans are thus by nature exploitable in confidence games from seers of truth, or from playwrights or film directors. John defines his craft and its purpose in terms that further confuse con man and filmmaker: "Very simple, really. . . . If one is allowed to believe . . . Our job is not to guess, but to *aid* . . . to . . . create an atmosphere . . . As I just did with *you*. . ."[24] John's job is to present and control a series of images or impressions to bring about a preordained reaction from his client.

John's parlour, where he works persuasive "magic" on Miss A, is strangely anticipatory of the card room where Mike and Joey attempt the swindle of Margaret Ford. Both rooms are dark, artificially lit. A woman enters a world unknown to her and sits at a table with men who are strangers. "You are safe now, no harm can come to you here,"[25] John assures Miss A. Like Mike, John places a premium on the giving and receiving of confidence. Miss A must have "one moment's faith"[26] and "must trust"[27] that he can detect both physical and spiritual scars. Ford is foreseen in John's invocation of Miss A's "psychic ability"[28] and her buried pain: "And it was traumatic, and so you repress it. We repress so much. But it all casts its shadow, and the things which you would know are all in you and all . . . *available* to you."[29] Recall Mike's contention: ". . . there's many sides to each of us: good blood, bad blood, and somehow all those sides have got to speak. The burden of responsibility's just become too great."[30] The women suffer both psychic sensitivity and repression concerning parents.

John's methods are unique in that he is able to remain within his sanctum, awaiting customers drawn to the web by need; the House of Games, in contrast, serves primarily as a base and meeting place for hustlers who work the streets, men whose effectiveness is dependent on their marks' lack of knowledge of their reputation. John, however, anticipates future clients, where an established trust "creates confidence in them."[31] It is the difference, in a sense, between the short and long con. John is a priest stationary in a sacred place, empowered to see, intuit, grant peace. The solemn authority of his particular brand of confidence pitch creates the soothing trust of the confessional. "And the questions of the spirit rise. And troubled, you come here. And we will *lift* your troubles. And answer your doubts. As all is open."[32] He explains to his lover Charles: "And you can do nothing till you have their trust. . . . Their question is: can They Confess to *You*?"[33] John plays at being a pagan, rather than Christian, priest. From the beginning he evokes an ancient past, a vague yet essential connection to those before him. "And we look at the stars. As they did."[34] When he later attempts to strip Charles of any belief in his mystic ability, John employs the same metaphor used in *House of Games*: "And there is no mystery. And then you can go. 'The Secret of the Pyramids?' No."[35] Like Mike, John is "a man proud of his craft,"[36] cognizant of deep and old traditions. The confidence games in *The Shawl* are part of a greater pattern of trust and release, perhaps accounting for the dialogue's "ritualistic and even unnatural sound."[37]

As *House of Games'* poker room may retrospectively form our opinion of the charlatan John at work in his parlour, so do *The Shawl's* sacred space, absolution, and echoes of antiquity bring new dimensions of significance to the confidence trade. Even poker may assume an almost mythic importance in such a context, symbolically telling of both author and material. "If one can know a man by his rituals," writes Samuel G. Freedman, "then the poker night reveals something essential about David Mamet."[38] Mamet hints at the centrality of habitual behavior in humans, and by extension its importance in his work: "There is a certain learned, habituated, perhaps even genetic need for the ritual of the culture in which you exist and which is your culture."[39] To ignore this need, he warns, "You have to pretend to be something that you are not."[40] Such pretense may speak to the necessity of role-playing, to psychological repression, and to the unending supply of needful victims and con man to take them. Dennis Car-roll believes that *The Shawl*'s five scenes form a pyramid, in which "the central scene, a séance, is like the apex"[41]; the play's entire structure, as well as its story and lead character, celebrates "the lyricism and mystery of the unknown"[42] with a unity of style and function typical of Mamet.

Acts two and four of *The Shawl* offer John's "behind-the-scene" explanations of his divination to Charles. These encounters are most reminiscent of the "off-stage" scenes in *A Life in the Theatre,* where older thesbian Robert is struck by an audience's discernment: "Perhaps they saw the show tonight . . . on another level. Another, what? another . . . plane, eh? On another level of meaning. Do you know what I mean? . . . A plane of meaning."[43] In his redundancy and indecision, Robert tries to credit a mystical quality of insight to the stage. Inversely, the mystic and his client proceed in a staged performance. Mamet argues that the skills of the theatre—for him philosophy, morality, and aesthetics—"cannot be communicated intellectually. They must be learned firsthand in long practice under the tutelage of someone who learned them firsthand."[44] He feels *A Life in the Theatre* is about "the necessity, the desire, the impossibility of communicating wisdom. It is about the relationship between young people and old people."[45] In *The Shawl,* a similar difficulty in communication occurs. As "John's words strip away the magic of his first-act performance,"[46] he detects Charles' disillusionment:

> I *show* you the trick "from the back" and you're disappointed. Of course you are. If you view it as a "member of the audience." One of the,
>    you will see, the most painful sides of the profession is this: you do your work well, and who will see it? No one, really. . . . If you do it well."[47]

John has appropriated the theatrical metaphor, attempting to sway Charles with the "beginnings of a craft,"[48] causing the young man's dismayed response that "that's all there . . . that's all there is."[49] Of course, John's lamenting of hidden craft is more appropriate for stage magician or confidence man than actor. Ironically, talent remains hidden only if unerringly employed, which is seldom the case in Mamet. Robert is a second-rate actor who bungles lines; Mike botches his elaborate con of Ford and pays with his life; John is tricked into exposing himself by a photograph. Such failures are in line with a Mametic tradition of incompetent crooks and failed relationships, a recurrent pattern exemplifying a human impulse toward exposure, to be punished or forgiven—"...you sought this out..."[50] Mike accuses Ford.

By the end of *The Shawl* John has dismissed Charles by denying him any possibility of true magic—i.e. any mysteries in life—forcing instead a prosaic explanation of all ostensible intuition. "I TOLD YOU. IT WAS A *TRICK*. ARE YOU *DEAF*? ...I'd *wished* we could be something more to each other. It was not meant to be."[51] Like many of the play's phrases, "It was a *trick*" is repeated with an almost incantatory efficacy; likewise, "trust," "confidence," and "belief" are repeated. For Charles, however, the suggestions do no good. Lacking training, interest, and tradition to either receive or impart qualities of belief, he is merely—rather than craftsman, priest, or physician—another petty grifter, "obsessed with himself as a commodity."[52] For John's part, the moment he denies mystical causes he places himself again in a theatrical sphere. Says Mamet: "Drama is basically about lies, somebody lying to somebody."[53] Of course, a definition of theatre so extended as to include all deception, exploitation, and role-playing becomes essentially a model of human existence. *The Shawl,* through its gradual release of information, clarifies the relationship between con game, mystery story, and existential enigma. While Charles considers, "How will the money *come* to us?"[54] John's questions hint at an abstract subtext, at resistance to trust:

> Should she contest this will in courts. Is this a question for the mystic? No. It hides a deeper one: this: how can I face my betrayal. How can I obtain revenge. Against the dead. Or: why did my mother not love me more? And so we help her. To *answer* that *last* question.[55]

John is not only concerned with ancient first principles, he also addresses the "last" question. His darker concerns—humiliation, betrayal, vengeance—end in periods rather than interrogatory marks, as if answers reside implicitly within the very articulation of the question. John's goal is to help Miss A "*face* herself . . . and she *will* reward us."[56] Her repression, a deep-seated anxiety toward her parents, is obviously analogous to Margaret Ford's illness. Similarly, Mike helps Ford to face herself. The confidence man is curiously both exploiter and physician of these ancient, inevitable disorders.

*The Shawl* achieves a unity of theme, style, and presentation comparable to Mamet's best film work, representing the writer's "never-

**David Mamet (1988).**

flagging fascination with the two ideas I discovered as a student: (1) every aspect of the production should reflect the idea of the play; (2) the purpose of the play is to bring to the stage the life of the soul."[57] This *"unified aesthetic"*[58] could easily substitute the words "film" and "screen"; Mamet applies the same energy and scrupulous methodology to his movies. The "life of the soul" seems at least partially bound to rituals of trust and mystery found in the magical/theatrical con artist roaming Mamet's work. Criminal exploitation by commerce, so common in his plays, is reborn in the hustler's even more explicit social role — as existential broker of the human sub- and unconscious. Occasionally even a weary hopefulness is exposed.

Carroll contends that the "power of John's prescience can only be effected through a development of trust between him and his client."[59] Throughout, however, John is also a persuasive performer, "mesmerizing in his particular confidence game."[60] His approach, like other Mamet men, is based on trust, apprehended through language. *The Shawl*, set primarily at a table, is especially passive except for its speech. As the séance commences, John instructs them to "be *silent* a moment,"[61] yet he continues to speak, droning and hypnotic. Part of his linguistic power, again shared with most Mamet protagonists, is storytelling prowess. Through John as medium, a female "spirit" relates a lurid tale of interracial infidelity, violence, betrayal, and, importantly, a woman's murder. Again *House of Games* is anticipated in women as willing victims in a world of men: ". . . you say that I reaped the desired result, that I won, stabbed, stabbed in the belly, ripped out with his dirk, bloodied the sheets, wiped it upon the wall. . . ."[62] A "dream" of feminine murder, its procreative denial in the destruction of the belly, its image of virginal despoliation in sheets stained by a murderer's blade, is shocking coming from the ordinarily benevolent John. Perhaps his supposed possession by such a tragic female spirit also signals his speaking for the repressed elements of Miss A's psyche. Mamet proposes a subtle balance between drama, dreams, and the mind:

> We respond to drama to that extent to which it corresponds to our dream life.
> The life of the play is the life of the unconscious, the protagonist represents ourselves, and the main action of the play constitutes the subject of the dream or myth. . . . The play is a quest for a solution.[63]

John specifically inquires as to Miss A's dreams, hence her unconscious: "In your dream . . . she said, 'What did you dream? And what did you dream that night?' And you told her your dream."[64]

The clairvoyant serves the function of psychologist as clearly as hustlers do in *House of Games*. Indeed, by having a private space, and by his method of direct interrogation, John's meeting with Miss A assumes an appearance of therapy.

MISS A: What, I . . .
JOHN: You hear a knocking. Your mother, "I called your name." But no faith. You *heard* her. She came to you, *say* it.

MISS A: I . . .
JOHN: Your apartment. And you heard a knocking at the. . .
MISS A: I don't. . .
JOHN: Yes! You *heard* her? The *wind* blew. SHE WAS CALLING YOUR NAME!!!
MISS A *(pause)*: It was my name I thought. . . [65]

Whether John is proceeding from legitimate insight or charlatan cleverness, to Miss A he serves as purgative clinician. Her inability to articulate, the undeveloped "I" followed only by an ellipsis is appropriate for her indefinite character. "Miss A" — and for that matter "John" — is a vague, incomplete name, implying a desire to be made whole. The realization of John's confidence tricks is rendered all the more painful by Miss A's admitted need: "If you can't *help* me, NO one can help me . . . why did I *come* here. All of you . . . Oh *God*, is there no . . . how can you *betray* me . . . You . . . you . . . God *damn* you . . . for 'money'. . .? God. . ."[66] In this instance the hustler's violation is the rape of a vulnerable and trusting spirit. Miss A's lack of alternatives accentuates her essential loneliness; her faltering speech fails in its desire to damn, instead repetitively evoking the name of a sought holy authority.

In light of John's earlier comments concerning craft, his slip-up appears almost intentional, a display of talent. Shortly after her outburst he has a seemingly genuine vision of Miss A's mother: "'Are you asleep my lamb?' And she thinks of you still. And calls to you. And she calls to you now. And I saw her by your bed. She Wore The Shawl."[67] That is, just after John appears to have irrevocably botched the con, Miss A is offered pacifying assurance of his powers and of a higher order affirming her beliefs. John justifies her trust and wins her commitment. His speech is confident and fluid, distinguished from hesitant, elliptical phrases earlier in the scene. Schvey sees this as John's "real moment of self-awareness as a result of her anguished cry of betrayal,"[68] while Kolin believes the shawl is ultimately "a cover for John's tricks"[69] which implicates the audience in a desire for genuine magic. "The shawl," he continues, "is a rich symbol for the multiple levels of illusions Mamet exposes,"[70] convincing Miss A to contest the will and presenting itself as "a mantle appropriate for a shaman such as John purports to be, especially in its ornate design. . . ."[71] Whatever the true nature of John's revelation, the moment is auspiciously timed; in that instant his dependence upon Charles seems finally overcome. He denies the young man's methods and draws closer to Miss A. Ironically, as Kolin points out, his actions also salvage the con and further its plausibility. In their final scene together, Miss A seems wholly dependent upon the older man.

Freedman notes the "search for a father figure"[72] in Mamet, using this idea to explain the frequent mentor-protégé dynamic. Surely this is applicable to *The Shawl*. Finally, John and Miss A sit alone together in his parlour. Their conversation recalls the fragile father-daughter probings of *Reunion*. Charles has been rejected and dismissed. Miss A is determined to have further proof of John's prescience. He replies, "... but still skeptical. Good. We can't overcome our nature. For it protects us. You ask what you wish to ask."[73] His later simple, unequivocal affirmation of a spiritual encounter is the very answer he so adamantly denies Charles. The argument that John has abandoned Charles' ways for a higher ideal is, however, open to debate. In the end John possesses a quiet and convincing mastery not unlike the opening scene. His language is again coercive, perhaps the tone for a successfully completed therapy. "Yes. Now. You seem ... you've *decided* something, for you seem in better *spirits* today. Something has been ... And a *burden* has been lifted from your mind. Good. I see *clarity*."[74] He pushes her gently toward closure, toward payment, toward the decision Charles requested from the start. Recall in this context Mike's "burden of responsibility"[75]; John still employs the rhetoric of the con game. When the conversation turns to fees, he invokes the language of the second scene, designed to exploit a mark's guilt, indebtedness, responsibility, and fealty: "To help with our work. Some would leave fifty. Some would leave nothing. It's completely up to you."[76] Whether or not John is truly clairvoyant, he overlooks neither commercial interests nor his methods from before he divined the shawl. He seems to accomplish both of his primary goals: to assist Miss A and to accommodate his fiscal benefit.

"The theater," writes Mamet, "is not the imitation of anything, it is real theater," and "human beings must concern themselves with the truth of the individual moment, and recognize and ratify their coconspirators' existence and desire."[77] John and Miss A exemplify such a reciprocity; they each ratify the other, in a situation which elaborates many elements of theatrical performance. Mamet's term "coconspirators" implies a mutual incrimination by action; everyone attempts transactions of exploitation and need. Miss A's "ambivalent hatred and jealousy of her mother"[78] is surely recognized by John and anticipates Ford's slips concerning her father. As a side note, Anne Dean reports that Mamet has subsequently considered revisions to *The Shawl*, "changing the homosexual pair at the center of the work to a heterosexual couple. Thus, John could, without much hindrance, become Joanne!"⁷⁹ This would render the play even more similar to *House of Games*, particularly in its conclusion. A woman forsakes a petty confidence thief and returns to another woman for communion. The overriding idea of denunciation of the male—or anyway the masculine—is the same. "Drama is really all about conflicting impulses of the individual," explains Mamet. "What you are doing, just as in a dream, is taking one individual and splitting him into two parts."⁸⁰ John is quiet and effeminate; generally in their relationship, Charles represents the masculine/aggressive and John the feminine/passive.

If, as Mamet contends, drama is the quest of the protagonist toward his goal, and at the same time characters are split from a whole, then that journey may often constitute an attempt at reunion. John perhaps enjoys one moment of true psychic power, a moment sufficient for both him and Miss A to continue. She had burnt the shawl in rage five years earlier. Perhaps this is feminine rage, Electra repression, or in itself a denial of the shamanistic powers she so craves. If Mamet's proposed reunion is one more basic than the sexual, is an attempt to reintegrate the very nature of humanness, then trust in the soothsayer is vital, even if by this trust the exploiter profits. In both *The Shawl* and *House of Games*, the mark does gain what appears to be a restorative self-definition; in both, the hustler fails. Mike is murdered by that prideful will which he awakens; John fails to bring his lover into the fold and is exposed as deceiver—Miss A never ceases to question him. If the life of the theatre and the soul, dream life and human unconsciousness are all synonymous, as they seem to be by Mamet's reckoning, then as viewer, as mark surrendering trust to the writer, director, or actor, one recognizes the protagonist's struggle and undergoes his own ritual of repression, trust, awareness, and, perhaps, betrayal. The Aristotelian process of recognition and reversal Mamet claims to be "the essential celebratory element of theatre"⁸¹ is shared between the artist and his audience of conspirators.

## *The Spanish Prisoner, Prairie du Chien,* and *Vint*

*The Shawl* has been produced with complementary shorts. In its premiere, in Chicago, the play was opened by the enigmatic *The*

*Spanish Prisoner,* in which three pairs of characters—differentiated only by letter-names—recall elaborate stories of a Spanish galleon, an unrequited love in port, and a southern black boy who is killed. Richard Christiansen reports that the play "gets its title from an old confidence game and . . . is also about the search for meaning and balance. It is a word play, similar to Mamet's recent radio dramas, in which understanding is elusive."[82] *The Spanish Prisoner* is indeed abstruse, calling to mind the author's comment that only "if the question posed is one whose complexity and depth renders it unsusceptible to rational examination does the dramatic treatment seem to us appropriate. . . ."[83]

And yet within the play's probing, stuttering density are the omnipresent themes of dominance and control. Another storytelling framework, where characters achieve identity solely through fabrication, develops the embryonic hustler. "Dreaming. In this hell in which we live . . . the sole gift which we . . . I will not say endorse, for it goes *so, so* far be . . . *accept.* And the rest, we say the test of *life,* the final: THE WILL TO EXPLOIT."[84] Time-honored traditions of craft and history, may only be a boundless human "gift" for exploitation. *The Spanish Prisoner* sweeps from the Escorial to, again, Egypt, to Alabama, unhampered by geography or time. "You see: one needn't have confidence, because it is also possible to lose—so there is a result to your actions *whatever* you do. . . . And you cannot combat human misery."[85] The passage foretells Mike's delivery to Ford during their first "short course in psychology," linking "confidence" and "human misery."[86] The play also adds another word to the psyche-psychology dynamic, the more malevolent "psycho" in context of the parent: "It is a tale that we know. The psych, the psycho . . . the unconscious aspect of one dead parent."[87]

The piece's ending is intriguing: "The man who aids her escape will reap her love and share her fortune. Who would not support her? And so he does so. You know the rest."[88] The rest is, presumably, another tale of dominance and abuse, as the similarity between "reap" and "rape" suggests. The same speaker, "F," earlier posits that continual human misery *seems* to be lifted "by an act of love,"[89] while the closing tale concerns a woman on the run, her father's fortune stolen from her, and a man who will return it to her for commercial gain. The happy ending of this "love" story is suspicious. "You know the rest."[90] Carroll ponders another reading, seeing the antidote to such bleakness in *The Shawl,* "a play which deals with the transcendence over the will to exploit."[91] While an attractive notion, the ambiguities of *The*

*Shawl*'s conclusion problematize such an optimistic view, especially when a will to exploit is considered beyond mere monetary gratification.

In *The Shawl*'s New York production, *The Spanish Prisoner* was replaced by the revised radio play *Prairie du Chien*. Set in a train at night, the piece develops two stories concurrently: a violent gothic tale recounted by a traveling salesman and a card game which explodes into accusations and gunfire. The play, writes Robert Brustein, "unravels on the stage like a Faulkner short story"[92]; Connie Booth remarks on "the Storyteller's tale gaining impetus from the movement of the journey...."[93] These favorite themes of Mamet—the raconteur/salesman, the game of chance—are related here only through implications of juxtaposition. Carroll contends that transferring the play to stage even more apparently dissociated the two actions. "The violence in the story and that in the card game just happened to manifest themselves at the same time—which made the play even more disturbing."[94] Conversations, however, subtly overlap. The Storyteller appropriates gambling phrases such as "I'll bet it is,"[95] while the Dealer interrupts, for the audience, the tale with such revealing commentary as "Takes the queen."[96]

Mamet writes: "Working for radio, I learned the way *all* great drama works: by leaving the *endowment* of characters, place, and especially action up to the audience."[97] Uncharacterized drama is thus like a camp fire story, or a fairy tale as defined by Bruno Bettelheim:

> a fairy tale loses much of its personal meaning when its figures and events are given substance not by the ... imagination, but by that of an illustrator. The unique details derived from his own particular life, with which a hearer's mind depicts a story he is told or read, make the story much more of a personal experience.[98]

In *Dark Pony*, as a father drives his daughter home he tells her the simple, unendowed tale of vulnerable Rain Boy and his savior Dark Pony, a story more moving and efficacious for the adult than the child. A lifetime of disenchantment provides a subtext that, for the father, renders the story crucial. "He looked up above him. Dark Pony was standing there. ... 'Oh, Dark Pony,' he said. ... 'I thought you had forgotten me.'"[99] *Prairie du Chien* is even more explicit in a tale's "overt and covert meanings" for "the sophisticated adult."[100] Bigsby notes that in much of Mamet's work "fiction is a fundamental strategy and consolation to characters who could scarcely survive the knowledge of their own marginality."[101] The "Storyteller" continually confirms that the "Boy" of the "Listener" is asleep before adding another gruesome detail. As their generalized names suggest, these characters find identity only through specified roles in either performance or game of chance ("Dealer," "Gin Player").

*Prairie du Chien* stands as a bridge between *The Shawl* and *House of Games*. The story of a woman's betrayal and violent death echoes John's séance, while both short and film share extended card games. By *Prairie du Chien's* stories being intertwined, the two other works are quietly associated. In *Prairie du Chien,* the burning red shawl is replaced by a "pretty red dress. . . . And it was burning."[102] If the shawl approximately represents a loss of maternal security, then the dress is betrayed female sexuality. John's vision of Miss A's shawl and the grotesque Boston of 1840 share image and tone with the Storyteller's recollection of lust, murder, and despairing loneliness. The card game, meanwhile, escalates in violence and denial.

> DEALER: No one was cheating you. You're *crazy*, friend. *(Pause.)* Eh? You're *crazy*, fellow.
> GIN PLAYER: He was crimping cards.
> DEALER: Where? Where? Show me one card. Show me one marked card. *(Pause.)* Eh? You son of a bitch. They ought to lock you up. They ought to take a *strap* to you. *(Pause.)* If you can't lose, don't *play.*[103]

The words are close to *House of Games*:

> MIKE: You sonofabitch, you've been steamrolling over me all night. . .
>
> . . .
>
> VEGAS MAN: The man can't *play,* he should stay *away.*[104]

Whether the Dealer has been cheating is impossible to determine, although his vascillation earlier in the scene and the vehemence of his defense seem incriminating; the Player, however, outnumbered and lacking proof, is ridiculed and finally shamed, although he may well have identified a hustler at work.

Another brief, recent play of Mamet's, *Vint,* concerns yet another card game. In this adaptation of Chekhov's story, Commissioner Persolin catches his clerks in a late-night game where dossier files substitute for cards. He overhears them bidding his wife. Soon Persolin too is involved: "Let me *profit* from it, *please.*"[105] He demands clarifications—

"Yes, yes, yes, and so my wife's the queen of clubs"[106] — and scorns poor play — "Wasted. Yes. Who taught you to play?"[107] The languages of government and gaming grow interchangeable; individuals — including one's spouse — are merely representative commodities to trade or discard. Political acuity is demanded for success in the game.

> PERSOLIN: You know ... you're laying the whole ministry open to—
> NEDKUDOV: That's what *I* said.
> PERSOLIN: Look — look — can I get in?
> KULAKEVITCH: Sir, we'd be honored to—
> NEDKUDOV: Give him the cards.
> ZVISDULIN: Deal him in.
> (Persolin *is dealt in*)
> PERSOLIN: All right. Now: Let's get back to *you*.
> PSUILIN: I bid your wife.[108]

Mamet capitalizes on his shared concern with Chekhov of dehumanization, exploiting a story set in his own arena of cards and male initiation. He explains the importance of card games in his work: "Poker is a game of skill and chance. Playing poker is also a masculine ritual. . . . Poker will reveal to the frank observer something else of import — it will teach him about his own nature."[109] Such a game, for Mamet, is educational, where "improvement can be due only to one thing: to character. . . ."[110] A game needing both skill and providence, cards offer a microcosm of the life of men, where success is founded on courage, bluff, and appearance, those same talents constituting the hustler.

## Speed-the-Plow

*Speed-the-Plow* opened on Broadway in 1988 amid much interest and excitement, due partly to the casting of Madonna as Karen. The play's subject: the inherent, almost spiritual corruption and venality of Hollywood producers. Mamet was returning with a report of his adventures in the Wild West. William A. Henry III reports the characters were based on Ned Tanen, head of production at Paramount, and Art Linson, producer of *The Untouchables*. In short, this time the scam was entertainment. Bobby Gould (played by Joe Mantegna in the 1988 Broadway production) and Charlie Fox (Ron Silver) — like men in *Glengarry Glen Ross* characterized only by age — are "tribal hustlers"[111] clearly in the Mamet tradition, yet "characters who are more articulate and amusing than some of his earlier ones."[112] But more than a simple Hollywood story told with the author's typical humor, brio, and salesman rhetoric, *Speed-the-Plow* has apocalyptic concerns. Mamet says the play is "about the end of the world.... It's all going to come down."[113] Christiansen concurs: the play is Mamet's "most specific dramatic comment yet on his belief in the inevitable decline of our civilization." It is a work "of profound stoicism about our decaying culture."[114] This subject of imminent collapse has persistently intrigued Mamet, who sees in the end a restful peace. "People get oppressed by the heat and humidity, it's got to rain before it's going to clear up. There are ebbs and flows in any civilization. Nothing lasts forever. We had a good time.... Now you've got to pay the piper."[115] Against a bleak superficiality of movie commerce, Mamet juxtaposes his headier themes. Kroll sees this contrast as the play's genius: "Mamet's master stroke is to shove these self-satisfying, self-loathing clowns smack up against the Big Questions of Our Time."[116]

Gould and Fox are descendants of all Mamet con men, although education and success set them apart. Their pure relishing of vice, the lack of any ethical standard beyond revenge or profit, is exceptional. While *Speed-the-Plow* is one of the writer's funniest plays, it is also among his darkest, partly due to the men's joy, satisfaction, and awareness of their decadence. They are, as Fox says, "Young Americans at WORK and PLAY,"[117] whose days carry full agendas of deception, exploitation, and willful mockery of any belief not bankable. In a "world built on greed and cynicism wasting its opportunities for doing good, its spirit collapsing in violent death throes,"[118] rarely have waste and collapse been so fully, enthusiastically embraced by the participants.

Gould establishes his place in the confidence tradition by imparting trust—ultimately in a too great degree—to the temporary Karen. Another of the play's Mametic signatures is the inevitable justification of swindle as business. "It's a business," says Gould, "with its own unchanging rules."[119] Such business is interchangeable with robbery, depending upon one's situation in a deal: "You get a Free Option on a Douggie Brown film, guys would walk in here, hold a guy up..."[120] While Fox readily agrees, presumably Karen is slower to understand Gould's euphemisms for deception:

> GOULD: Yes. No one has any intention of making the book, but we read it, as a courtesy. Does this mean that we're depraved? No. It's just business ... how business is done, you see?

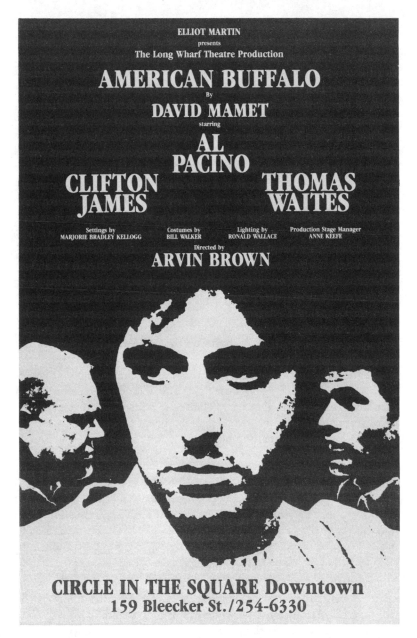

The Off Broadway revival of *American Buffalo* with Al Pacino (1981).

KAREN: I think.
GOULD: A business. Start to close.[121]

There are numerous other similarities to earlier plays. Fox has a voracious, almost existential need for coffee in act one. He is drinking coffee when Brown comes to his house with the film option; throughout the initial office scene Fox demands coffee—"I, I need a cuppa coffee. . ."[122]—to compose and "calm" himself; Karen has difficulty finding the machine and delays the drink's arrival; and Gould, jokes Fox, "takes his coffee like he makes his movies: nothing in it."[123] Coffee seems a trivial motif until one recalls Don's advice to Bob in *American Buffalo*: "You know how much nutritive benefits they got in coffee? Zero. Not one thing. The stuff eats *you* up. You can't live on coffee, Bobby."[124] And yet Fox and Gould *do* seem to subsist on it, suggesting not only a natural energy so high it can be regulated by caffeine, but also their symbolic existence without nutrition, coupled with an addiction to a "black" substance that destroys from within. Karen, meanwhile, has difficulty supplying this for them. Apparently, she is not a coffee drinker.

Mamet's association effect of recurring actors is repeated by Mantegna's presence as Gould, "a more laid back and upscale version of the salesman he portrayed in *Glengarry*. . . ."[125] David Blum writes of the Mantegna-Mamet synergism: "What it is that I am telling you is that Joseph Anthony Mantegna is the voice and Mamet is the words, and that is what this is all about."[126] Mantegna adds: "David tells people he writes with me in mind, which I guess means that I'm The Guy."[127] Henry extends the comparison between Mantegna's characters in *Speed-the-Plow* and *Glengarry Glen Ross*, two "salesmen who have no skill except persuasion, no talent but for heightened, theatrical speech and naked yet manipulative outbursts."[128]

Gould has achieved a financial success only vaguely dreamed of by Mamet's earlier hustlers. He is among an elite pantheon of Hollywood moguls not only pandering to America's baseness, but propagating its illiteracy and sadism. Mamet presents Gould as a parodic, inverted Christ figure, savior son of the studio. Gould's opening line has a mock-biblical diction and concern that will persist: "When the gods would make us mad, they answer our prayers. . . . I'm in the midst of the wilderness."[129] Ironically, the wilderness is his own life, while the tone foreshadows temptation shortly to follow. Fox's role is in service to this "prince among men."[130] Many of the deific allusions are puns or ironies.

Gould thanks Fox for setting off his new job as producer—i.e. creator—"with a bang,"[131] obliquely suggesting the men's "Big Bang." Gould purports to possess unearthly power—"It's done"[132]—and wisdom to impart—"The two things which are always true."[133] The irony of this caricature is its appalling triviality: green-lighting a picture and the non-existence of net profits constitute the extent of Gould's godly beneficence and wisdom. Yet he recognizes the metaphor's applicability: "Hey, hey he sends the cross, he sends the strength to bear it."[134] The father figure to Gould's Christ is studio head Richard Ross[135] who wields absolute power, rules on matters of creation, and speaks, by phone, only with appointed son Gould. Ross can "fly," leaving without notice while others' fates dangle. He appears neither benevolent nor well-informed of the lives within his control. Fox is no more than a possible messenger to Ross, an idealized "Bringer of Good *News*..."[136] The pantheon of power-elite contains its own hierarchy of influence. And even Ross, by his sudden unexplained departure, must respond immediately to unknown priorities. Fox, as subordinate, acknowledges Gould with proper rude humor of camaraderie: "My job *is* kissing your ass."[137] His long-range goal seems attainment of Gould's level of authority, followed by extensive revenge: "But, but ... oh maan ... I'm gonna settle some fucken' scores."[138] However, he keeps aspirations in check, throughout act one pandering to Gould's vanity, frequently addressing him with conspicuously biblical diction. "Lord, I believe, aid thou my unbelief."[139] Note the inversion of trust and Christian necessity. When Gould informs Fox of their lunch date, the response is, "Thy will by done."[140] Between Gould and Fox such conversational heresy is self-conscious satire, an ongoing celebration of the collapse of traditional values, of the worship of Nothing.

When Gould is alone with Karen, his self-styled deification assumes new earnestness; like a good salesman, he adapts pitch to audience. In the woman's presence he stresses the responsibility and martyrdom of his position. "To *make* something, to *do* something, to be a *part* of something. Money, art, a chance to Play at the Big Table..."[141] In his attempted seduction, Gould addresses Karen much as Mike does Ford—directly, conspiratorially, unearthing her repressions, desires, and needs. "That's what makes life exciting, *addictive, you* know what I'm talking about, you want a *thrill* in your life?"[142] In his circular nihilism, he closely resembles Roma: "A tree fell in the forest, what did I accomplish? Yes. You *see*? There is a way things are."[143] Gould suggestively comments on Ross' power over him: "And he has a button on my console."[144] Gould must agonize over the decision of when and whether to "push the button," a situation again ironized yet made ominous by the Hollywood context. In whose hands does judgment await? Gould continues to Karen:

> Can we keep ourselves pure? I prayed to be pure. . . . I did, I said God give me the job as Head of Production. Give me a platform to be "good," and I'll be good. They gave me the job, I'm here one day and *look* at me: a Big Fat Whore.[145]

Gould is ambiguous, neither convincing nor *un*convincing in his confessions to Karen and his abrupt conversion. Determining his sincerity seems an impossible task since the man himself is clouded in confusion. The god he prayed to for his job is likely only Ross, although Karen touches him significantly.

Act two is Gould's mock-temptation. In the inverted reality of *Speed-the-Plow,* the seductions he must resist are love, belief, and forgiveness: "Down below the bridge, I'll tell you: written with such love . . . *Such* love . . . God. A thing to be thankful for. Such love."[146] Karen, as temptress, strikes where Gould is most vulnerable. Earlier, he acidly replies to a Fox insinuation: "Naaa. Nobody Loves Me. Nobody loves me for myself. Hey, Big Deal. . . ."[147] Note the men's tendency, especially Gould's, to speak in capitalized phrases, suggesting both self-assumed justification and the easy, transient banality of their profundity. Nearly every action, no matter how crass or venal, is rendered inalterable creed by capitalization: "Get The Asses In The Seats,"[148] says Gould, expounding criteria of a "good" film. Fox's "I Could Of Gone Across the Street"[149] interprets even desertion as dogma.

Karen's long, mystical speeches in act two recall John's meditations in *The Shawl.* She proselytizes, pleads, coaxes, demurs. Critics rightly center on Karen as a key to the play's mystery: "Her crafty innocence makes a nice contrast to the cynicism and incidental treachery and open greed of the men,"[150] notes one reviewer, and others similarly label her "a more consummate con artist than the two aces themselves"[151] and "an enigma within an enigma, in the manner of the Lindsay Crouse heroine in *House of Games.*"[152] Karen *is* reminiscent of Ford, particularly in her hesitant, theatrical shrugging off of naïveté: "I, I, I've been depraved, too, I've been frightened. . . . *I* know what it is to be bad, I've been bad. . . ."[153] Intentionally, she seems both hustler and victim. Director Gregory Mosher explains: "The audience is meant to go out asking one another: Is she an angel? Is she a whore?"[154] Certainly Karen would prefer the former association: "We needn't feel frightened. The wild animal dies with pride. He didn't make the world. God made the world. You say that you prayed to be pure. What if your prayers were answered? You asked me to come. Here I am."[155] Thus she concludes act two, which begins and ends, in the technique of the con artist, with her words. Her offer is to alleviate Gould's suffering of a decimated land with a deity of hope and omnipotence, a deity other than Ross. Ironically, in Gould's cosmology—founded in the pantheon of Hollywood—he *is* culpable for furthering the world's pain. Moreover, any attempt by Gould to film the radiation book would be futile; Fox points out that Gould's "name will be a *punchline* in this town,"[156] the film would probably never be made, and if so, in all likelihood would be a financial disaster. An incriminating subtext of *Speed-the-Plow* is that Fox and Gould are almost certainly right in their narrow perception of the "Movie Going Public."[157] Mamet, writes Frank Rich, "pitilessly implicates the society whose own fantasies about power and money keep the dream factory in business."[158]

Is Karen the angel she professes or, as Fox suggests, "What is she, a witch?"[159] His accusation that Gould is under a spell seems justifiable; Gould is quiet and dazed throughout the final act. To Fox, Gould has been emasculated: ". . . you're going to *run* all over everything, like something broke in the *shopping* bag, *you fool*—your fucken' sissy film—you squat to pee. You old *woman*. . ."[160] Such an attack is perhaps the most leveling, most crass and violent Fox can muster during a "tantrum that is equal parts rage, hurt, con-artist scam and genuine grief at a betrayal."[161] Gould's symbolic transformation to woman explains his vulnerability to Karen's manipulations; Mamet's ordinary male-female alignment of dominance and subservience is reversed. Karen's mistake is admitting the potency of sex in her hustle, sending Gould back to a world of men and movies—inversely, a comparable confession occurs from Mike in *House of Games*. Mel Gussow places Karen in the context of the author's women:

> As with other Mamet heriones (the few that there are), the character has an other-worldliness. In that sense, she is related to the protagonist of the movie *House of Games*, played by Lindsay Crouse, and to the character that Ms. Crouse portrayed in an earlier Mamet play, *The Shawl*. In both of those cases, a woman is drawn into a confidence game. With Madonna, it is the confidence game of Hollywood.[162]

Gussow's exchange of Madonna's name for Karen is telling, and the association with Ford goes beyond mere victimization by con artists; these women execute their own cons, adapting men's rules. For example, even a rhetorical gimmick like Gould's endless politeness is turned against him. "Thank you," he tells Karen. "No," she responds, "I thank *you*."[163] Karen is quite good at exploitation. Gould, by contrast, is, because of his job, as prone to conniving advances as a beautiful woman: "Everyone Is Trying To 'Promote' Me . . . Don't you *know* that? Don't you *care*? *Every move I make*, do you understand? Everyone *wants* something from me."[164] Karen is oddly both yielding and dominant; Brustein notes that Gould's "conversion to higher movie values occurs, in Chekhovian fashion, between the acts. . . ."[165] Presumably, Karen's best work happens off-stage in bed.

Moira Hodgson argues that Mamet's women, including Karen, "always seem to function more as plot elements, as sources of complication. . . ."[166] Such a comment seems odd considering the centrality of recent characters Miss A, Ford, and Karen, all of whom actively participate and are catalysts for thought and change. Karen is essential to *Speed-the-Plow*'s deeper concerns; she is no less a definite character— albeit refined, sifted, idealized—than the men. Walter Kerr's interpretation of Karen draws her into the Mametic realm of the play's psuedo-religious fascination:

> We're dealing with a woman to whom all words are awesome. In a way, the play is *about* self-consciousness in the presence of language. . . . Anyway, she is a priestess of the cult up there, and well able to wreak her own private magic on the man pursuing her.[167]

Nearly as essential to the con artist as psychological intuition is mystical perception—Karen possesses both. She is as ready a candidate as Ford for an assault on the citadel of gender exploitation. John Simon discusses *Speed-the-Plow* in terms of such linguistic efficacy. Mamet's plays, he says, "show how power translates itself into language and how language, in turn, translates into power. . . . It is more than a metaphor yet not quite a causal relationship, which gives a Mamet play its dreamlike quality."[168] In *Speed-the-Plow* the dominance of language is apparent, from the playful, paranoid brutality of the men to Karen's rhythmic, soporific earnestness.

Rich credits Mamet as being a superior storyteller to "most people working in the movies, and his new play is full of the unexpected twists that have distinguished *Glengarry Glen Ross* and *House of Games* from much of his earlier work."[169] He seems to attribute Mamet's plotting skills to Hollywood involvement. However, *Speed-the-Plow* is a deceptively simple story, even when considered a "morality play with huge themes," its characters "both normal and mythic."[170] Karen's manipulation of Gould's basic human impulse toward union shows her as guilty as the men in establishing "God Himself [as] just another exploitable concept — or con — in the greedy machinations of American commerce...."[171] This is appropriate for a play which joyfully organizes its own temporal hierarchy. Again, Mamet implicates audience in its support of base entertainment — the Fox-Gould repartee itself offering a prime example? — over significance. If Hollywood is the dream factory of America, how poor those dreams are. Another irony is that *The Bridge,* the radiation study both scorned and admired in the play, is actually a short story by Mamet, published in *Granta.* Mamet mocks his own seriousness, and whether or not *The Bridge* is intended as meaningful, it is drudgery compared to the hilarious vulgarity of Gould and Fox. Finally, might art and entertainment hold equally selfish motives? "One may seem pecuniary, the other profound. In the scheme of things, does that make any difference?"[172]

Mamet's short story isn't the only off-stage cleverness surrounding *Speed-the-Plow.* Much attention was given to the casting of Madonna as Karen, and as Gussow's synonymous usage of names suggests, the singer brought potent, conflicting preconceptions of virgin/whore/saint to the role. Brustein comments on a Pirandellian effect, with "one of the play's themes — the vulnerability of art to commercial manipulation — being realized behind the scenes."[173] Other critics reported that the opening night audience "seems charged. Has the audience come to see Mamet or Madonna, or both?"[174]; "flashbulbs during the show were almost as profuse as the applause at the end."[175] How typical it is of Mamet to assure the success of his first major play since *Glengarry Glen Ross* in such a way as to comment ironically on the play itself, indicting audience by its very appreciation.

There is no doubt Gould, like the audience, is strongly affected by Madonna/Karen. He stumbles through act three confused, monosyllabic, entranced. He reads from *The Bridge* as if from scripture:

> "'Is it true,' she asked, 'that we are always in the same state of growth, the same state of decay as the world in which we live? If it is true is it not true that the world is then a dream, and delusion?' All this being

true, then what remained to him was this: Nothing." *(Pause.)* "Nothing but God."[176]

Karen's words are indistinguishable from the text; for Gould to accept responsibility for the world he endorses is to take from him his beliefs and his nihilistic power, to leave him dazed and as indecisive as a child. Paradoxically, "truth" brings delusion. "Like many a cheap-jack hustler, he momentarily finds religion. But his faith in the book, and the woman who made him believe in it, seems to be still more illusions to be stripped away."[177] Enlightenment, moreover, is no more compassionate than earlier greed. "You ruined my life,"[178] Fox tells him simply and pathetically. Gould replies: "Be that as it may.... Now, I have a meeting."[179] The conversation continues, Fox unconsciously punning on the uncommerciality of Gould's new enterprise, Gould cold and dismissive:

> FOX: Would you tell me why?
> GOULD: I told you why. Because I've found something that's right.
> FOX: I can't buy that.
> GOULD: Then "why" is because I say so.
> FOX: And eleven years down the drain.[180]

Gould forsakes male friendship for a vision of mystery and meaning perceived in the body and voice of a seductive young woman. Fox warns, cojoles, threatens, commiserates, and echoes Gould's own words: "She *wants* something from you. You're nothing to her but what you can *do* for her."[181] Reunited with Fox, Gould again waivers, and Karen seems to lose much of her magic in the "morning after" setting of act three. Small slip-ups disclose her, like the past tense in her reference to what "was a temporary job"[182]; in the context of the office, her motivations seem increasingly suspect. Fox spits at her, "you and Bob, you became 'Lovers,'"[183] the latter term ironized by capitalization, trivialized by quotation marks. On short notice, Fox must recover his advantage, and through language *casts* language—specifically Karen's speciousness—into a slippery and deceiving role. "It's only words, unless they're true,"[184] he offers with chilling ambiguity. He continues to dismantle the previous night: "And this is serious. Forgive me if my words seem to belie that, but I'm doing all I can, 'cause I love this guy too."[185] Clearly Fox and Karen contend for Gould's soul—manifested as his authority to approve a project—and Fox's language initially places

Charlie Fox (Ron Silver) interjects himself between Karen (Madonna) and Bobby Gould (Joe Mantegna) in *Speed-the-Plow*. **Photo by Brigitte Lacombe.**

him at a disadvantage. Fox and Gould, "masters of movie business cant,"[186] usually share a discourse of abuse, designed for humiliation, irony, and dissembling hatred. Fox's initial outburst of rage is followed by an apology of having been frightened, not only recalling Karen's earlier sermons against fear, but showing his gradual realization of the situation; when he resorts to his forte, cynical interrogation, Karen's "naïveté" cannot withstand it. In other words, by coaxing Gould back into the male rhetoric of happy corruption, Fox wins back both man and movie deal. Gould controls the first act and Karen the second, but Fox dominates the play's finale.

Fox's repetitive language, often in threes, suggests at times a deceptive shielding, at other times almost mystical evocation: "Ross, Ross, Ross isn't going to fuck me out of this...?"[187] he chants in act one. Later, his repetitiveness seems a ritual denunciation of Karen and her power. After identifying her as witch, he repeats: "And my, and my, and *my* chances with it..."[188]; then to Gould as if casting out demons, "*Fuck* you ... *Fuck* you ... *Fuck* you. Get up."[189] In effect, Fox assumes a priestly responsibility. The tripling of phrases resonates with vague religious significance, perhaps the trinity of Ross, Gould, and himself he attempts to restore. *The Bridge*'s query "How are things

made round?"[190] represents Karen's effort to smooth angles of authority. Fox articulates his support of triangle over circle: "'That silver is
more powerful than gold; and the circle than the square or the
triangle.' . . . I wouldn't believe this shit if it was *true*. . ."[191] Earlier,
Gould tells Fox, *"You Brought Me Gold,"*[192] whereas silver is traditionally used to ward off evil. During his struggle with Karen, Fox
reminds her, ". . . honey, you're at the Big Table, and, I'm done, then
*Bob,* the Head of Production, is going to say what's what."[193] Fox's conception of such a table is not the round construction Karen would
prefer, but a polygon with a clear hierarchy. Fox, one could say, knows
"angles," while Karen is the "rounded" female critics have sought in
Mamet.

Brustein contends that *Speed-the-Plow* "establishes friendship
between males and personal loyalty among the corrupted as virtually
the last remaining values in an increasingly hypocritical and decaying
society."[194] This is no new idea to Mamet and even brings a kind of
hopefulness to the play's ending. At least a last value *is* preserved;
Gould escapes the female, the witch / angel / priestess enigma. Yet the
play sends a bleak, apocalyptic message, signaling both the world's end
and the impossibility not only of heterogeneous love but of compassion, of union beyond vapid pursuits of commerce over art.

> Well, Bob, you're human. You think I don't know. I know. We wish
> people would like us, huh? To Share Our Burdens. But it's not to
> be. . . . And what *if* this fucken' "grace" exists? It's not for you. You
> know that, Bob. You know that. You have a different thing.[195]

Fox "saves" Gould and forgives him his transgression. The Hollywood
pantheon is re-established, reordered with Fox in a surer position. The
messenger has saved the messiah. Gould turns to a language of the
fallen — "I wanted to do Good . . . But I became foolish"[196] — but his
friend redirects him:

> FOX: What are we put on earth to do?
> GOULD: We're here to make a movie.
> FOX: Whose name goes above the title?
> GOULD: Fox and Gould.
> FOX: Then how bad can life be?[197]

A male order is restored, Fox assumes top credit, and a vacuous production machine continues.

Gould's "Oh, god, now I'm lost,"[198] in response to Karen's exposed betrayal, is an earnest and primal cry of the forsaken. One can only speculate how quickly and completely he will recover his greedy energy, although with Fox's encouragement he may soon return in full. Like other Mamet protagonists, Gould and Fox show courage by their mere dedication to survival; they are fueled by linguistic power and bitter conceits. In *Speed-the-Plow*, this vision seems at its bleakest. The men are intelligent, fully self-conscious, and highly successful; they belong to a class Mamet characters frequently rage against. Who is culpable? The play's last line — "Then how bad can life be?"[199] — is an unrivaled celebration of darkness. Only a constant, consummate verbal assault, like Fox's, may keep the abyss disguised. If such is a predominantly "male" position — difficult to dispute in light of the Karen-Fox battle — then *Speed-the-Plow* is certainly a step back, in terms of hopefulness, from *The Shawl*'s attempted union or even *House of Games'* therapeutic exorcism of the male. In *Speed-the-Plow* Woman is vanquished; con men win the world without compromise or mitigation.

Gussow notes that Mamet has written "about other media, namely theater and radio. In both cases, his attitude was one of great affection."[200] *Speed-the-Plow* thus seems opposed to *A Life in the Theatre* and *The Water Engine;* at best, the presentation of Hollywood is ambiguous, resigned to destruction, but hardly celebratory for an audience. Yet, as usual, Mamet enjoys his hustlers, their vitality and durability. Finally, Fox is presented as vastly more attractive than Karen and her self-serving pretense. This may be yet another manner in which audience is implicated; like the creator, we prefer hustler to prophet, embrace corruption over banal and hypocritical virtue. How much *Speed-the-Plow* may be taken as serious criticism of Hollywood is hard to say, as is Mamet's place in a system he has increasingly served. Henry calls Mamet a "superb entertainer"[201] — an epithet rendered suspect by *Speed-the-Plow*'s ambivalence toward art and entertainment — then attempts to unravel the inherent contradictions of writing such a play: "it is hard to say whether *Speed-the-Plow* is an outcry against Hollywood or a cynical apologia from a man who, in real life, is finishing one Hollywood film and about to start another."[202] Rich credits Mamet with additional cleverness — creating "riveting theater" that with its minimal cast and set would "probably make terrible cinema."[203] In other words, although Mamet's recent efforts have been primarily cinematic — the mastering of image and action — he reminds us that he remains our premiere language playwright. As expected, he's playing games; Hollywood superficiality is juxtaposed against modern apathy and societal collapse, and the result is entertaining yet provocative drama. As to Hollywood, Mamet presents himself as careless, sly, and as satisfied as Fox: "It's the old Jewish joy of the deal. . . . Besides, the people in Hollywood are so funny. It's a place full of gamblers, hucksters, and con artists, including me. We're all rug merchants."[204]

# CHAPTER III

# *Things Change*
## Finding a Family

*Things Change,* released in 1988, is a departure from the darkness of *House of Games* the previous year. Mamet describes his second film as director as a "fable that's a lot gentler than my other work."[1] David Ansen agrees the movie "unfolds with the pixilated simplicity of a fable," but finds *Things Change* a logical progression from Mamet's premiere in its joy of rediscovered storytelling, "the old-fashioned art of spinning and twisting a tale. These are funhouse movies, planted with narrative trapdoors."[2] Ansen's comparison agrees with Mamet's own perception of himself as filmmaker: "I'm having a great time. . . . It's like creating 10-second plays. Basically what it all comes down to is storytelling."[3] The author's comments tend to highlight the playfulness of directing—"You get to play dollhouse every day"[4]—a job which includes not only tale-spinning but an enjoyed authority. Directing is "more fun than writing plays,"[5] although he retains the comparison.

Such light-hearted job descriptions are partly exuberance, partly coyness, complementing a paradoxical role of blue-collar artist, erudite, confident, and simply direct. Mantegna likens Mamet to "being a general of an army. So when you've got a guy with that much confidence, it's a natural kind of job."[6] Studio press releases for *Things Change* stress the relaxed, encouraging environment of a Mamet set, the director "constantly circulating, cigar in hand, talking with the actors, getting opinions from the crew, joking with the extras. . . ."[7] Like *House of Games, Things Change* is an ensemble effort, stocked with many of Mamet's long-time friends and troupe. For example, a flurry of heavy betting in a casino scene is undertaken not by actors, admits Mamet, but "guys from my poker game in Vermont."[8] Other cameos

Jerry (Joe Mantegna) begins to appreciate the simple wisdom of Gino (Don Ameche) in *Things Change.*

include Mamet's agent and his family babysitter. The publicity releases report that the film's core of actors "lovingly refer to themselves as 'The Mamet Family.'"[9] Mantegna sees the group as an extension of stage practices, when he "used to work in a theater with a theater company. You build up a working relationship and can look at each other and say things and understand."[10] The film set develops an ease and subtlety analogous not only to stagecraft, but reminiscent of hustling criminals' communication and skill. The concept of the Mamet family is eerily appropriate for *Things Change,* a film concerning the Mafia. Mamet is clearly the "Don" of his family, and the director's word, despite all equanimity on the set, is final. A powerful man can afford to be generous. For Daily, the role is a culmination of Mamet's career-long thrust for success: "A movie director is larger than life, the creator of a fictitious universe . . . minions hanging on his every decision. He is in control."[11] Mamet, the critic adds, "is clearly a man who relishes his celebrity."[12]

In *House of Games,* the intricacies of the con game become, finally, inextricable from activities behind the camera. The film's cogency and success rest on a beautiful, organic unity of style and substance, text and subtext, with Mamet's own comments demanding the director-con artist comparison. *Things Change,* while different in tone, offers in its family concerns a similarly striking unity. In creating a film about honor, friendship, keeping one's word, and the longing for tradition and tested values—a film, in short, about locating a family for oneself—Mamet works with his friends. Labeling Mamet as Don is more than amusing, it is as crucial as the director-hustler analogy in *House of Games* to understanding the film's themes and purpose. As usual, the world depicted is predominantly male and operates outside the law. Whereas the confidence trade is here still an identifiable subculture, the Mafia represents a different sort of crook, existing openly, not below but *beyond* prescribed law, yet politically and socially integrated. Both types, mobster and con man, share a defining group identity; perhaps together they roughly exemplify society's ambivalent treatment of the artist, who is socially and morally castigated (con man), yet held above, apart, in awe for his individual authority and refutation of tribal law (mobster).

Mamet's fascination with criminality continues in *Things Change* as a study of its organizations. Mamet explains his, and the American public's, insatiable curiosity:

> There's a fascination with the Mafia. That's why the *Godfather* movies were so popular. We assume that it's a society that functions by its own rules; that it has its own sanctions and rewards. And we find that very satisfying. Which is why Hollywood usually depicts the mob as a benign organization . . . certainly no less so than the God of the Old Testament.[13]

The pantheon suggested in *Things Change* is surer of its power and enforcement than *Speed-the-Plow*'s hierarchy. The Cosa Nostra is old, quiet in an authority backed always with potential for devastating violence. In Chicago, Mr. Green's peaceful, ornate, palatial home, protected by gates and muscled guards, is in contrast to the chaotic bustle and noise of the surrounding city. Don Vincent's mansion/fortress nestles undisturbed amid alpine spendour. *Things Change* is in one respect a movie about the American Dream, about Old and New Worlds. The imperturbable calm and dominance of the Mafia represent, perhaps, the only means of realizing that dream: authority, brutality, exploitation, and a far-reaching network—a family—of cooperative support.

Part of the cinema–Mafia paradigm is realized in the authority of the director-Don; at the same time, Mamet has always shown great interest in fraternal associations. "Legacy is one of Mamet's persistent themes. In his films he writes about surrogate families: con men, salesmen, actors. His characters search . . . for a sense of tradition that spans the generations."[14] Obviously he found such a bond and continuity in theatre and brought these relations with him into film. Such loyalty is a common element in the American Mafia myth. Don Vincent explains: "It's good to know one's family. . . . A good man prides himself on knowing those who are connected to him."[15] As the menace in his words suggests, those *not* of the family, those without clear affiliation, are thereby threats, enemies until shown as otherwise. Such a system of loyalties, paranoid but pragmatic, is constructed to endure. Once established as "friend"—a frequent euphemism in *Things Change*—one is treated with reverence and privileges of royalty. Mamet knows his subject. What greater gift to grant loyalty, in a cinematic equivalent, than film stardom? He may reward fealty with prestige.

As discussed earlier, *Things Change* features many Mamet regulars—Nussbaum, Ricky Jay, W. H. Macy . . . —and one of the leads is again played by Mantegna, Mamet's inimitable voice. The Mantegna-Mamet relationship is the best example of Mamet family loyalty. "Against studio protest," reports Glenn Lovell, "Mamet has continued to push Mantegna."[16] Mamet is a huge fan of his friend and co-conspirator: the actor "has fantastic depth. If you look at the great leading men—Henry Fonda, Jimmy Stewart, Cary Grant. . . . You feel that there's nothing in the world that would induce them to do anything that's false, sentimental or manipulative. Joey has that quality."[17] Mantegna's earnestness, his ability to extract trust from an audience, makes him ideal for Mametic salesmen and con artists. His appearance of integrity is subversive. Daily contends Mantegna is "perfect for Mamet's work. He is the quintessential Mamet actor, bringing a certain veracity to the blue-collar characters he plays."[18] In turn, Mantegna is highly supportive of his patron: "He's so concise, so precise. Ninety percent of what's up there is there to begin with. He's a natural as a filmmaker."[19] The actor recalls an evening backstage after a performance of *Glengarry Glen Ross;* Mamet glumly informed Mantegna he couldn't guarantee the lead in a film version of the play due to contractual restraints. "Then he dropped two scripts on my dressing room table. They were *House of Games* and *Things Change.* You can't ask for greater frankness and loyalty than that."[20] Mantegna, brightest and best of Mamet's troupe, is thus granted its greatest boon: stardom.

Mantegna has his own opinions on Mamet's identification with hustlers and the appreciation they share of a crook's brand of dishonesty. "It's a little bit of the honor-among-thieves. In a way, you'd rather be taken to the cleaners by the kinds of guys in *Glengarry* than by, let's say, a politician or somebody that's *supposed* to be doing good. . . ."[21] The Mafia, unacknowledged royalty of America, is arguably more honorable—in its traditions, rituals, family base, and unapologizing severity—than an elected and secretly depraved government. Daily notes that Mamet not only writes of criminals with admiration, but resembles them in personality. "They are all characters with tremendous confidence in their abilities, performers who depend on an audience for their success."[22] While the Mafia is ostensibly covert, and therefore not as dependent upon audience as the hustler, still the mobster needs participation of family and servants for, like royalty, ritual verification. The mobster of film, in any case, is a curious mixture of public and private.[23]

Mamet views the director as a jack-of-all-trades; or, perhaps, as a Renaissance man: "You have to be a little bit of a generalist, I think, to direct a movie. You have to know a very weensy bit about a lot of things: a little bit about acting, a little bit about rhythm. . . ."[24] Still, a director must surround himself with specialists and be a mediator and psychologist. Mutual loyalty and tested rapport are efficient, reliable methods of assuring necessary service. "He has a very good instinct, and he's very good with people,"[25] says Mamet's producer, Mike Hausman. Mantegna speaks of a sort of general courage Mamet possesses to undertake the many facets of filmmaking: "He's of the same ilk of the Hemingways and those kinds of guys that were complete kinds of men. . . . He's always had an incredible confidence in what he set out to do."[26]

Mantegna's "complete man" points to another time, before specialization limited skills. The comparison is simple: the director, like mob boss, salesman, or hustler, is a natural leader of men, with the perquisites of sureness, acuity, and verbal facility—the components of influence. The leader, meanwhile, remains most accomplished of his players: "I am a showman," concedes Mamet. "I'm a peddler too. . . . I love the process."[27]

*Things Change,* though co-written by Shel Silverstein, is pure Mamet. The story's superficial gentleness is a ruse. Kehr argues that "Mamet and Silverstein summon up the obvious only to undermine it, working almost exclusively on the delicate fringes of the frayed material."[28] He notes the film's stylistic similarity to *House of Games:*

> Mamet retains his own serene distance from the material, avoiding any
> overt expression of emotion. The actors once again speak in slow, precise
> monotones (though Ameche, a wily old pro, occasionally circumvents
> his director to slip in a direct, sentimental appeal to the audience), and
> the images once again have a highly formal, pared-down quality.[29]

The accusation of Don Ameche's subversion is especially interesting;
the already subverted, by Mamet, is thus returned to approximately
traditional sentimentality, creating a kind of self-referential surreality.
Ameche is not ordinarily of the Mamet family, and outsider status
would account for any deviant agenda. Ansen elaborates the effect of
*Things Change*'s self-consciousness: "Mamet's preference for spare,
almost ritualistic dialogue and stiff, rather theatrical staging heightens
the movie's fablelike nature."[30] The film's Mafia bosses often speak in
complete sentences, as if following ingrained rules of protocol; in contrast, Jerry stammers uncertainly. That he frequently attempts, and
fails, to appropriate a "ritualistic" speech exposes his desire for family
integration. Travers places *Things Change* in a definite Mametic context: "...the characters ... move across the venal, violent landscape
Mamet knows best.... Some things don't change: Mamet is without
peer at harvesting wit from a wicked world."[31] *Things Change* unques-
tionably contains a subversive intent, no less intricate and elusive than
that in *House of Games*. Pauline Kael amplifies some of Kehr's comments while trying to pinpoint the method and purpose of the director's distinctively flat style:

> Mamet cons the audience. He brings it into a hip complicity with him.
> He gives people the impression that in making them wise to the actors'
> games he's making them wise to how the world works — that he's letting
> them in on life's dirty secrets. And flatness of performance seems to be
> part of the point. Mamet's minimalism suggests a knowingness, disdain
> for elaboration or development.... People can feel one up on the
> action....[32]

Kael's comments are insightful, if harsh. As in much of Mamet's best
work, the audience's relationship with art — perhaps the play or film
itself — implies a greater, existential dynamic concerning the nature of
the world. One soon anticipates the author's cleverness, his convolutions. In the case of *Things Change*, says Kael, one waits "for the plot
to be more clever than it is.... Mamet sets up a story with a buried
theme: the yearning for a day when men kept their word."[33] Although

she inexplicably finds this theme unfulfilled, Kael points out a recognized concern: a basically simple, essential story of honor in a society which inhibits and even punishes such behavior, and the difficulty, significance, and inherent deceptiveness of keeping one's word.

*Things Change* begins focused on a delapidated photo album, its leather worn by decades. As the main title progresses, a hand removes a silver coin from the album cover and turns pages. Inside the book are yellowed, rolled photos — family, children, a boat — representing generations and tradition. The movie partly concerns reunion with old ideals and, thus, concerns memory and dreams. The boat has an increasing, clarifying significance as the plot unfolds. A melodic tune from an older world is played on acoustic guitar, mandolin, violin, and accordian. The picture fades to black, which becomes the jacket of a man playing a mandolin in a music shop. The instrument will not tune; he trades it for another. Past him, motionless at the window, stand two men in overcoats. They are Frankie and Silver, intruding Mafia muscle. The sequence is graceful, stylish, and as Kauffmann suggests, makes one "hungry for what's to come."[34] The men recognize Gino outside and follow him; the shop's music gives way to a train's metallic screech. Succinctly, the film's key themes are introduced: the importance of a dream-life and the tranquility of persisting wishes, nostalgia for lost friends and family, contrast between Old World and New, between artistic sensibility and harsh "business" interests, the soothing of the private, the rushing disharmony of the city.

Gino's meeting at Mr. Green's mansion begins to elaborate these concerns. The old Sicilian sits in his clean but worn suit, his face sad and thoughtful, his back straight. His shoebox, symbolizing values of economy, service, and skill, is beside him. Silver and Green enter; their names warn of profit and greed. *"They step forward. Green goes and sits down on the couch. Silver steps forward and stands behind Green at the back of the couch."*[35] Such a theatrical entrance suggests ceremonial movements of royalty and its attendants. The chamber is silent, disturbed by neither Old World music nor urban noise. Nussbaum, in a menacing portrayal, resides as Green. At the proper time Silver begins to speak, calmly, repetitively, in methodic, complete sentences, a manner that throughout the film represents certainty, authority, and ritual, often before a stranger.

Two weeks ago a man named Aaronberg was shot to death, at the corner of Racine and Belden — this is public knowledge. Two people saw the

crime, and this was also in the papers. This is public knowledge. What
I'm going to tell you now is not public knowledge. Do you understand?[36]

Gino lowers his head and nods. What he knows, perhaps, is not the
meaning of the words as much as the sense and intention of their tone,
a hierarchy of success and wealth in which he occupies the lower end,
or perhaps a first inkling of "justice" and "friendship" as business terms,
financially negotiable. Silver—i.e. money—keeps talking: "To prevent
a grave injustice from being done. To protect an innocent man . . . .
someone must confess to a crime. . . "[37] Silver speaks with a practiced
monotone easily mistaken for earnestness; he displays no knowledge of
the corrupt ironies his clichés rest upon, that justice is served by pur-
chasing a murderer. They extend the offer as a business proposition—
scapegoat assumption of guilt for the price of Gino's dream:

> MR. GREEN (shrugs): You could say you were in a prison now. (He nods
> sympathetically.) In three years . . . You must have a dream . . . do
> you have a dream?
>
> . . .
>
> GINO: A fishing boat.
> MR. GREEN: Your dream is a fishing boat.
> GINO: In Sicily.
> MR. GREEN: In three years, you could have that fishing boat. You could
> earn yourself that boat. If you stay in your shoe store, what will you
> have in three years?[38]

Through the guise of shared knowledge and integration into a
group, the mobsters intimidate Gino with a vicious exploitation of his
private dream-life. The thing which remains unspoken throughout the
film, although apparently known by everyone, is that Gino, quite an
old man, will never survive a prison sentence. Green's coercion is
therefore doubly insidious. Gino will get nothing in return for his life
beyond preservation of the *dream* of a fishing boat, with its values of
solitude, relaxation, rest, union with nature, and return to the old
land. Writes Mamet: "Thorstein Veblen informed us that status (and,
thus, domination) was achieved not through direct display of wealth,
but through display of that commodity priceless beyond wealth, i.e.
time—through display of leisure."[39] It is this wealth of leisure for which
Gino dreams, yet he is asked to trade the time that is irreplaceable to
him. Further, Green invokes the "earning" of one's desired goal, with
the irony that the signing of a false document which admits murder will

suffice where a lifetime of integrity and work have failed. *Things Change* is another Mametic study of the poverty of the American success myth, where criminals prosper and law-abiding immigrants labor as peasants.

When Gino—who, without surname, must suffer as servant—denies their request, he is immediately relegated to a menial social position. In one deflating mimicry Green reduces Gino to both shoeshine "boy" and laughable foreigner: "Shine 'em uppa, Joe. . . "[40] Gino, confused, moves to light Miss Bates' cigarette; in the screenplay she *"notices his dirty hands and draws back."*[41] In the film, she doesn't get that close, seeming to assume the dirtiness of his type. As in *House of Games,* the lighting of the cigarette is sexual in connotation, and Miss Bates' hurtful rebuke denotes her loyalty; she takes a match off her master's desk. Green continues his abuse, feigning offense at Gino's refusal of "friendship": "Tell 'em I need a guy, I need a friend. . . And call Plesetska in the twenty-eighth district. . . . Let's go, let's go, boy. We wanna get you back to your shoeshine stand . . . (*Gino kneels down and opens his box*)."[42] Gino will be returned, ostracized, and again made to rely on the austere values of shoeshine tools he refused to surrender. He is excluded from a subsequent flurry of activity, spheres of influence including the police. Only after Gino bows, acknowledging his subservience, does Green promptly leave the room.

Muttering ostensibly to himself, his back to Gino, Green unleashes a tirade of bigotry and hatred, condemning Gino's many supposed offenses:

> A man comes into my house. What does he want? I tell him, whatever you want. Says buy me a boat. Fine, I'll buy him a pushcart. I'll buy him an organ and a monkey and he can put a bandanna on his head. Son of a bitch immigrant said he wanted a boat. I'll give him a boat.[43]

Why Gino succumbs to such ethnic slurs and stereotypes is unclear, but the main cause seems the effective totality of the group's alienation techniques combined with any imagined violation of honor or protocol. The old man surely desires integration into such apparent heights of influence and familial community, however dubious, and this weakens his unarticulated resistance. And, of course, the problem of Gino's boat remains; only by desultorily pursuing the dream's possible fulfillment may he preserve the integrity of his desire for return and liberation. The lives of both Gino and Jerry, writes Richard Corliss, have been studies in "obsequiousness, shining the shoes and licking the boots of the powerful."[44] "Don" Ameche says of his character: "He is a man who has never used anyone in his life. He is a man of total honor and total honesty."[45] He is, in essence, the antithesis of Green, which makes their partnership—the signed confession, the held gun, the toast—only more regretful. Once Gino accepts, Green immediately reverts from bigoted expletives to rhythmic cadences of bestowal. He gives Gino a coin from their shared Sicilian past, an insincerity which will ironically, ultimately, be Gino's salvation. For now, however, Green controls; the script addresses him for the first time as "The Don,"[46] identifying him as both criminal and family lord. "To my new friend,"[47] he toasts, employing the film's incriminating euphemism.

Within the same labyrinthine corridors Jerry is introduced. The appearance of Mantegna brings Mametic associations of hustler, street rhetorician, and confidence craftsman. In *Things Change,* such expectations are repeatedly subverted, often for comic effect. Jerry is an inferior mobster on probation, reduced to a woman's position of wearing an apron and washing dishes while other men collect pay envelopes. As in *The Untouchables,* Mamet has his hoods use a baseball analogy to emphasize failure to the group:

> FRANKIE: We got a . . . what is this . . . Jerry something or other working here? . . . I thought we sent him down to the farm team. . .
> RAMONE: Why was that Frank?
> FRANKIE: It seems he can't follow orders. . .!
> *Laughter from the group. They look at Jerry.*
> RAMONE: Can't follow orders? What, is the guy a team player or what?
> FRANKIE: No, it would seem not.[48]

Jerry's dilemma is comparable to Gino's in that both desire but lack a nurturing family; both are ridiculed and reduced—to boy, to woman—due to reluctance to follow group mandates. "No pay, no pals, no prospects,"[49] a faceless flunky says of Jerry. Advancement is based on obedience, a submission of individual will; otherwise, all privileges are withheld—payment, male companionship, hope for the future. Frankie asks: "What does a guy get who can't toe the line?" The answer, in unison: "Probation."[50] Probation in this context is not an intermediate period between imprisonment and freedom, but rather a sort of purgatory threatening permanent displacement from the family, used to extort continual proper service. Ironically, throughout the film mob henchmen frequently gather, eat, and gossip in kitchen areas, implying their low though prideful position in family structures. They are only muscle, guards and messengers and bullies, but at least they belong.

Appropriately, Frankie assigns Jerry the task of watching Gino. "Hey Cinderella . . . comeere. . . "⁵¹ he orders, anticipating Jerry's fairy tale adventure and ensuing transformation. Jerry, in response, removes his apron. The three-day length of the assignment alludes to biblical rebirth. Gino and Jerry leave together. *"The bodyguards close the gate and go back into the house."*⁵² An ultimate and worst consequence is suggested: in a lawless world of Mafia ritual and service, to be locked *out,* without contacts or connections, in rootless isolation. Jerry, says Mantegna, "is a person who is not quite sure where he fits in. He is looking and thinks he knows what he is looking for but he really doesn't."⁵³

Jerry and Gino's first scene is set in the dim confinement of an unadorned hotel room. The theme of performance, so common in Mamet, is present in Jerry's feeding Gino details of his confession; Gino is a quick, adroit study of his role as criminal. Jerry is an efficient line coach:

> JERRY: Yeah, don't get it too pat, three or four. . .
> GINO: Three or four times I shot him. That son of a bitch.⁵⁴

Soon bored by this routine, Jerry decides to exercise his control of their situation by granting Gino three days of enjoyment before prison. Ironically, Jerry's act of authority renders him Gino's servant. This is typical of the younger man's ineffectiveness and the reversals his actions cause. Attempting the idiom and manner of his group, he sets in motion processes and reactions he can neither anticipate nor control. He exemplifies what Bigsby finds in Mamet, "a life performed with ever-decreasing confidence and competence."⁵⁵ Problems are initiated by Jerry's ignoring of the team priority: "They? There *is* no 'they.' *I* am they. What do you want to do?"⁵⁶

The two men step off a plane into the sunshine of Lake Tahoe. *"They breathe in the air."*⁵⁷ Clearly this natural, nutritive beauty is in contrast to the city's congestion and dim rooms. However, the private jets, bodyguards, and exclusive Galaxy Hotel show a nature bought and co-opted by the power elite. Jerry continues as servant—"Here to make you happy. Anything to please, that's me"⁵⁸—then recovers a tough façade: "And when I say it, out here, *do* it. . . . I *am* the boss. You keep that clear, we're going to get along fine."⁵⁹ If Jerry believes "out here" to be beyond family constraint, he is immediately shown his error by the appearance of mob driver Billy Drake and an ironically white stretch limousine. Drake again introduces the subject of service and punishment, substituting a metaphor of schoolboy for minor league player: "I heard you had to Stay After School. You couldn't obey *orders*."[60] Jerry shows himself to be an atypical, one could say inferior, Mamet protagonist: he is habitually awkward in speech and incompetent as a language hustler. Here he is mastered by a mere chauffeur, salvaging the conversation only by casting Gino as enigmatic Mafia head, a variation of the old man's assigned role. "Who *is* it. . . ?" Drake asks nervously. "If you *don't* know, then you *shouldn't* know,"[61] Jerry replies, cloaking himself in the murky knowledge of a true insider. He assumes a role for himself that reflects his desire: to be a trusted and unquestioned second man to a family leader. Once Jerry has initiated his fabrication, he relishes its layers of privileged mystery: "Babe, this is the guy, *behind* the guy, *behind* the guy . . . But what I got to *tell* you, is, I cannot *talk* about it."[62] Jerry is most fluent when perpetuating his troubles.

Gino is silent throughout the encounter with Drake. Like Jerry, he is not an aggressive linguist; as a foreigner he seems to have difficulty expressing himself. *Things Change* develops the idea of an *other* language, obscured and partly forgotten, which speaks truest of old things; it is this second tongue, of the Old Country, in which Gino is fluent. His English is idiosyncratic, marked by a heavy accent, yet with a kind of austere dignity. But Gino is most effective when communicating only with his forlorn eyes. Denby elaborates:

> In *Things Change*, Gino's uniform is silence, which is perceived by the hoods as the reticence of power. . . . In a formal, impenetrable society, a man who says nothing can never be found out. Gino *looks* dignified—he has a thick Sicilian mustache, he stands still, and he's too sad to smile.[63]

Gino plays his unanticipated role naturally and well; better, certainly, than Jerry his. In the back of the limousine, he calmly eats a grape from his sack, perhaps foreshadowing the "Roman" extravagance soon to follow. Much of the film's humor, notes Kehr, "resides in Gino's perfect, gentle equanimity. His abrupt shift in fortune seems neither to surprise nor intimidate him."[64] Such underplaying is also key to a convincing portrayal as crime boss.

The old man's calm continues during his ascendency to the Criterion floor of the Galaxy. "Please call upstairs," the manager informs an assistant, "and tell them our friends are coming."⁶⁵ Such figures of power as the men represent are naturally assumed as friends. The scene that follows is a satiric reenactment of the Old World's discovery of an American Dream of opulence, excess, and service. The sexual innuendo of the names — Gino as "Mr. Johnson," their twenty-four hour butler "Randy" — sets the tone. The men are led into *a magnificently appointed, huge duplex hotel suite.*⁶⁶ *"Stai calmo, lo paccio io,"* Jerry advises, and Gino responds, *"Come vuole lei."*⁶⁷ These travelers in an unfamiliar land revert to their old language; as Jerry struggles to maintain a semblance of control, the two men share the adventure. While Randy lists the hotel's services, Gino searches rooms, a mock-explorer on *"his voyage of discovery."*⁶⁸

Randy informs the men their "money is no good in this hotel" and *"bows himself out."*⁶⁹ The men's reaction to their altered circumstances is typical of the film; they don't exchange even a single word, merely *"look at each other."*⁷⁰ The most significant communication in *Things Change* is nonverbal — gesture, expression, or ambiguous silence. The screenplay often stipulates a particular look or motion in terms of unspoken dialogue. In a situation where the main player doesn't know his part, the most effective improvisation may be a subtle expression. Mamet and Silverstein, continues Denby, "amuse themselves with the grave ceremonies of Mafia style — the elaborate protocol, the codes and traditions enveloped in silence."⁷¹ Gino's reticence takes him far, especially among those serving him. Kehr suggests the film's unspoken lines are the crux of its humor: "The gags in *Things Change* lie in what isn't said (the punchlines are left for the audience to supply) and in what doesn't happen . . . it asks the audience to participate in its creation. . . ."⁷² As in *House of Games,* the audience is given an active role. Within Gino's silence is a wisdom of recognizing the tenuousness of the men's masquerade. Other means than verbal facility may signify a hustle. The elaborate giving of coins, for example, is a method of offering trust, demonstrating *Things Change* as another variation of confidence games, one predicated on *un*spoken codes.

For both Jerry and Gino new roles are a realization of authority, prestige, and respect denied by a lifetime of service. In effect, they realize a power transcending economic wealth, although Jerry's airline tickets serve as a reminder that seizing the American Dream *is* merely dream, vacation, fluke. The irony persists that only parading as criminals assures fruition of their desires; they hurry to be "tailored" to their roles, equally enjoying being served. As the plot complicates, the men increasingly seem peers, mutually dependent. *"Gino buttons his jacket. He looks at Jerry, who is also completely reattired in new and very expensive clothing. Jerry rises, goes and stands by Gino. He picks off a piece of lint. He turns to the door. The two of them leave in unison."*[73] The elaborate leisure of their movements shows the extent of enjoyment as they acclimate both to the style and appearance of the roles. "What complete serenity," Mamet writes of fashion, "in the knowledge that one is momentarily immortal — that one's very appearance must inspire respect." We search "for the totem that will allow us to be judged by our cover, and to be judged as *good*."[74]

The casino sequence is crucial in establishing the true nature of the Jerry-Gino relationship. "I'm here to gamble,"[75] says Jerry, apparently without ironic reference to the danger of their situation. He reminds Gino of the real world waiting: "Two days, then we go back to Chicago . . ."[76] That Jerry believes they will so easily escape Tahoe suggests his ignorance of Mafia protocol. Gino repeats his confession, and then, both men having paid homage to "reality," they gleefully proceed with current illusions. "If you got the Name," Jerry gloats, "go get the Game . . . let's gamble."[77] The absolute respect and obedience they receive from the casino's employees question, of course, the worth of such obsequiousness. The man who *appears* powerful *is* powerful, and as usual Jerry's words imply more than he knows — the inherent corruption of a culture predicated on greed, fear, and homage. Jerry is impressed by the attention. He attempts both to awe Gino and to serve him — to be, in short, deified by the old man.

> GINO: I never win nothing.
> JERRY: Well, maybe we can fix that.
> GINO: Oh, no, Jerry, not even *you* can fix something like that.
> JERRY: "Not even me," eh . . .?
> GINO: Not even you.
> JERRY: Not even someone like me . . .[78]

This doubt of Jerry's power sounds like teasing. A difficulty of *Things Change* lies in determining Gino's intelligence and cognizance. Since he never articulates more than is necessary, he is genuinely elusive. One begins to feel, however, a calm and sure intelligence, certainly more aware, humorous, and assertive than his partner's. Gino pours quarters into a slot machine, foreshadowing a more significant and beneficial later use of Don Vincent's gift. He sees in his hand the Sicilian coin, and the dark subtext and destructive motive of Green's "friendship" shows in his face.

Jerry is meanwhile arranging fate and fortune in the form of a private roulette table for Gino's gratification. While the screenplay has each man betting his own number, in the film they share "number twelve." Gino insists: "We partners, whatever happens, we go Fifty-Fifty. Okay?"[79] Jerry, by agreeing, seals their fraternal contract. He is momentarily in the role of expert he loves — describing the game and its subtleties, directing action, controlling destiny — but is shortly distracted by comedian Jackie Shore's complaints to the assistant manager. "We gotta lose the lighting guy. He's napping up there."[80] Shore's comments are pertinent. His problem is a lack of team effort, an inability to stay in his stage light due to poor help. "A beautiful show, a fine show, well thought out, but if you don't have the support . . . you see that's my theme in what I'm telling you . . . support. . ."[81] The analogy to a mob team is apparent; however, Shore's problem is the opposite of Jerry and Gino's, whose desire, continually frustrated, is to stay *out* of the spotlight.

While Jerry listens to the conversation, Gino wins thirty-five thousand rigged dollars of the casino's money. Once again, Jerry's attempts at subtlety and control backfire. Gino, impressed with Jerry's betting savvy, quotes his simple wisdom: "You fly Number Twelve, you play Number Twelve."[82] Jerry succeeds too well in manipulating fortune and Gino's opinion; like all his schemes, it quickly surpasses his control.

Jerry stammers, hesitates. He tries to explain to Gino, without sacrificing prestige, why they must return the money. He stutters through an exploratory, nonsensical speech: "Yeah, but listen, it's, it's, it's a thing of 'hospitality.' We're um, we're 'guests' in their hotel, we sure, we could take the money, it's not a question of the 'money' . . . It's just for the sake of, um, of 'honor,' to be an honorable guest. . ."[83] Jerry likes the sound of "honor" and repeats it. Gino seems to respond to the intention, if not the sense, of Jerry's dissembling, intuiting the younger man's desperation. In the Wheel of Fortune he finds an opportunity to return the money without embarrassment and still acknowledge Jerry's effort.

WHEEL OF FORTUNE LADY: Just as advertised, Sir, the wheel of fortune, the Pride of the Galaxy, never refused a bet of any size.
GINO: How much I win if I bet thirty-five thousand dollars?

WHEEL OF FORTUNE LADY: If you bet thirty-five thousand dollars and
your number wins, you'd win three million five hundred thousand
dollars.

. . .

GINO: I bet thirty-five thousand dollars. Put it on number twelve.[84]

His bet in essence restores natural odds, where winning is merely a
dream. Placing on twelve shows support for Jerry and symbolic grati-
tude for the gambling set up.

The roulette table, like the weekend, is a temporary indulgence
set in motion by Jerry and corrected by Gino. Lady Fortune works heavily to the casino's advantage, though the purpose of her wheel for the
duration of its turning is the perpetuation of dreams. Gino enjoys,
briefly, a potentiality of three million dollars, a sum to make a weekend's fantasy a life's reality. In *Things Change,* the *dream* remains more
important than its realization, imagination and memory more valuable
than promised reward. Gino acts honorably; he returns the casino's
money and, in the first of several instances, rescues Jerry. The younger
man begins to realize the delicate inversion of their relationship; for the
audience, another Mametic mentor-protégé dynamic is operating.
Gino drinks a Scotch, tips the waitress; he is all deliberation and
graciousness. *"He walks over to Jerry."* Again, words are inadequate.
*"They look at each other. Gino smiles."*[85] The smile is not at Jerry's ex-
pense, but in recognition of their adventure and emerging friendship.

Presumably, Jerry needs until evening to consider their partnership. In a telling juxtaposition, his words of appreciation are followed
by Jackie Shore's on-stage Mafia joke:

JERRY: Well, you handled yourself very graciously back there.
GINO: When in Rome, we do what the Romans do.
JACKIE SHORE *(monologue)*: My theory is—criminals want to get
caught. The reporter says eighteen of twenty suspects arrested are
known to have organized crime ties. If they don't want to get caught,
don't wear the ties. You know what I'm saying?[86]

In the film, Gino's line is more accusing: "When *you* in Rome, *you* do
what the Romans do." In either case, the Mafia is comparable to the
Roman Empire. Shore's joke further comments on Jerry and Gino's
predicament. The men have flaunted their supposed crime "ties."
Shore literally catches them in the spotlight and speaks of an imagined
relationship with Gino. "One thing that doesn't change is friendship,"[87]

Director David Mamet relaxes with the star of his "family," Joe Mantegna, on location for *Things Change*.

he adds, friendship here equaling fealty to crime. The Mafia indeed wears its ties of tribute and loyalty.

Jerry attempts to accost Shore backstage, but two showgirls distract him: *"Cherry and Grace dressed in very abbreviated Egyptian costumes. Gino and Jerry ogle them."*[88] Egypt connotes another ancient, powerful, and mystical power curtailed to Tahoe enjoyment. As in other Mamet works, the secrets of the pyramids represent a world of magical potential, as do the girls for Jerry and Gino. Ironically, these showgirls symbolize purity, virginity (Cherry), and benevolence (Grace).[89] In their *"Roman Bath Hot Tub,"*[90] amid busts and marble, the men, wrapped in togas, romance the bathing women. Again, much of the communication is gesture. "I always wondered where I was meant to be,"[91] sighs Jerry, langorously accepting his good fortune; Gino, relaxed as storyteller and philosopher, answers with the "Ant and the Grasshopper,"[92] an amusing parable revealing much of the film's harsh ethical orientation, where hard work is rewarded with death and where the irresponsible flourish. "The grasshopper, he eat-a the ant,"[93] concludes Gino, and all listeners nod appreciatively. He succeeds who is strongest, who may devour the other.

After the story, Gino sings a love song in the old language; Jerry, as partner and mediator, translates. "Return to me. My darling. I adore you. Only you. Only you. In my heart."[94] The younger man congratulates the older in the same tongue, noting the beauty and appropriateness. "Sentimento Perfecto. Bravo, Gino. *Canto bello.*"[95] Their companions are moved not merely by the song's loveliness, but by the men's sincerity. In the film's most touching and sentimental moment, the women, moving in the water like graceful, magical animals — and accompanied by soft, ethereal lighting — invite the men to fish at their cabin. Boats and fishing, in *Things Change,* represent communion, reunion with nature, leisure time reflecting both success and an older, purer time. The scene's sadness is in the impossibility of the proposal and the regretful yearning of the men. Such a rendezvous would require a dropping of masks that would axiomatically prevent its occurrence. For the men, who know Gino will die in prison, their Roman bath is a bittersweet climax to the weekend's dream cycle. Gino quietly, simply laments: "We gonna be gone for quite a while, dear girls."[96]

The next morning Jerry unsuccessfully tries to reestablish his authority. "Hey Gino, wake up and smell the coffee.... Listen and learn something,"[97] he adds, appropriating the discourse of his hoodlum boss Frankie. Surprisingly, Jerry shares a dilemma with *House of Games'* Margaret Ford: he is torn between two mentors, one enervating (Frankie and the mob team) the other nurturing (Gino). Jerry is panicked by the time he finds Gino down the hallway with Randy, the elder continuing a role of instructor from the night before:

> GINO: And you can't make a good shine unless...
> RANDY: ...the shoes are clean.... The shine comes from underneath.

GINO: That's right.
RANDY: I wonder why I never noticed that before.
GINO: Hey, if everyone knew everything, there wouldn't be no school, eh?
RANDY: Yes?
GINO: Shine-a shoes like anything else...[98]

Shoes and their shine are symbolic of Gino's integrity and honesty. The heightened significance given his craft recalls the directness of Chance the gardener in Jerzy Kosinski's *Being There;* practical lawning advice is interpreted as sage commentary on how to save a nation: "'I know the garden very well,' said Chance firmly. 'I have worked in it all my life. It's a good garden and a healthy one; its trees are healthy and so are its shrubs and flowers, as long as they are trimmed and watered in the right seasons.'"[99] At times, Gino seems as unsuspecting as Chance; certainly the people around him are as needful of hope and guidance.

Jerry fears an irrevocable loss of control, hence the severity of his reaction to Gino's minor infraction, evidence the old man "can't obey orders,"[100] an ironic comment in the context of their situation. Jerry exercises his last measure of power: he threatens to return them to Chicago immediately. He employs the Mafia's definition of friendship as servitude and claims to break all ties with Gino and his values: "I was *your* friend, but you weren't *my* friend. The hell with you. Go back to Sicily, go back to prison, I don't care...."[101] In the screenplay, Jerry invokes his affiliation to the team: "You belong to the Organization, you belong to *me*."[102] Such a pretense is too late, however, and the two men are soon reconciled. Gino spouts his confession as affirmation for Jerry, then he suggests they see the showgirls. Jerry attempts to discount the women's affections and the previous time together; by undercutting the validity of the men's shared experience, he may yet emerge as the blasé commuter of wisdom: "Yeah. They liked us real good — everybody likes you when you're somebody else."[103] While both men and audience long to believe the genuineness of the women's offer, Jerry poutingly reminds that friendship and affection are founded upon roles.

Billy Drake interrupts their reconciliation to introduce "two *friends* of ours,"[104] echoing Jerry's recent use of the same word. *"Two burly, well-dressed organization men enter the room."*[105] Their sudden appearance, in conjunction with Jerry's taunts, almost argues an unlucky summoning of brute forces to which he claims allegiance. Their hulking, vaguely concealed menace is in visual contrast to Gino's fragility. Jerry stands, so to speak, between the two. Rather than the kind patience of Gino's shoe instruction, the mobsters deliver monotonous, programmed sentences similar in tone to Silver's. "Joseph Vincent sends you greetings and welcome to Lake Tahoe. He extends to you this invitation: to be his guest at his Estate at Lake Tahoe for luncheon today.... We'll be waiting for you in the lobby."[106] The scene cuts to Jerry and Gino *together* in the rear of the Don's limousine. Again Jerry is unable to speak coherently—as a traditional Mamet protagonist—instead displaying his inability to control or even pretend control. His advice to Gino falters: "...Let *me* handle it. Whatever it *is*, I'll, I'll..."[107] The extremity of circumstances throws Jerry and Gino together as a newly formed, if unpracticed, team, yet *Things Change*'s only fluent speakers in English remain the Mafia thugs with their flat, redundant, and ritualistic deliveries. Mamet's causal relationship between language and power persists, but here perhaps power precedes and enables, rather than stems from, persuasive speech.

Once again, Gino's simple honesty, rather than Jerry's scheming, saves them. In Don Vincent, Gino finds a surprising soul mate, a man appreciative of old ways and values. "It's good to know one's family," offers the Don. "A good man prides himself on knowing those who are connected to him."[108] Robert Prosky analyzes his role: "He is an unexpected man. He is a man of sensitivity and compassion—all the things you would not expect of a Mafia 'Don.'"[109] Yet he commands a threatening position. Before Gino may be accepted, he must be satisfactorily identified. Don Vincent assumes the stilted diction that has come to be associated with menace: "We'll talk business *later*. But I must know. What brings you to this occasion?"[110] Ironically, Green's coin—by its represented values—saves Gino's life. Don Vincent remarks on the coin, *"as if throwing him a cue,"*[111] and Gino luckily recalls the aphoristic response which designates him as family.

> DON VINCENT: What a lovely old coin.... Is There Anything That You Can *Tell* Me About It?
> GINO *(beat; nervously)*: A Big Man Knows the Value of a Small Coin. *The Don moves to Gino.*
> DON VINCENT: It's always good to make a new friend.[112]

The Don uncovers the coin's face tattooed on his forearm, thus revealing the two men's closeness. They drink together, and Gino's toast in the old language moves the Don as his song touched the women. "... *L'amicu mui du me cori.*"[113] Again Gino evokes the heart, its intuition as basis of friendship. "I haven't heard that in thirty-five years,"[114] responds the Don, proving himself a sentimentalist with a past similar, and similarly distant, to Gino's.

Outside, the Don's boat and his offer of fishing the next day begin to seal their sympathetic bond. An ambiguous conversation concerning shoes follows, which the Don interprets as metaphoric wisdom:

> GINO: You have beautiful shoes.
> DON VINCENT: Even the best shoes wear out. Things change.
> GINO: With care they last a long time, you watch closely . . . you watch
> for the crack.
> DON VINCENT: And then. . . ?
> GINO: And then you watch more closely.
> *Beat. The Don considers, nods.*[115]

While Gino certainly seems to be complimenting the Don's character, again his simple delivery renders it impossible to know how fully he intends his advice against erosion of character. At least instinctually Gino associates shoes with values. Chance the gardener reasoned hopefully that "everything will grow strong in due course. And there is still plenty of room in it for new trees and new flowers of all kinds."[116] Gino would seem to share his natural optimism.

In many ways Don Vincent is living Gino's dream-life, although he needs the old man's reminder of the value of boat and leisure. They have obviously shared a profound afternoon. Inside the men embrace, and shortly afterwards Don Vincent implores Gino with the language of lovers: "You'll stay tonight, stay with me, tonight. After dinner we'll talk. Will you stay?"[117] The exchange of coins, Gino's old for the Don's new, is the "consummation" of their bonding. Ameche sees one theme of *Things Change* as that "you don't have to be born a blueblood to be a man of total integrity, which is what Gino is. . . . Gino *makes* changes, but he doesn't change. He also sees things in . . . others that they don't see at all."[118] For Don Vincent, Gino recovers a lost memory of the Old World. *"Da un'amico a un'altro."*[119] In turn, the Don empowers Gino with a wish in the New World, a small fulfillment in an otherwise frustrated dream. The Don says of his gift: "But it, too, is a symbol. And should you ever need my friendship, you put this coin into a telephone. . . . Whatever you wish, if it is within the power of your friend, that wish shall be granted."[120] Unlike the coinage clanging futilely through slot machines, Don Vincent's quarter, backed by the muscle of that same corrupt society, is guaranteed not to fail. The men

Gino (Don Ameche) finds an unlikely friend from the Old Country in Mafia head Don Vincent (Robert Prosky) in *Things Change*.

walk toward the house, laughing, arms around each other. Don Vincent has also renewed Gino's anticipation of fishing. "We'll have a nice dinner," says the Don, adding, "we'll talk about 'shoes'"[121] as if to affirm Gino's prominence. Gino has performed his role as crime boss consummately, relying not on threat and bluster, but sincerity and truth. He plays the part, that is, with a mythic largeness which has always appealed to and convinced American audiences, stressing values of family, tradition, loyalty, and nostalgic loss of innocence. Set in a gorgeous landscape of forest, lake, and snowcapped mountains, the meeting of Gino and Don Vincent affirms an American Dream founded on independence and meditative appreciation, yet denies the dream's plausibility. The Don is, finally, a criminal lord, and Gino is an imposter.

Meanwhile, Jerry is restricted by a role that he himself chose — assistant, muscle, organization man. The Don accepts both Jerry and Gino in their presented parts, thus eradicating Jerry's presumption of control and concretizing Gino's authority. Jerry has no latitude to either alter events or argue. The Don's inquisitive henchman Kenny tries to pry information from a sulking and worried Jerry: "I mean, I never seen the Don pal *up* that close with someone like that before.... What are they? Friends from the *Old country*?"[122] The interrogation, both in its nervous tone and limousine setting, echoes Jerry's earlier encounter with Drake; the scenario Jerry initiated has become only too true. Events have escalated so far beyond his control that even he must acknowledge the mortal danger. Ironically, Jerry quiets the driver Kenny by silence, a rare instance in which he doesn't exacerbate his predicament by speaking.

Although Jerry demands their escape that evening, Gino effects its success. Don Vincent welcomes the country's Mafia heads — including Green — all of whom bring gifts of homage, pistols and knifes, praises of admiration and for health. *"Spero che tu viva per mille anni,"*[123] wishes the Italian Don as he presents a mandolin. The instrument recalls the film's first scene, lost craftsmanship, celebratory music. This is a meeting of royal courts, well represented by conflicting values — arms versus art, violence versus honor and praise. Don Vincent seems unexcited by the ceremonies, describing it to Gino as "a life full of business, eh?"[124] thus establishing a typical Mametic context. Gino, unable to offer a proper explanation or farewell, must breach etiquette and flee. He leaves wearing the Don's hat, which Jerry tosses aside as he resumes sufficient control to engineer their escape from the man-sion/fortress. Jerry, however, is such an inadequate crook even the sim-ple procedure of stealing a car eludes him. "How do you hot-wire a car? You, uh ... you, uh ... you cross the, uh..."[125] Again Gino is sav-ior, acquiring "grace" by the direct actions of his goodness and dependency. He picks up a dashboard Madonna to pray; a key falls from it. Gino starts the engine and *"smiles at the Madonna."*[126] Such an immediate reward for faith suggests the anachronistic intimacy of a folk religion.

Predictably, their escape is not smooth. "What...?" Jerry begins, in disbelief: "We're out of gas. Guy's the head of the Vegas mob, he can't keep gas in the car. What kind of country is this...?"[127] His Teach-like associations recall the comic inversions of *American Buffalo*. In contrast, Gino's mood takes a laconic and regretful turn as he considers what lies ahead and the inexcusable manner in which he betrayed Don Vincent's hospitality. "We was going fishing tomorrow,"[128] he laments. Meanwhile, Jerry's ineptness with the gas station attendant shows not only his utter ineffectiveness as bully, but the end of the Tahoe ruse: "Do you know who this *is*...?"[129] he says of Gino. "Don't know," replies the attendant, "and don't care, but you owe me four dollars."[130]

A blue-collar laborer, immersed in American values yet distant from the leisure of a ruling mob class, threatens to turn Jerry in to local authorities; values are so subverted and skewed that even Jerry can't miss the irony. From the attendant: "...treat a workingman like that ... *you* didn't work for that gas, *I* worked for that gas, I gotta *pay* for it.... Lemme talk to th' sheriff. I'll hold."[131] Away from the mountain resort, where hierarchy and mannerisms are understood, Jerry and Gino's roles no longer hold; on the common earth, a practical economic system for goods still operates.

Gino enters with a handful of bills, in a habitual pattern of rescue. He is a martyred savior in this instance, as the money only facilitates his return and imprisonment. Throughout the film Gino's passivity, generosity, acceptance, and sacrifice suggest a Christlike demeanor, if sometimes for comic purposes. The old man's sad, watery eyes express unusual loss, regret, and spiritual understanding. As the men pull from the station, the camera discovers the source of Gino's money: *"The two showgirls, Cherry and Grace dressed for fishing, along with Randy, standing by their jeep. The two girls wave to Gino."*[132] Acquiring cash for Jerry's salvation costs Gino heavily, presumably his pride and appearance before those who care for him. The women's waving is a symbolic farewell to Gino as Don and to marginal hope of fishing, companionship, and independence. Gino's order to Jerry to "take the money"[122] implies crucifixion of one, betrayal by the other.

Driving to Chicago is appropriate, as their night on the road supplies a time of transition and reflection, perhaps a last supper before the end. They maintain the illusion of Gino's release from prison; Jerry attempts to pacify him: "The time passes, you got the right attitude, the time passes by very quickly."[134] For Gino, the passage is his allotment of time on earth— "... It goes by quickly..."[135] They affirm their friendship, reminisce, and, sadly, persist in illusion:

> GINO: An' I get *out,* an' you come see my boat.
> JERRY: Yeah. I'll come see your boat.
> GINO: The sun come up we *fish,* the sun go down we *drink* ... we talk about old times. We talk about Number Twelve!!!
> JERRY: Yeah. Okay.
> *Beat.*
> GINO: Is not such a long time...
> JERRY: No.
> *Beat.*
> GINO: So what's the big deal?[136]

The distance between language and knowledge here is dramatic, between the dream of a life lived to natural rhythms, like the grasshopper,
and the reality of a feeble and innocent old man dying in prison. *"Long
shot. The car, alone on a desert road, a billion stars above, the car driving away into the distance."*[137] Their isolation, a yearning for basic
human decency and comfort, is heightened by a sky of stars, limitless
impossibilities in an unattainable "Galaxy."

The Chicago hotel room to which the men return, with baggage,
is a poor reminder of Tahoe's Criterion suite, its dim confinement instead foreshadowing Gino's imminent prison cell. The gray overcoat of
his role as confessor hangs conspicuously by the door. A great deal of
time, much more than three days, seems to have passed. Jerry stammers
again, this time with reluctance and affection: "Whaddaya want to
do...? Naaaaa ... I don't ... I ... Hey, hey, I ... I wish you didn't
have to go."[138] During these difficult words, Gino removes his tie, his
"Crime tie," as he begins to exchange one role for another. Again he
will portrary a criminal, this time accepting society's censure rather than
its awe. First, however, he has a last and crucial lesson to teach his unwitting pupil. In the ensuing argument, Jerry is scared and uncertain,
Gino calm and consoling, a rare man of honor:

> GINO: I got a deal. Three year in prison, I get out, I go back, I buy my
> boat.
> JERRY: You buy your boat. *(Shakes his head sadly.)* You know what
> your money's goin' be worth in three years? It won't buy a *tooth-
> brush,* whaddaya, you, whaddaya, you. THREE YEARS OF YOUR
> LIFE...??? You're ... NO. This is not a *deal....* It's a hustle ...
> they *hustled* you. Three years for three *days...*
> GINO: I give my word.[139]

The exchange is telling of both men, but particularly of Jerry's
growth. To let Gino escape, as he offers, would assure castigation by
the "family" and could cost him his life. He both admits his feelings
for the old man and attempts to return one of Gino's rescues. Linguisti-
cally, the Mafia has become "they" rather than a team "we." Jerry's
breakthrough, however, is still marked by naïveté; he will learn his true
job is, and has been from the beginning, to kill Gino. The stressing of
three days is again an association with Christ — three days in which Gino
has risen from a death of servitude, perhaps? Gino repeats Jerry's name
as if speaking to a child. He agreed to the deal for preservation of his
dream, not in any genuine expectation of survival and leisure. The men

argue, in other words, on different levels of meaning: Jerry incompetently practical, Gino unwaveringly idealistic. "They'd break their word to *you*," Jerry adds, resignedly. Gino replies, still instructing his disciple: "Maybe yes, maybe no. What they do no matter. I give *my* word. . . . I give *my* word. . . . I'm going to miss you."[140] Gino preaches for honor maintained on a private level, rather than acting for the team. He exits to the bathroom to groom, shave, *don* his accepted burden of guilt and sin. When he returns, he moves his shoeshine box from floor to bed—his values are intact. The men's silent sharing of cigarettes is interrupted by Frankie's early arrival; that is, the team comes between the two individual friends. Frankie puts the gray overcoat onto Gino's shoulders and follows them out. The door closes; fates are sealed.

Outside, the men adjust their new coats—i.e. roles. Gino walks ahead of the others, as if into ambush. He takes out the letter from Grace and Cherry and rereads it. He slaps the folded note along a black wrought iron fence as he passes; both children's games and imprisonment are suggested. Frankie offers a different route: "Hey, I thought we'd take a walk by the lake. Give him some air in his lungs."[141] A walk by the lake is what Gino originally requested of Jerry, but here it is another Mafia euphemism; "air in his lungs" is a peculiar but undoubtedly lethal phrase, implying perhaps drowning or perforation by bullet holes. Something irrevocable has passed. Gino tears the letter in half and discards it; nothing more than memory will survive. Frankie pointlessly asks Gino if he knows his confession, heightening religious overtones of the execution. A beautiful sequence follows: Gino, brightly lit, descends alone into an underpass; Jerry, in shadows, attempts to retain an innocent belief in promises, denying his own revelation of the mob as hustlers and thieves. Frankie speaks *"softly, explaining the obvious"*[142] and *"shrugs, as if to a child"*: "The whole thing was, Set This Guy Up, get his prints on the gun. . . ."[143] Jerry disavows the team's deceit: "You sonofabitch! What the . . . who *are* you, all of you . . . make a *deal* with the man, you. . . ."[144] He denies such a family but is still too dull to anticipate Frankie's last surprise: *"You're* gonna kill him, pal. . . . You wanted to square yourself. You got off probation. . . ? . . . THIS is the job."[145] The price of redemption and reintegration is the murder of Gino, betrayal of the old man's values and denial of their shared experience.

Denby notes that "as Jerry, Mantegna starts out with his usual confidence. But Jerry is too stupid, and finally too decent, to be a good

criminal...."[146] Jerry shows Gino the gun; immediately, the old man
intuits the situation and Jerry's choice. He nods and says nothing. Jerry
is panicked; he reminds Gino of his former opportunity to escape, to
which Gino again replies, unequivocably, with the same sure simplic-
itly, "I gave my word."[147] This is Jerry's pivotal moment of crisis and
decision. Frankie goads him from a distance; Gino is silent. *"Overcome
by frustration,"*[148] Jerry is hysterical: "I SAID I'D DO IT, I GAVE MY
WORD, EVERYBODY GAVE THEIR GOD DAMN WORD."[149] In a sense,
Gino's word of honor *has* damned them both, forcing Jerry to irreversi-
ble action. He inadvertently, perhaps, hits the approaching Frankie in
the face with the gun, dropping the hoodlum to his knees in a mock-
penitent position before them. "Oh God..."[150] Frankie groans, then
tells Jerry he has just killed *himself,* suggesting that any assault on a
family member is effectively suicide.

Jerry's response is to run, presumably with Gino: "Great, now I'm
dead, you're dead, we're all dead. You got the keys to the car...?"[151]
His alliance with Gino is affirmed, even if accidentally decided. "What
he finds in this old shoeshine man," Mantegna says of Jerry, "is this guy
who is at ease with who he is and who lives by these basic kinds of rules.
And I think by the end of the movie Jerry comes to some realization
about himself and about honor."[152] Ameche adds a corroborating view
of Gino: "He sees the natural goodness of Jerry and in the end makes
a change in him."[153] If Gino's goodness dooms Jerry to action, it also
saves him a final time. Rather than car keys, Gino produces Don Vincent's quarter and phone number. Possibility shines in his eyes, reward
for right action and Jerry's dedication. "I'm gonna make a call,"[154] Gino
announces. "If Ever You Should'a Need My Friendship..."[154] Those
dreams of the Old World shared with Don Vincent pay off in Gino's
one moment of potency in the New World. As often in a fable or fairy
tale, the granting of a wish accomplishes only restoration of original circumstances. Frankie, who botched his assignment by trusting Jerry,
performs Gino's courtroom confession. Functioning as scapegoat *for*
the scapegoat—"...the guy, *behind* the guy, *behind* the guy..."[156]—
Frankie is sentenced not to three years, but "to the maximum allowed
by law, a term of imprisonment of twenty years to life."[157] Whereas
Gino's references to the heart are founded on friendship (Don Vincent)
and romance (Grace and Cherry), Frankie's assault on that organ is only
cold, uncontrite violence: "I shot the sonofabitch three times in the
heart."[158]

The scene cuts. *"Sicily. The sea. White house. A fishing boat. A hand reaches through the picture and comes back with a shoeshine rag.*"[159] Gino and Jerry's fate is the shoeshine store; a dream that makes life bearable has been preserved. Gino shines Jerry's shoes. As master, he is also anxious to serve. Both men take shoes from pairs awaiting restoration of lustre. They do not speak, yet communication is unusually complete. *"They both look at each other, shrug—'It could be worse.' They both turn back to shining shoes."*[160] The "worse" would be either both of them dead or Jerry having slain his savior. As it remains they are together, less lonely than before, pursuing a profession that in its usefulness and service is not incomparable to the skills of the carpenter. The sounds of the city intrude, then a violin resumes as the picture fades to black. *Things Change* is gentle and optimistic only on the personal level. Basic values of male friendship, craft, and a healthy dream life persist only in isolation. Things, indeed, change, and indeed stay the same. The individual may retain honor, identity, and dreams if these are held quietly and in poverty; economic and political prosperity are left to the criminal fraternity.

Ameche and Mantegna provide a moving and sympathetic chemistry. They shared the Volpi Cup for best actor at the Venice Film Festival for their performances in the movie. Ansen says the men "discover a delightful and touching dance of the Old World and the New"[161] Mamet is no less successful with a film so wistfully different in tone from his other work.

> *Things Change* offers convincing evidence that Mamet is on his way to developing a voice in film as distinctive as his voice in the theater. Amazingly, it's a voice that draws on few identifiably theatrical devices—on language, performance or emotional projection—but instead on the more mysterious, film-proper qualities of point-of-view, pacing and visual placement. That Mamet is at home in both worlds is enough of an accomplishment; that he can operate with such adeptness in both seems nearly miraculous.[162]

Kehr's exuberance seems largely justified. Perhaps in *Things Change* Mamet stages a struggle between his own conflicting impulses of old and new; between, broadly, the ancient directness of stage and nascent cinematic form. Hollywood, in its venality, authority, insularity, popular appeal, and ritualized codes and signals may be a viable analogy to the embedded brutality of a criminal New World.

CHAPTER IV

# The Screenplays
## Crime, Lawlessness,
## and the Quest for Grace

### *The Postman Always Rings Twice*

Mamet's theory of directing is, by his own admission, a particularly *writerly* approach, "concocted out of my rather more extensive experience as a screenwriter."[1] He continues: "I saw and see the director as that Dionysian extension of the screenwriter—who would finish the authorship in such a way that (as always should be the case) the drudgery of the technical work should be erased."[2] The directing method apparent behind *House of Games* had, then, been years in development. Mamet began his screen adaptation of *The Postman Always Rings Twice* in 1978; his earliest comments on film, from the perspective of screenwriter, already suggest the montage theory he would espouse as director. "The script makes the audience ask what happens next and makes the audience care about the answer to that question"[3]; *Postman* "is structured in the screenplay almost along classical lines of suspense and no question is really answered in any single sequence. It makes a very productive use of the medium of cutting...."[4] Also present is the basis of Mamet's later association of film with dreams and the unconscious: "Films are a symbolic medium. Movies succeed when they are symbolic, when we can make the jump between cuts."[5] Virtually all of his more recent theories concerning cinema are contained in such earlier opinions, although the vocabulary isn't yet fully in place. Mamet the *director* would add that "there is a trade to screenwriting and there is a trade to directing a movie. They're very much the same trade"[6]; and "directing is just a technical skill. Make your shot list."[7]

91

Such demystification of the director's art, and its close association with screenwriting, Mamet recognizes as personally limiting:

> There are some directors who are visual masters—who bring to moviemaking a great visual acuity, a brilliant visual sense. I am not one of those people. So the answer I'm giving is the only answer I know. I happen to know a certain amount about the construction of a script, so that's what I'm telling you.[8]

Thus Mamet admits his limitation, casts himself in the blue-collar craftsman role he prefers, and offers an approach to film founded on the *writer's* imagination, application, and honesty. Eisenstein's style of montage is appropriate because it implies a psychic conception of the world: "It is the nature of human perception," writes Mamet, "to connect unrelated images into a story, because we need to make the world make sense."[9] A correctly designed film both manipulates and compels its audience to continue involvement. "The audience is ordering the events just as the author did, so we are in touch with both his conscious and his unconscious mind."[10] In 1980, Mamet as screenwriter also perceived film's implicating coercion: "I tried to put the audience in the same position as the protagonists: led forth by events, by the inevitability of the previous actions."[11]

Mamet's expertise as writer is largely undisputed. By constructing his directing on natural and already honed skills, he has been able to apply a writer's confidence to filmmaking: "Almost no one in this country knows how to write a movie script."[12] Such conceit—of the touted *dramatist*—was Mamet's platform from the beginning of his Hollywood association, allowing him to freely criticize the creative poverty of West Coast movie factories. He explains the tepid response to his first draft of *Postman*: ". . . it dawned on me I wrote it the way I wrote my plays. . . . To me, the dialogue is self-explanatory. So I added 'savagely' or 'feelingly' after each character's name—and they said it was a great screenplay."[13]

The writer admits to having learned much from Bob Rafelson, director of *Postman*. "He consulted me about casting, sets, costumes. He taught me about movies."[14] His appreciation of Rafelson's precision and judicious use of camera anticipates Mamet's own later preoccupations as director. "Rafelson is a great perfectionist, in terms of planning and logistics. . . . He's not patronizing. He *becomes* part of the audience. . . . In terms of style, *The Postman* is classical. Rafelson's style is always the motivated camera; it doesn't move gratuitously."[15] On that first film, Mamet was impressed by the unity on the set: "...it's like the atmosphere on stage when one is dedicated to a project. That's one thing I like about Hollywood—about this movie, anyway...."[16] Years later, the attraction would manifest itself as the Mamet family. In fact, the troupe's later comments on Mamet's precision as director echo Rafelson's reciprocal appreciation of his fledgling screenwriter: "He gave a great, great clarity of intention to the characters. That's what he had learned from [James M.] Cain, and that's what I wanted. It's all in the directness of the behavior."[17] When a critic says of Rafelson's films that "every frame is a trap,"[18] there can be little doubt of an influence on Mamet's work. Economy, clarity of intention, irrevocability of action, all of these must have appealed to the young screenwriter and been recognized as shared imperatives by the accomplished dramatist. Diane Jacobs writes that in *Postman* "Rafelson enshrouds the most casual event with an aura of inevitability" and "crime is simply fated to happen."[19] Mamet's later demand for plot is that it contain "the two essential elements that we learned from Aristotle, *surprise and inevitability*."[20]

Why Mamet was attracted to Cain's novel is as apparent as the attraction to Rafelson's directing. He was surely impressed, stylistically, with Cain's directness, purity of intention, and basic story. "It's like he learned to write reading [Aristotle's] *Poetics*," Mamet observed. "I was struck by his honesty, his frankness about his problems, his personal perceptions of the world."[21] The elements of Cain's plot appealed to a love of immemorial concerns: "It's a 4,000-year-old story: the aging man with the young wife, who wants to precipitate some violence, sexuality, regeneration and so takes on a younger, more virile stranger to their house."[22] In a more abstract account, Mamet described Cain's story as "screwing and betraying each other—and under all this very cynical vision is a crying need for human contact in a bad, bad world."[23] If *Postman* is centrally "about people deluding themselves,"[24] then it is indeed an ancient story and one eminently appropriate for a Mametic treatment. Critics' comments on Cain's bleak world highlight the novelist's philosophical proximity to Mamet's perceptions of a society morally adrift, untrustworthy, and rushing toward its end. Kauffmann, for example, assesses Cain's desire to "dramatize the immorality of egotism, the fact that there is no reliable bar between gratification-as-ethics and murder."[25] The term "dramatize" is itself telling of technique, but this comment applied to, perhaps, the conclusion of *House*

Frank (Jack Nicholson) and Cora (Jessica Lange) initiate a fiery relationship in *The Postman Always Rings Twice.*

*of Games* shows an eerie applicability. The moral indeterminacy of Mamet's hustlers is easily located in Cain's vagrants: "They have desires and impulses, which blow them about like trash in the street, but they utterly lack balance wheels to keep them consistent, if not necessarily straight."[26]

Such characters—"sleepwalkers in a night of the soul"[27]—are certainly not unique to Cain and have immediate relations throughout the American school of hard-boiled fiction. Denby finds "ungovernable female sexuality working on men's violent impulses" as the "juicy paranoid premise"[28] central to such novels. Cain creates, he continues, a world "in which people are stripped of everything but sexual and criminal impulses."[29] As much as Cain's simplicity and directness must have appealed to Mamet, perhaps the themes attracted him even more. Sexuality and criminality are the cardinal drives in Mamet's work, as perhaps they are in humanity. These basic concerns anticipate the coalescence of sex and murder in a play such as *Edmond,* where the protagonist is "forced" to kill the waitress Glenna. "You stupid fucking . . . *now* look what you've done. . . . Now look what you've bloody fucking done."[30] That is, shortly after completing *Postman,* Mamet presents *his* depiction of Cain's scenario: waitress, stranger, an ensuing and inevitable sexuality that leads to murder. Mamet's Cora chastises Frank: "what are you, an animal?"[31] Edmond also ponders an idea of human bestiality: "Maybe *we* were the animals."[32] According to Corliss, *Postman's* characters are trapped "by the grim imperatives of the Depression and . . . search for the deepest sense of identity through sex"; their "rutting passion . . . offers them both the reckless hope of transcendence."[33] Such self-definition through sex is one of Edmond's attempts and also defines such Mamet plays as *Sexual Perversity in Chicago* or *All Men Are Whores: An Inquiry* — a centrality of frustrated relations and failure to be thus ratified. Even in a play without women, such as *Lakeboat,* sex's definitive power can predominate: "I mean in a flash all this horseshit about the Universe becomes clear to me, and I perceive meaning in life: I WANT TO FUCK. I want to stick it inside of her."[34] Perhaps more than sex, crime has been key in all of Mamet's film work. A conspicuous omnipresence of jails, courts, law struggling with lawlessness, and criminal activity argues these as more than Hollywood plot staples, but symptomatic of a diseased community.

Mamet makes some interesting alterations to Cain's story. In the novel, Frank Chambers is a young man, twenty-four years old, not overly clever, prone to placing outbursts of passion in a religious context of salvation: "I kissed her. Her eyes were shining up at me like two blue stars. It was like being in church."[35] Mamet's Frank, a hardened drifter and con artist *"in his late thirties,"*[36] indulges no such romanticism. The change may have partly been to accommodate Jack Nicholson in the role, but Mamet's depiction continually recasts the novel's emotional youngsters as bitter adults. One especially Mametic addiction is a bus station craps game, where Frank's overwhelming excitement for gambling disrupts his and Cora's initial attempt to depart together. Male camaraderie, an unspoken code of values and behavior, specialized jargon identifying the group, and attraction to games of chance to test one's divine approval, these familiar Mamet themes constitute the scene. Other than Frank, the participating men are identified only by male roles: Sailor, Salesman, Shooter. The following confrontation, edited in the film, foreshadows in its menace and protocol the card games of *Prairie du Chien* and *House of Games:*

SAILOR: You're leaving with the *money?*
FRANK: Well, I *won* it.

SAILOR: Hey—I want a shot to get it back.
*A beat. The Sailor pushes Frank slightly.*
FRANK: Fuck you, Captain. I'm *leavin'* now.
*The Sailor goes into his pocket, as if to draw a knife or a razor or something.*
FRANK: Well, you bes' come out with a *battleship,* Jim, if you wanna go around with me. You see? I *won* this money.
. . .
FRANK: Huh. . .? . . . All right? *(a beat)* Good meeting with you.[37]

Such a conversation, while trademark Mamet, could never happen to Cain's Frank, who in a comparable scene hustles $250 at pool only to promptly lose the money to a superior shark.

*Postman,* in both novel and film, features much of the tension between male and female that has characterized Mamet's work. Even the Mamet-Nicholson Frank, sardonic, knowledgeable, and disillusioned, is no match for Cora. "As Cain saw it," describes Corliss, "woman was the temptress, and Cora was a wailing siren—Circe in a highway diner."[38] Dan Yakir contends that "Rafelson and Mamet have made Cora much more sympathetic than Cain intended"[39]; nevertheless, she is hard, aloof, and the instigator of murder. Mamet says of Frank: "He tries to exploit her and leave her, but can't. He finds himself bound to her."[40] Cora is the enchantress; in her arms, for Frank, is both sin and redemption. Frank "fancies himself a sharp and desperate fellow," writes one critic, "and never sees that Cora is pulling the strings. She sets him up to rape her, since that's how she likes it. She puts the idea of murder in his head. . . ."[41] Arguably, *Postman* is Cora's story, just as *House of Games* is finally Ford's. She is, in agreement with Mamet's definition, the catalyst: "The story can only be interesting because we find the progress of the protagonist interesting. It is the *objective of the protagonist* that keeps us in our seats."[42] Cora's immediate objective is to murder her husband, but broader goals seem based on simple, traditional values of commitment, love, security, and family, thus her staunch refusal to "go on the road"[43] with Frank. Her inability to realize such modest dreams, the desperate criminality that carries her inevitably beyond return, renders her pathetic. In the novel, Frank, from his death row cell, tries to unravel the enigma of Woman as represented by Cora: "She wanted something, and she tried to get it. She tried all the wrong ways, but she tried. I don't know what made her feel that way about me . . . . I never really wanted anything, but her."[44] Frank's musings are sadly vague, confused, and lost. In a final obfuscation of

Cora (Jessica Lange) and Frank (Jack Nicholson) unsuccessfully attempt to go on the road together in *The Postman Always Rings Twice.*

love and religion, Frank wishes, also pathetically, with a basis only in faith, to be reunited in another place. Like Mamet's intention with screenplay and audience, Cain's last line curiously involves readers in Frank's muddled, hopeless wish for grace: "Father McConnell says prayers help. If you've got this far, send one up for me, and Cora, and make it that we'll be together, wherever it is."[45]

Ironically, behind Cora's entrapment and disappointment lurks an indictment of Hollywood, a subversive ambivalence Mamet shares with Cain. In the screenplay, Cora explains the cause of her situation: "I won a beauty contest. First prize was this screen test. I got off the Super Chief and guys took pictures of me. Ten days later I was working in a hash house. . . "[46] By these few words Mamet connotes the essence of American celebrity worship, its vanity and lies. Hollywood, whose business is fabrication and illusion, extends a tantalizing promise to a pretty, naïve woman from Iowa. She is torn from the heartland and thrown into a melting pot of corruption; this is the prize for her beauty. One senses that the amoral power structure of *Speed-the-Plow* is already inflexibly in place. Cain is more explicit in elaborating the decimation of Cora's hope and self-respect, but Mamet is clearly sympathetic.

Mamet calls Cain's novel "quintessentially American,"[47] an observation that in context — of Cora's plight, for instance — is as much
criticism as compliment. His alterations stress an American Dream
motif in the story, particularly in modifications to the husband, Nick
Papadakis: "He's very much the prototype of the first-generation
American: he wants to succeed, is good at business, but feels a bit of
an outcast. And enjoys it."[48] Mamet transforms Nick into a philosopher, lamenting the failure of America's promise: "Frank . . . dis country . . . eh. . .? Is no . . . *Ideas* here. . . . Opportunity . . . Yeah! Dey
got. But no happiness."[49] In the novel, Nick is a greasy, distasteful
stereotype, and, ironically, Frank likes him. But the film's older,
hardened Frank despises the Old World Greek for criticizing America's
lack of joy and intellect and the true poverty of its economic benefits.
Nick is in some ways an ancestor of Gino in *Things Change.* Their ac-
cents are similar, language barriers that symbolize a societal rift in
values. Both suffer racial slurs and lack full integration into American
culture. Both toast to the anachronistic value of friendship and are
betrayed by that bond — Gino by Mr. Green, Nick by Frank. Obvious
and important differences separate the men — Gino is a quiet, honest
Sicilian, Nick is boisterous, lascivious, and greedy — yet the similarities,
and the concern with a bigoted and disintegrating America, are compelling.

Jacobs argues that "the greatest *film noir* directors were Hollywood
emigrés (Fritz Lang, Hitchcock) whose work has been interpreted as
subliminal social criticism,"[50] offering a thematic reason why Mamet,
in his first film as director, would turn to subversive *noir* conventions
linking violence and disenchantment. Jacobs continues:

> Cheated of the well-being they perceive all around them, these strong
> men and women unleash their frustrations in crimes of greed and
> passion.
>     Rafelson and Mamet take this idea an interesting step further. In *The
> Postman Always Rings Twice,* it's not the wayward murderer, but his
> entreprenuerial victim who is discontent with America. . . . Thus Rafel-
> son and Mamet add a new dimension to the genre's social-Darwinism
> cynicism: a suggestion that America weeds out the contemplative man
> as inexorably as it weeds out the failure.[51]

Thus Mamet's persistent interest in the immigrant's isolation and
dissatisfaction complements his explication of confidence games and
predatory business — the target is a foundering America.

The ambiguity of the film's ending, where the caustic irony of Frank's arrest and conviction for the "murder" of Cora is omitted, was treated harshly by most reviewers. Carroll notes that Mamet's finale, an auto accident caused by Frank's distraction during an embrace, underlines a cautionary tale: ". . . untrammelled and adulterous sexual gratification leads to even worse crime, and crime does not pay."[52] But the effect of Mamet's ambiguous ending, as Colin L. Westerbeck Jr. points out, is to render the death of Cora not inevitable, as Cain the moralist designed, but arbitrary, unexplained, and tragic, a conclusion "more shocking than anything ever dreamt of in Cain's philosophy."[53] In Mamet's screenplay, but altered in the film, Cora ridicules them mutually: "We're scum, Frank. You and I. I knew it when I first met you, and we will never change."[54] Continually, they have betrayed both each other and the love they hoped would save them. Nick, embodiment of foreign motives, is dead, but a realization of domestic contentment is thwarted by their *own* worthlessness in a society which breeds such. In short, they have no notion of a proper way for humans to treat one another; they lack dignity, respect, and tradition. They are animals, like the lion cub birthed, in Mamet's telling, by Frank's faithlessness, and the habitual action of the diner is only deadening and imprisoning, its rejuvenating potential long exhausted. Michael Sragow comments that Cain's "lowdown characters have the same grand passions as Romeo and Juliet but have no idea how to express themselves except with wisecracks, lust and murder."[55]

The marriage of Cain-Rafelson-Mamet may have come about accidentally, but seems as fated as Cain's novel. Thematically and stylistically consonant with Mamet's concerns, the project greatly influenced him as filmmaker. Nick instructs Frank to "never mock a man talk funny. I talk English better than she talk Greek. Eh?"[56] Frank rejects the lesson. Mamet supplies his murderous couple with their own American language, but with articulation comes the perception of an irretrievable dream, half-forgotten because only vaguely known. These are not impulsive young lovers, but jaded criminals. Their words serve only as proclamations of guilt.

## The Verdict

*The Verdict* was released late in 1982, shortly afterwards garnering an Academy Award nomination for Best Screenplay Adaptation. Mamet

took more interpretive liberties with Barry Reed's novel than he had
with Cain's, resulting in a harrowing script and a well-received film.
Sidney Lumet, like Rafelson, undoubtedly influenced him as director.
*The Verdict* is a somber movie, with a physical darkness to match its
subject. In an overview of Lumet's career, Kroll summarizes a concern
with deep-seated corruption, an unmanageable culpability for the individual close to that in Mamet's work:

> Lumet reflects his awareness that in today's mass societies the tragic flaw
> so often lies in "the system," those huge aggregates of power that can
> neutralize and crush the individual. These Lumet movies don't exempt
> the individual responsibility; they show how difficult it can be for or-
> dinary, decent, flawed people ... to exercise that responsibility.[57]

Even more apparent is Mamet's response to something in Reed's story
of a dogged, boozing Irish lawyer who sees in a malpractice case his final
chance for redemption, which is *The Verdict*'s primary theme. Several
critics have elaborated similarities between *The Verdict*'s screenplay
and *Edmond,* written consecutively. To Carroll, the two works trace a
mythic journey as delineated in Joseph Campbell's *The Hero with a
Thousand Faces*: "A hero receives a 'call' to adventure, is tested,
undergoes initiation, experiences apotheosis, and returns to the world.
The pattern is one of disintegration, enlightenment and enhanced integration."[58] Carroll also likens both *Edmond* and *The Verdict* to *The
Shawl* in that the protagonists' affections for a woman "cannot take
hold ... until the man receives an insight or makes a decision which
will allow him to consolidate an earlier process of self-growth...."[59]
Dean, moreover, notes a comparable style in script and play:

> Mamet's recent experience in filmmaking had a direct influence upon
> his writing in *Edmond.* When he began working on the play, he had
> just completed the screenplay for Sidney Lumet's film, *The Verdict,* and
> the extreme economy of means used in *Edmond* reflects his desire to say
> as much as possible in the briefest scenes. There is, in *Edmond,* a very
> filmic interest in moving the action with as little hindrance as possible.[60]

Stinton corroborates *The Verdict*'s impact on the playwright: "[Mamet]
became more conscious of getting what you want out of a scene as
rapidly as possible, of constructing it so that it accomplishes a specific
objective and makes the audience want to know what happens next."[61]
Stinton anticipates almost verbatim Mamet's opinion years later on the

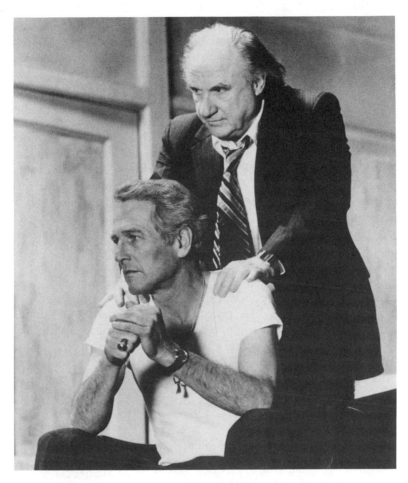

**Frank Galvin (Paul Newman) shares his uncertainty with mentor Mickey Morrissey (Jack Warden) in *The Verdict*.**

responsibility of the director: "Get into the scene late, get out of the scene early, tell the story in the cut."[62] Again, Mamet's success as director is founded upon screenwriting techniques. Kael remarks, further, on *The Verdict*'s "(deliberately) stale and repetitive language,"[63] foreshadowing the stylistic flatness and studied pace that are Mamet's most noticeable traits as filmmaker.

Comparison with the black, vitriolic *Edmond* is useful in clarifying *The Verdict*'s ambiguities. Both works, Carroll recalls, were criticized by some for a "fuzziness in . . . indictment of specific causes of social corruption."[64] The allegorical and spiritual imperatives of *Edmond* reflect back to illuminate, darkly, the journey of Frank Galvin in *The Verdict.* Generally critics were moved by the bleakness of Mamet and Lumet's vision; Denby, for example, appreciates the film's "dredged up details of the boozing, derelict life — life after the crack-up. . . ."[65] Kroll adds that the script is "strong on character, on sharp and edgy dialogue, on the detective-story suspense of a potent narrative," in a film which deals "powerfully and unsentimentally with the shadowy state that ideas like good and evil find themselves in today."[66] Kael, like Carroll, finds in *The Verdict* "a sensitive hero's struggle to regain his self-respect"[67] presented in the guise of a realistic study of institutional corruption.

Among Mamet's alterations to Reed's novel, a theme of anti–Semitism is largely erased. The mentor figure of Moe Katz is replaced in the film by Mickey Morrissey. The story's bigotry is simplified, perhaps essentialized, to include only the Boston Irish community, again a concern with immigrants not quite accepted and assimilated into their chosen community. The male drinkers at O'Rourke's bar — around whom Galvin feels sufficiently relaxed to deliver a dirty joke in thick brogue — are not merely extensions of Mamet's male tribe, but a society offering ethnic recognition and acceptance. By his jokes, Galvin identifies himself as storyteller, as performer, even as dramatist. "Remember," writes Mamet, "that the model of the drama is the dirty joke"[68] in simplicity and clarity of purpose. When Galvin addresses his mentor as "Mick. Mick. Mick. . . ,"[69] there is no doubting the novel's concern with anti–Semitism is still present, recast in a focused yet subtle presentation of a displaced community of Irishmen, moderately successful yet not quite at ease. Perhaps another reason Mamet deleted the irascible Katz was to distance himself from *The Postman Always Rings Twice,* where he had coincidentally developed a Jewish lawyer of the same name.[70] Finally, he varied the material while retaining *The Verdict*'s ethnic concern. The novel itself associates Irish stubbornness with Jewish tenacity; Katz kids Galvin, "'You have no talent for surrender. Are you sure there isn't a little Hebrew blood in your background?'"[71] Mamet makes such a similarity explicit, indeed indistinguishable, by introducing "Mick" Morrissey and eliminating a comparison of races. In his screenplay, he changes Frank's name to Joe, although the name is returned to its original in the film. Perhaps, again, Mamet hesitated to write consecutive screenplays for lost "Frank" protagonists.

Mamet's lawyers are indisputably related to, and a form of, confidence artists. Kenneth R. Hey comments that Galvin, despite degrees and honors, "makes his living exploiting misery. . . ."[72] Mamet's opening sequence, of Galvin invading funerals for potential mournful clients, is shrewdly developed from a brief mid-novel reference; this is the salient opening impression Mamet requires from his "hero." In the film's first scene money surreptitiously changes hands, introducing a corruption which will permeate the film. Dean sees a central concern in Galvin's relation to the bereaved, one immediately incriminating: "Galvin's hypocrisy and his piety . . . are nauseating; Mamet's dialogue establishes the hushed tones of sincerity and, at the same time, points to Galvin's duplicity."[73] The screenplay distinguishes the sorrowful and exploited as *"working-class people,"*[74] important in a film where criminal corruption stems from professional classes and "the mark of villainy is a well-cut three-piece suit."[75] Galvin's attempt at suave manipulation fails when a son at a second funeral home asks a question of character to be echoed throughout the movie: "Who the *hell* do you think you are. . . ?"[76] Dick Doneghy, *"a workingman,"*[77] husband of Galvin's client, later asks him the same question of identity, shortly afterwards adding, "You ruined my *life,* Mister . . . Me and my wife. . . ."[78] Kael labels Galvin an "incompetent . . . untrustworthy lawyer; he risks leaving his clients penniless because of his faith in the common man. . . . This lawyer appears to be going into court to strengthen his own character."[79] Her comments stress the qualifying, obscuring ironies behind any journey of redemption or reintegration.

Galvin's funeral antics aren't his only association with con games. Mickey reminds his ward, "I get these people to trust you,"[80] suggesting that lawyer and hustler share a central tenet of manipulating confidence. Galvin is not a thief or criminal, but simply, naturally, and in a noticeably Mametic fashion he fabricates and dissembles as a general method of interaction. His "con" of a forged secretarial letter, taped to the office door to convince gullible Sally Doneghy of a thriving law practice, is the kind of low-rent scam Frank *Chambers* might appreciate.[81] This hustling approach, ingrained from a long association with a duplicitous profession, continues throughout the film. When his key testifier Dr. Gruber (money-*grubber?*) inexplicably disappears to the Caribbean, Galvin's first instinct is to ply the sympathies of the doctor's maid: "I . . . please. My wife . . . my wife's pre*scrip*tion has run out. If I can *call* him . . ."[82] Galvin nevertheless fails, as he usually does. Later in the script, he and Mickey go through the New York City directory trying to locate a possible witness. In another example of confidence role-playing, Galvin suggests to the older man a method of approach to strangers:

> GALVIN: . . . tell them you're Dr. *Somebody* . . . you have to find this *nurse* . . .
> MICKEY: . . . yeah . . . good . . .
> GALVIN: . . . you need some old *forms* that she had . . . somebody's *dying* . . . [83]

Again, the exploited emotion is personal tragedy. The use of such deception often seems unnecessary, but Galvin's paranoia is so deeply imbedded that such cons have become habit. Aristotle's notion, dogmatically applied by Mamet, that "there is no such thing as character other than habitual action,"[84] casts Galvin into a suspicious light. Perhaps the incongruity between the lawyer's actions and his supposedly good intentions accounts for that nagging existential question from his blue-collar dependents—Who are you?

One effect of returning Galvin's name to Frank is the continual references by those intimate with him, especially Mickey, to "Francis," with its saintly connotations, or often by contrast his distance from such behavior. *The Verdict* is so drenched with Irish ethnicity, and the Catholic Church so constantly present, that such an association is not farfetched, but unmistakeable. Mamet supplies conspicuous dialogue to support his "saintly" satire. Galvin says to Laura, in context of a bet for a dinner date: "Now tell me the truth. Because you cannot lie to me"[85]; the syntax is peculiar, vaguely Christlike. "Truth" is a key word in *The Verdict,* as often evoked, and as abused, as "friendship" in *Things Change.* If in that later film Gino is a comic Christ in his simple and unadulterated goodness, then Galvin represents a tempted, burdened savior, surrounded by darkness, corruption, and ever-present venality. Appropriately, his loftier comments are usually underscored either by their delivery or the actions simultaneously performed. Paul Newman is exceptional in this regard, creating an ambiguity between word and action, word and presentation. Before Galvin commits to a "purer" path which will also endanger his clients, he speaks soothingly into the phone, presumably to Sally. The words seem heartfelt, moving, reminiscent of sentiment found in *Edmond*'s conclusion, yet they are delivered monotonously, almost somnambulantly, with more an effect of the practiced banalities constituting much of John's mystic prattle early in *The Shawl*. As he speaks, Galvin sits alone in his room lit only by a single light; he drinks whiskey and circles dollar figures on a pad. The words contrast with the action: "Well. Well. Well. Finally we're *none* of us protected . . . we . . . we just have to go on. To seek help where we can . . . and go *on* . . . I *know* that you love her . . . I *know* you're acting out of love."[86] The content is priestly in its kindness, saintly in prescience, yet the subtext is greed. He blesses her and hangs up. For Denby, Mamet's screenplay obscures church and state:

> an essentially religious conception of the law. For Galvin is like nothing so much as a parish priest who has lost his faith. He's gone past cynicism, yet he's not quite dead. The spirit of the law has died in him, but he knows that it's still alive in other people.[87]

Where Galvin separates himself from others sinking in *The Verdict*'s mire of corruption, and from many Mamet hustlers, is in his willingness, indeed necessity, to ask for help. If Galvin is a priest, then his inverted mission is understanding, forgiveness, and assistance *from* those around him. His unabashed vulnerability is eminently more effective in eliciting sympathy and help than are his manipulative attempts. He pleads with Mick not to leave him alone to prosecute an impossible case: "I have to do it, Mick. I've got to stand up for that girl. I need your help . . . Mick, will you help me . . . ? . . . Will you help me . . . ?"[88] His intrinsic dependency renders him almost childlike; or, perhaps, his need is indeed his most saintly characteristic. In an opening statement to the jury, Galvin's use of a generalized "I" extends his own longing to them all: "'How can I be *pure*. How can I be impartial without being cold. How can I be merciful and still be just?' And I know that most of you have said some sort of prayers this morning to be *helped*.'"[90] In court, he is both minister and theatrical performer. For a film audience, the effectiveness of such a sermon lies, as Carroll notes, in how the "social conviction of Galvin's words are counterpointed by the low-key uncertainty with which they are delivered. . . ."[91]

The Catholic Church is implicated in *The Verdict*'s hierarchy of self-justification and criminal malpractice. Bishop Brophey works closely with insurance investigator Alito, doesn't "want the Archdiocese exposed,"[92] and is concerned if they will win the case. Brophey personally offers Galvin pay off money, pontificating on balance and reputation from *"behind his beautiful desk.'*[93] He considers an easily divisible bribe "just."[94] His rooms are luxurious, sedate, and calming, warmed

Ed Concannon (James Mason), the "Prince of Darkness," cross-examines Caitlin Costello (Lindsay Crouse) in *The Verdict*.

by a fireplace. In this sanctum sanctorum of righteous opulence, Galvin, clutching his briefcase as if it were a failing totem, is clearly out of place. He pleads with Brophey as priest to understand the implications of his accepting the money — "If I *take* the money I'm lost"[95] — but the clergyman's ears seem unaccustomed to matters of the spirit. In the following scene, Galvin finds a listening ear, if not a sympathetic one, in the Mametic environment of lawyers playing cards in the courthouse. Mickey is confounded over Galvin's refusal of settlement money and delineates the ludicrousness of the younger man's Christlike conceits: "Are you *nuts*? What are you going to do, bring her back to *life*. . . ?"[96] Mickey clarifies who the saintly lawyer and his dubious disciple face as opponent, setting up the courtroom as metaphysical battleground: "You know who the attorney is for the Archdiocese, Eddie Concannon. . . . He's the Prince of Fuckin' *Darkness*. . ."[97] In *The Verdict*'s world of skewed values, Satan himself represents the interests of the church. In Reed's novel, Brophey is even more explicit with Galvin as to his position: "'You can *afford* to lose. You're one man. It's one man's destiny. We cannot afford to lose. We have two thousand years and eternity to protect.'"[98] However, Mamet's script is in the end even more fatally critical of the church; while Reed has Brophey ultimately intercede in support of truth, in the film the church's loss is answered only by an unsettling, brooding silence.

In *The Verdict,* doctors constitute much of the church's modern authority. Surgeons represent God's healing work; they are in essence deified both by co-workers and a general populace of believers. Mickey understands how crucial this preception is to their case: "*. . .and* they got depositions from the nurses, everybody in the operating room, the *scrub*-nurse. . . 'All these guys are God. I saw them walk on water. . .'"[99] The novel makes clear a connection between the fraternal medical order and organized crime which must have appealed to Mamet, reiterating a preference for an outright criminal over one ostensibly serving the public. Again, from the intrepid Moe Katz: "'But with doctors,' he continued, 'it's worse than the Mafia. They have a conspiracy of silence. A code. The man in white is a folk God. . . . At least, the Cosa Nostra makes no pretense about its benevolence. But these guys are full of pious shit.'"[100]

Mamet also develops a metaphor of courtroom as theatre. Galvin's roles throughout the film may be partly confidence ploys, but also represent a mediocre actor at work. He interacts poorly with prospective jurors at their selection, his first court "performance" in some time; Mamet refers to Galvin's *"flop sweat."*[101] Mickey notes his partner's nervousness—"Been a long time, huh. . .?"—to which Galvin responds, like an old stage professional, "I'm getting it back."[102] In the novel, Katz explains that "lawyers are like the players. They come into court wearing fancy suits and old suits."[103] He then elaborates various acting styles and refers to the jury as audience. Galvin, once he relocates his talent, has the actor's charm of part rhetorician, part magician: "Hypnotic. Forcing their attention upon him, and then casting a spell before they even knew what was happening."[104] Still, he retains the actor's ancient uncertainty: "He paused again. Did they get it? Did they understand?"[105]

*The Verdict*'s consummate performer, however, scientifically, almost omnisciently prepared for court, is Concannon. In parallel scenes, as Mickey and his opponent prepare witnesses for the stand, the men are clearly more than actors; they are also directors of their court plays. Concannon is expert as acting instructor—coaxing, abusing, suggesting, and finally creating an acceptable, playable approximation of truth. He drills Dr. Towler at length, displaying both mastery of the man and thorough knowledge of the audience: "Don't equivocate. Be *positive. Just tell the truth.... Answer affirmatively. Simply."*[106] In fact, Concannon's directions to his witness are not far from Mamet's mandate for effective acting: "...to accomplish, *beat by beat*, as simply as possible, the specific action set out by the script and the director."[107] In the novel, Concannon conflates law practice with medical and religious culpability: "...the courtroom is *my* operating theatre. I know how the operation is performed. There are rules and ceremonies..."; he adds, revealing his closeness to a hustler's motive, that his "aim is to give you the confidence to tell the truth."[108]

Many elements of *The Verdict* screenplay are tellingly Mametic; the venal Judge Sweeney, for example, announces from his finely furnished chambers that justice is a "business"[109] and settlement negotiable. He tells Galvin he himself would have taken the offered money and "run like a thief."[110]

In contrast, the small role of Dr. Thompson is compelling. Thompson, hired witness for Galvin, object of ridicule for both his color and his age, speaks the truth with a quiet, persistent dignity. His testimony is discredited by a harrassing Sweeney, and the two seem representative of opposing spirits, with the brashness of corruption overpowering the comparative humility of truth. Even when all seems lost, Thompson remains hopeful: "You know ... sometimes people can surprise you. Sometimes they have a great capacity to hear the truth."[111] Although he appears only briefly, Thompson presents a sad but unrelinquishing belief in humanity's compassion. Likewise, Galvin's last words to the jury call upon whatever remains of the individual: "If. If we would have faith in *justice*, we must only believe in *ourselves*.... And *act* with justice.... And I believe that there is justice in our hearts."[112]

Galvin's closing statement conspicuously ignores the "facts" in the case of Deborah Ann Kaye. The film has continually shown the fragility and malleability of evidence; Sweeney, in his most damaging gesture, disallows the entire testimony of Caitlin Costello due to a legal technicality. Thus Galvin's final words — and his switch to "we" indicates mutual responsibility — call up a spiritual imperative which is the true subtext of the trial. His request for right action, based on inherent human knowledge of justice, is another application of a "character as action" axiom. Perhaps he also begins to answer the nihilism throughout Mamet's previous work. Compare Galvin's summary of the world's suffering with Teach's violent despair at the close of *American Buffalo*:

GALVIN: You know, so much of the time we're lost. We say "Please, God, tell us what is right. Tell us what's true. There is no justice. The rich win, the poor are powerless. . . ." We become tired of hearing people lie. After a time we become dead. A little dead. We start thinking of ourselves as victims. *(pause)* And we *become* victims.[113]

. . .

TEACH: My Whole Cocksucking Life. . . . The Whole Entire World. There Is No Law. There Is No Right And Wrong. The World Is Lies. There Is No Friendship. Every Fucking Thing. *(Pause.)* Every Godforsaken Thing.[114]

Teach is the very victim Galvin describes, but while the sentiment is similar, the tone is dramatically different. Teach is violent, barbaric, and denies any survival of values; Galvin seems after all to be the opposite. Standing in a court of law which should, ideally, represent the highest attainment in the justice and civility of mankind, Galvin delivers his speech; he is still hesitant, still disappointed, and again he asks for help, calling upon what he hopes to be a common desire for truth. A hope which "in effect, is a prayer . . . a fervent, and a frightened prayer"[115] founded, perhaps unlike the prayers of a Bobby Gould, in sincere need.

Mamet's screenplay, however, denies a happy conclusion; corruption proliferates, continuing to choke faith. Galvin, in his willingness to request and accept help, receives a small portion of a grace for which he longs. Yet an additional change by Mamet vitiates Galvin's satisfaction. While in the novel the betrayal of Laura is discovered early and taken almost as a matter of course, in the film her deception is devastating. Robert Hatch notes that "Galvin's joy in his courtroom victory is offset by a personal blow that subverts the happy ending which has been dangling like a sugarplum before the eyes of an expectant audience. Galvin is a flawed man, and he wins a flawed reward."[116] Laura is turned from Reed's confident young hustler, protégé of Concannon, to another lost soul entrapped by the habitual wrongness of her actions. Galvin is unable to respond with forgiveness to her literal calls for help. The film's very end, while not in the script, reiterates their mutual defeat: Laura slovenly on her hotel bed, liquor glass in one hand, telephone in the other; Galvin, off liquor and drinking coffee, awkwardly at the desk in a dingy office, the phone ringing, ringing, a prayer *he* hasn't the strength and grace to answer. "The positive ending of *The Verdict*," writes Carroll, "still leaves it a moot point how generously Galvin will be able to act to those who have betrayed him in the past—

even with his newly-won self-knowledge and confidence."[117] Kael is even more skeptical of any legitimate growth or education: "It's a story of a man who was disillusioned and became a drunk; by the end he has regained his illusions."[118] In tone, Frank and Laura's relationship resembles that of Nick and Ruth's in Mamet's *The Woods,* a play written just before *The Verdict.* Like Nick, Frank comes for nurturing, for sympathy, for sexual healing; like Nick, he is unable to return such favors. The jury's ruling in favor of Deborah Ann Kaye is a brief victory for Frank Galvin, who even during his finest moment is alone. He cannot compensate for the charity he lacks and for which the company of men is no substitute.

## The Untouchables

In 1985, producer Art Linson approached Mamet, who had recently won the Pulitzer Prize, about scripting *The Untouchables.* Linson is reported to have reasoned, "Don't you think the logical career move would be to do a remake of a TV series?"[119] That Mamet quickly agreed speaks to the potential he saw in the contrast between Eliot Ness and Al Capone. Criminals have continually populated Mamet's landscape; hierarchies of organized crime are explored in both the screenplay for Linson and in Mamet's own film *Things Change. The Untouchables,* however, is a different sort of story, although possessing some of the same fable-like qualities disguised in conventions of Hollywood genre. The film is a gangster period piece and, importantly, Mamet's greatest paean to the mythos of Chicago. Malone instructs the fledgling Ness in a ritual of retributive violence — he is both mentor in the omnipresent teacher-student duo and a Mametic salesman pushing an ideology of blood: "He pulls a knife, you pull a gun; he sends one of yours to the hospital, you send one of his to the morgue. That's the Chicago Way. That's how you get Capone. . . . I'm making you a deal. You want this deal?"[120] Mamet elaborates a nostalgia for his home:

> Nobody makes gangster jokes or thinks of the city as particularly violent (which it isn't). Yet we do make police jokes and take pride in considering the force *haimishly* corrupt (which it isn't). . . . It was and is a story of possibility, because the idea in the air is that the West is beginning, and that life is capable of being both understood and enjoyed.[121]

This comment contains much of the same complexity which keeps *The Untouchables* from being merely a formula cop film. The movie employs many elements of the Western, not as parody, as many critics suggested, but as a sad remembrance of a perception of reality based on hope and innocence no longer attainable except ironically. The film's ambivalence is achieved by conflicting pulls—also apparent in Mamet's essays—between civilizing strictures of domesticity and violent, definitive action in the company of men.

Mamet summarily explains his attraction to criminals: "'I guess I consider myself an outlaw as a writer,' he allows, rubbing that bullet-shaped dome. 'I'm good at writing criminals because A) I was born in Chicago, and B) I know a lot of these people.'"[122] A Chicago background is thus both explanation and justification, with more than a hint of bragging elitism. "I do not approve of your methods," barks a naïve Mountie, having witnessed his frontier's invasion by urban violence and presumably a cold-blooded murder by the "good" guys. Ness, advocating Malone's way, responds, "You're not from Chicago."[123] Mamet's celebration of his city is simultaneously an exultation of criminal violence and Old Testament vengeance—"Here endeth the lesson,"[124] jibes Malone—a legacy of brutality and corruption, American in scope, but still specifically Chicagoan. Mamet is without compunction in altering history to suit story: "That something is true does not make it interesting. There wasn't any real story. Ness and Capone never met. . . . So I made up a story. . . ."[125]

In his essays, Mamet develops the metaphor of artist as outlaw, casting himself as the pariah enchanted with order but compelled toward the other, a paradox marking much of his work. "I would like to belong to a world dedicated to creating, preserving, achieving, or simply getting by. But the world of the outsider, in which I have chosen to live, and in which I have trained myself to live, is based on none of those things."[126] He adds, "my *profession* of artistic vision arose, I think . . . to accommodate and embrace a deviant personality. . . ."[127] These thoughts seem equally applicable to either gunfighter or outlaw, highlighting Mamet's affinity for both figures; a hint of each, alternately protecting and threatening society, exists in the artist.

The clarity, simplicity, and tensions of the Western, and its ritualized patterns of regeneration through violence, must have appealed to Mamet, for he brought the genre's conventions to *The Untouchables*. Many passages from *The Six-Gun Mystique*, John G. Cawelti's seminal study, reverberate with Mamet's own artistic intentions.

Cawelti suggests that buried within the Western is a latent ambiguity toward America, a society it desires to endorse and praise, but does so only with increasing difficulty: "...the Western is effective as a social ritual because within its basic structure of resolution and reaffirmation, it indirectly confronts those uncertainties and conflicts of values which have always existed in American culture...."[128] Such a conflict echoes Mamet's own: an exploitative, profane enactment of stories, the frustrated cultural nihilist behind them, and a constant tension between hope and hopelessness, morality and its malleability. Consider *Glengarry Glen Ross* in the context of Cawelti's explanation: "...the closing of the spatial frontier has led to the closing of a spiritual and cultural frontier. There is no more free land; only real estate deals."[129] Indeed, a staple villain of Westerns is the banker, epitomizing Mametic avarice and perversion of the American Dream: "Instead of the pioneer's mutual respect and loyalty, the banker-villain possesses skill at manipulating and exploiting the townspeople to his own advantage."[130] Capone is easily exposed in such light, as well as a multitude of past Mamet hustlers who have traded character for commodities.

Mamet, of course, was not the first to tailor Western conventions to an urban setting. Cawelti cites the relationship of renegade cop films, such as Clint Eastwood's Dirty Harry series, to their predecessors: "...the inner city is a dark and bloody ground, and it is comforting to imagine a lone individual hero acting out the code of the West against gangsters, drug dealers...."[131] He goes on to remark about a sharper sense of "moral and social ambiguity"[132] in these urban counterparts, partly due to the harsh spatial landscape of the city and lack of a frontier or open prairie. But Mamet doesn't use Western formulae solely for obscurity, although *The Untouchables* contains many disquieting juxtapositions between straightforward, unblushing presentation and anachronistic value. Kauffmann adds:

> It used to be a critical commonplace to compare gangster films to Westerns.... But the gangster ... is not only still present in our society, his presence is swollen—so much that the underworld seems to be the real world while the rest of us dawdle in the deer park of criminal kings. Forty years ago Robert Warshaw wrote: "Most Americans have never seen a gangster. What matters is that the gangster *as an experience of art* is universal to Americans." The facts of our life and art experience ... make *The Untouchables* simultaneously relevant yet quaint. With its battle over mere booze, with Capone's brazen antics, De Palma's film seems in a ghastly way almost innocent.[133]

This is much closer to Mamet's intention than those reviews which saw the film as an attack on the banality of goodness and the saccharine sentimentality of family life. Rather, *The Untouchables* takes place in a mythic past, as a presentation of law and justice rendered precious by the ironic distance of current corruption—impossible rectitude, and fortitude, longed for but recognized as having existed only in a mythic national past or in the dream realm of story.

Perhaps in this way, as a fable of America's persistent hopefulness yet inevitable loss of innocence, *The Untouchables* resembles *The Water Engine* more than any other Mamet work. Both stories are set in an imaginary Chicago of the 1930s and both concern strict dichotomies of good and evil. "As Stanislavsky told us," reminds Mamet, "we shouldn't shy away from things just because they are clichés."[134] Denby hails *The Untouchables* as "a celebration of law enforcement as American spectacle,"[135] a comment connotatively akin to Mamet's own observations in his essay "Concerning *The Water Engine*":

> The only profit in the sharing of a myth is to those who participate as storytellers or as listeners, and this profit is the shared experience itself, the *celebration* of the tale, and of its truth. . . .
> Tolstoy wrote that the only time human beings treat each other without pity is when they have banded into institutions.
> Buttressed by an institution, he said, we will perpetrate gross acts of cruelty and savagery and call it "performance of our duty," and feel absolutely no necessity of judging our own actions.
> The code of an institution ratifies us in acting amorally. . . .[136]

He continues that *The Water Engine* is "an American fable about the common person and the institution."[137] Charles Lang's invention of an engine run on water, potentially of great benefit to mankind, causes only concerns of economic catastrophe amid the ominous higher powers of production and distribution. The play is by far Mamet's most elaborate, with a large cast and demanding intricacies of production and setting, all complicated by the artifice of telling the story through an old-time radio show. Like *The Untouchables,* the play comprises broadly painted characters, a hero of almost parodic virtue, romanticized conceptions of good and evil, and a highly self-conscious presentation.

*The Water Engine* is both celebration and eulogy for an earlier time in American myth-history, when an ideal of hopeful progress persisted. The play begins with singers' praises for, again, the Windy City—". . .

Til upon thine Island Sea/ Stands Chicago, great and free,/ Turning all the world to thee. . . ."[138] — segueing into a voice-over which establishes the play's ornate, ironizing framework of performance and self-praise: ". . . aaand welcome to The Century of Progress Exposition. Yes, the Second Hundred Years of Progress."[139] *The Untouchables* is more simply related than *The Water Engine,* lacking the play's overlapping representations of reality, but the stories share an elegaic tone. Lang's invention offers a threat to controlling powers comparable to Ness' dedication to upholding the "Law of the Land,"[140] made apparent by the messenger sent to tempt each man. The enigmatic Oberman explains to Lang, as if to a child, that "I represent some interests which are very much concerned with this machine of yours. . . . [I]t would be best for you quite quickly to avail yourself of aid."[141] Similarly, the oily "Alderman" approaches Ness, presenting threats as opportunity, smugly equating goodness with naïveté: "Mr. Ness: You're an educated man. Let me pay you the compliment of being *blunt.* There is a large, a large and *popular* business which you are causing dismay. Why don't you cross the street and let things take their course?"[142] In both, the threats are enacted; no one is untouchable. Two of Ness' group are slaughtered and he himself is compromised. Lang and his sister end as anonymous corpses. The reach of corruption is inescapable, but both stories maintain an improbable hope which identifies them as American fables. Plans for the water engine are delivered to a precocious shopkeeper's son; Ness sees Capone convicted. Yet these endings seem Pyrrhic triumphs, small in context, victories of spirit more wishful than convincing, perhaps in the case of the film accounting for Schickel's observation that *The Untouchables'* "pervasive mood is a strange and haunting sadness."[143]

An elegaic tone is shared, again, with the Western; Cawelti explains the feeling as a vague sense of loss, a sort of collective regretful dream, anticipating Mamet's assertion that the *"purpose of technique is to free the unconscious. . . .* The mechanical working of the film is just like the mechanism of a dream; because that's what the film is really going to end up being, isn't it?"[144] In the Western, this effect manifests, reasons Cawelti, because

> despite this ritual affirmation of the central values of American society, a tension remains which is never quite fully resolved. . . . Sometimes the tension shows itself as a definite sense of loss. . . . These qualities of feeling, which it is difficult to define precisely, reflect, I believe, that aspect of popular formulas which I defined earlier as collective dreaming.[145]

Malone (Sean Connery) stops Eliot Ness (Kevin Costner) from drawing a gun against Al Capone and his henchmen following the murder of Wallace in *The Untouchables*. Photo by Zade Rosenthal.

How surprisingly appropriate, then, genre conventions are for Mamet, who proclaims that "all film is, finally, a 'dream sequence.'"[146]

The ideal of progress—both social and individual—as explored in *The Water Engine* seems directly derived from the values of the Western; consider the sad, satiric treatment of the Century of Progress in such a setting: progress and development "celebrate leaving behind the past and the status quo for a better, richer, happier future," writes Cawelti. "Somewhat later, the westerning farmer was joined by the . . . inventor who struggled to bring the country to a new technological level."[147] *The Water Engine* questions the veracity of such an idealized past, meanwhile lamenting its extinction from viable beliefs:

> SPEAKER: What happened to this nation? Or did it ever exist? . . . did it exist with its freedoms and slogan. . . . In the West they plow under wheat. Where is America? I say it does not exist. And I say that it never existed. It was all but a myth. A great dream of avarice . . . The dream of a Gentleman Farmer.[148]

Even priests of progress preach a dream which for contemporary audiences sounds sadly naïve, stressing the emptiness of the country's myths and the failure of science: "Rocket travel, travel to the stars, the wonder of the Universe at last within our grasp."[149] Bigsby adds that "once coherent shapes of national purpose, moral endeavor, private and public ideals are now reduced to a ragbag of clichés, a few tattered remnants...."[150] The effect is comparable to Ness' "triumph" over Capone, in large part a symbolic victory over Prohibition, soon to be repealed, suggesting the circular whimsy of law, the smallness of the victory bought with Malone's and Wallace's deaths. What is lamented in both stories is not the passing of goodness, but the impossibility of continued *belief* in goodness, an indication of the death of "A National Dream-Life," as Mamet titles one essay. *Things Change,* Mamet's later mob-fable, concludes with a preservation of personal dreams, lives unfulfilled except in the sharing between Jerry and Gino of unattainable goals. The effect is a final feeling of dependency, wistful loss, and resignation. In *The Untouchables,* it is the *national* dream whose passage is mourned, hence the film's elusive sadness. Just actions reap impoverished results, cultural alienation rapidly overtakes hopes of a progressive community, and the audience is unable even to enjoy its conventional mythic types.

In both *The Water Engine* and *The Untouchables,* newspapermen hound the background as blasé forerunners of society's cynicism, drawn to the charisma of corruption, witnessing every humiliation of good and justice. In *The Water Engine,* the reporter Murray delivers patriotic platitudes which repulse him; he is equally disdainful of a concept of progress and of Lang's invention: "Thank God I don't have to sign it. What have I got on this evening?... Right. Right. Mr. Lang. 'They stole my engine.'"[151] Reporters are equally belligerent to Ness and skeptical of his enterprises, immediately labeling him an anachronism: "You consider yourself a Crusader, Mr. Ness...? Is that it...?"[152] If reporters are considered as audience or critics to Ness' brand of artistic rightness, then Mamet's own essays can be applied. Their jobs become "to *resist,* to the point where the determination of the artist overcomes their resistance. This is the scheme of artistic natural selection."[153] Significantly, the first and last people Ness speaks to in the film are journalists, implying the press not only reports news but in some way arbitrates social truth and change. Using the historical example of prohibition, today's hot news is shown to be tomorrow's trivia, and that which is interesting, colorful, and quotable is what is chosen to be offered a consuming public consciousness. Ness finally wins the press' sympathies for his ambiguous victory, which is reduced to a headline.

REPORTER: "The man who put Al Capone on the Spot."
NESS: . . . oh . . . I just happened to be there when the wheel went
around.

REPORTER: They say they're going to repeal Prohibition. What will you
do then. . .?
*Beat. Ness smiles.*
NESS: I think I'll have a drink.[154]

The script's closing title, deleted from the film, further ironizes Ness'
larger ineffectiveness, the persistence of corruption, and the culpability
of unfair legislation: "But the organized crime and disrespect for law
which Prohibition spawned are with us to this day."[155] The tone of loss,
of an irretrievable era in cultural consciousness, again recalls *The Water
Engine.*
    The reporters' initial response to Capone is dramatically different
than to Ness. They crowd around the crime lord like adoring fans, in-
quiring why, since he holds the power and prestige of office, he "has
not simply been *appointed* to that position."[156] Indeed, Capone's
primary thug, Frank Nitti, carries a note of friendship and protection
from the mayor. Mamet's opening title announces, "It is the time of
Al Capone."[157] The luxuriousness of Capone's rooms, the subservience
of press and employees, the elaborateness of his protection, all suggest
a position of royal celebrity. Mamet's criticism of movie fans' indulgence of stars is equally applicable to Capone's reception: "When
we read of their loves, their income, their foibles, their crimes, we shrug
and smile, and, in so doing, we commit an act of subservience."[158]
Capone possesses, moreover, many Mametic qualities: he is a consummate performer for the press, responding with humor and wisdom; he
is, tellingly, the most fluent speaker in the film, associating him with
con men/rhetoricians. Nearly every time Capone speaks, he delivers a
speech, addressing, through the press, the public's awareness of the un-
fairness of law and its romantic ambivalence toward corruption. From
the beginning, he establishes his Mametic ancestry: ". . . What is
bootlegging? On the boat, it's bootlegging, on Lake Shore Drive, it's
Hospitality. I'm just a businessman."[159] Ness' own man, Wallace,
allows that "Capone's organization . . . is incredibly diverse."[160] In a
deleted passage, Capone dictates a morality based on public need, opposed to Ness' perception of justice as ideal: "But law is nothing other
than a reflection of the people's will. And in this case, in the case of
Prohibition, it's a *bad* law, for it does *not* reflect the People's will."[161]

Capone's ingratiating charm is simply a means of insuring profit by pleasing his audience.

Mamet abandons one gangster tradition; however attractive Capone may be, he is singularly unsympathetic. In one of the film's most effective scenes, a camera follows Capone's butler through crimson opulence, up a labyrinthine staircase, through a bustle of activity and protection into Capone's deepest sanctuary, where the crime boss sits bloated, satisfied, and satanic in satin pyjamas. He unfolds the newspaper and laughs at Ness' humiliation. He doesn't utter a word, merely chortles behind a cigar. Capone owns the press, by virtue of supplying good copy, as surely as *The Verdict*'s Concannon manipulates his own reporters. Both men are demonic heads of elaborate, essentially rotted, organizations of power. Mamet explains in his essay "Corruption":

> We frequently idolize those who oppress us—the alternative is to feel the constant pain of their betrayal. The tyrant strikes a silent bargain with the tyrannized: "Identify with me, obey me unthinkingly, and I will provide for you this invaluable service: I will tell you how worthless you are."
> We idolize these people in inverse proportion to the extent that we believe in them. [162]

Following Ness' first successful liquor raid, Capone gathers his crime bosses for a formal dinner. Looming over a circular table, Capone is, as Kael suggests, in "his Camelot,"[163] and again Concannon comes to mind, righteous, daunting and undaunted, before his long table of minions. In *The Untouchables*, Mamet evokes the American pastime of baseball as analogous to crime's fraternal team order, just as he does in a less horrifying setting in *Things Change*. "A man become preeminent," offers Capone, "he is expected to have enthusiasms. . . . Enthusiasms. . . . What are mine? What draws my admiration, what is that which gives me joy? *Baseball*."[164] He stalks around the table, clutching a bat, elaborating his metaphor of teamwork versus individual achievement: "Sunny day, the stands are fulla fans. What does he have to say? I'm goin' out there for myself. But I get nowhere unless the *team* wins!"[165] The final "I" pronoun seems to be Capone speaking of himself, his *own* greed. The baseball/crime images converge for one terrible explosion of primitive violence; Capone swings the bat, smashing the skull of his "betrayer," staining the whiteness of the round table with blood. Mere failure of duty is sufficient for one's "release" from this team.

Such violence, in the Western scheme, separates Capone from the hero's aesthetic killing, aligning him with the savage: "...knives and clubs suggest a more aggressive uncontrolled kind of violence...."[166] Capone has an explosion after the confiscation of a Canadian whiskey shipment: "I want you to find this nancy-boy. Elliot Ness. I want him dead. I want his family dead. I want his house burnt to the ground, I want to go there in the middle of the night and piss in the ashes."[167] A typically ironic juxtaposition from Mamet shows Capone's dedication to team spirit as it serves his private ends: "AM I ALONE IN THE WORLD...?? DID I ASK YOU WHAT YOU'RE TRYING TO DO ...???"[168] In "A Speech for Michael Dukakis," Mamet shows Capone's enthusiasms to be utterly opposed to the proper public official, "elected *not to enact his own whims,* his own 'passions,' but to ... put the rule of law, and the will of the People *as expressed in Law,* above his own will."[169] In a society, however, where public will is not reflected in its laws, such an idea of service is greatly problematized.

The burning of the home and the destruction of family further associate Capone with a traditional Indian role, but his henchman Nitti is even closer to the savage. In Nitti's first scene he blows up a speakeasy, killing a little girl. Like the villain of many "sophisticated" Westerns, Nitti is not dressed in black, but "like a sepulchral angel, in gleaming white synthetics."[170] He openly threatens Ness' family, in an unfilmed scene acting as an unmistakeable parody of the Indian type circling the pioneer cabin: *"The window of Ness' daughter's bedroom, seen from outside showing the little girl asleep on her bed ... Reflection. The face of Frank Nitti ... Nitti looking in the window, moves down the side of the house. O.S. the DOG BARKS. Nitti hears it and retires to the woods."*[171] Cawelti remarks on the opposition between civilization and primitivism in the Western, with women as "the primary symbols of civilization. ... and implicit in their presence is the sexual fascination and fear associated with the rape of white women by savages."[172] Even more than a smirking Capone, the twisted, almost inhuman countenance of Nitti is *The Untouchables'* symbol of gleeful malevolence; he is the primary instrument of Capone's evil, endorsed by both official and unofficial rulers of the city.

Capone's reference to baseball is only one of the screenplay's several mentions of games and competition. Mamet at least suggests that the whole cops-and-robbers routine is an elaborate, ritualized game of machismo and death. After the murders of Wallace and the DA's star witness, Malone asks Ness if they're finished: "You're sayin' that we sat down in a game that was above our head?" Ness accepts the poker analogy: "It does appear so. It would appear so to Mr. Wallace."[173] Capone offers the press a boxing metaphor for his war with Ness: "I'll tell you one more thing: When you got an all-out prize-fight, you wait until the fight is over, one guy is left standing. 'N' that's how you know who won."[174] Ness, recognizing the perverse closeness of death to their actions, screams at the corpse of the first man he is forced to kill: "Didn't you hear what I said? Are you *deaf* ... what is this.... A game..."[175] Similarly in the Western, there have "evolved narrative counterparts to the primary characteristic of a game structure,"[176] including opposing players, rules for legitimate action, and a distinguishable field of battle. The goal of such a game, according to Cawelti, is "to resolve the conflict between the hero's alienation and his commitment to the good group of townspeople."[177]

Appropriately, the gunman Ness kills stumbles into the room muttering Italian; presumably he did not understand Ness' warning. Race and bigotry constitute a subtle yet nagging subplot in the film. The dialogue is littered with racial slurs, enough to convince that immigrant friction from other Mamet work is present. Broadly, opposition is between the "bad" Italians who have destroyed the American ideal and the Irish who watched them do it. The two groups ostensibly embrace different systems of order — the Italians are mobsters, the Irish are cops. Similarity between the names Capone and Malone suggests not only Malone's necessary knowledge — i.e. involvement — with crime and his allegiance to violence, but also that these men head the film's rival factions. A lone exception in this separation is Stone, the one "good" Italian, forced to change his name, Giuseppi Petri, to be assimilated into law-abiding culture. There is at least a hint here of the Western's traditional racism toward blacks and Native Americans. In the initial meeting between Malone and Stone, the seasoned cop tests the rookie's passion by attacking his race:

> STONE: Giuseppi Petri.
> MALONE: Well, that's what I thought ... *(to Ness)* That's all we need, get a thieving *wop* on the...
> STONE *(stunned)*: *What* did you say...?
> MALONE: I *said* that you're a lyin' member of a no-good race...
> STONE: Better'n you, you stinkin' Irish *pig*...[178]

In this instance, the men's ethnic hostilities are inverted to form a basis of *personal* respect and friendship. Later, Malone calls Stone by his real

Frank Nitti (Billy Drago) interrupts Al Capone's (Robert De Niro) evening at the opera with news of Malone's assassination in *The Untouchables*. Photo by Zade Rosenthal.

name, symbolizing his acceptance of the younger man but also recalling a background which cannot be escaped or altered — "You're a good cop, Giuseppi...."[179] A deleted scene in which Stone converses with a waiter in Italian lends a strong sense of submerged pasts being lived by men of both races. In contrast to Nitti's violence, Stone represents a tradition of Catholicism; in the screenplay, he speaks in Italian over the body of Malone, as if to a dying savior: "Holy Mother of God. What have they done to you — ?"[180] Stone's character is further testified to by his marksmanship; he is introduced as "a real prodigy"[181] with a gun. As well as a typical quality of the Western hero, this is for Mamet a sign of Hemingwayesque virtue, a metaphor of an artist's training and sensibility; marksmanship, he writes, "tests, under great pressure, those skills and principles we have developed in moments of calm."[182]

Other than Stone, Malone unequivocally detests Italians, whom he seems to see as inherently corrupt. He accuses a fellow Irish cop of betraying their race: "You're my people? You run with the dagos, and then you're my people?...THEY RUINED THIS *TOWN*, MIKE!"[183] Up to the moment of his murder, Malone derides Italians, noting their savagery: "Isn't that just like a Wop—bring a knife to a gunfight."[184] Even Ness is infected; he calls Capone a "guinea sonofabitch."[185] The Italians reciprocate the animosity not only by Stone's vitriolic response, but worse by Nitti's lie that Malone "died screaming like a stuck Irish pig."[186] This bitter racist theme, in a film superficially so regenerative and hopeful, is discouraging testimony to mankind's basic tribal hatreds and is left unresolved. Ethnic tension undercuts Ness' ongoing goal of a free and integrated American society, which, unattained, signifies more than a closing of the frontier, but the atrophy, through bigotry, of the nation's soul. In the essay "Liberty," Mamet expresses concern that America's revised opinion toward refugees will have a great cost: "And so a young nation's love of liberty has become a love of the power to control through the awarding or withholding of liberty. A love of liberty has become a love of power."[187] And yet, as *The Untouchables* demonstrates, the effect of the great melting pot is a hateful, bitter, and permeating corruption, where the police are murderers and criminals are unacknowledged legislators.

The film's central theme is a familiar one for Mamet: a celebration of the company of men and the rite of passage of young men under the tutelage of the wizened old-timer. The teacher-student relationship of Malone and Ness is perhaps the most congenial and loving of any in Mamet. Cawelti notes that in many Westerns "the central action is the initiation of the hero into the world of men...."[188] Racial complexities are involved in these relations: "Often the group of comrades represents a marginal or alienated social class with an ethnic or national background different from that of the hero: the WASP cavalry officer has his Irish sergeant...."[189] This last example is remarkably applicable. If Malone's code, like that of the West, "is in every respect a male ethic,"[190] then a crucial opposition in the film, as much as law versus lawlessness, may be the female domesticating impulse versus a male world's comradeship and physical action. Attainment of family and opportunities of home require "the repression of spontaneous passion and the curtailment of the masculine honor...."[191] The latter impulses Ness, as eminent family man, seems prepared to abandon. The irrevocable loss of such a choice is contained in Mamet's own reflections; his essay "In the Company of Men" notes the value of male camaraderie, a cohesive unit "directed to subdue, to understand, or to wonder or to withstand together, the truth of the world."[192] However, Mamet also possesses a strong desire for New England traditions analogous in their community and sedentary simplicity to the pioneer town: "The 'ringer' in the town is me," he exclaims proudly, amazed at local efforts "to secure the benefits of life, liberty, and the pursuit of happiness for ourselves and our posterity."[193] Mamet reminisces about Vermont without irony or apology, and the same odd amalgamation of hope and hopelessness, patriotism and cynicism, is present in *The Untouchables*.

The script introduces Ness in his home; his wife manipulates a scene in which the lawman does not speak. Oedipal impulses of the Western are quickly recognizable. Ness' hesitation in complying with his wife's directive to "go to work"[194] against Capone implies the young man's naïveté and reluctance to leave home. Kevin Costner plays Ness with a rectitude and directness comparable to Gary Cooper, but beneath a vague desire for undefined good Ness is unformed as a man. The first raid on Capone ends with Ness — parasol in hand — humiliated and emasculated by his innocence. The Malone-Ness relationship establishes itself immediately during their chance meeting: "Whaddaya want," growls Malone, "a free lesson in Police Work?"[195] Ness' primary strength in the beginning is his willingness to ask for help. Like Frank Galvin, he seeks those who can assist him; unlike Galvin, who has learned his lessons of corruption only too well, Ness must be initiated into the evil he seeks to end. "I need your help. I'm asking for your help,"[196] he pleads to Malone.

Malone, initially a reluctant tutor, deflates Ness' romantic notions of unequivocal good, meanwhile reciting staple Western clichés: "Well, maybe I'm that Whore With a Heart of Gold. Maybe I'm the Good Cop in a Bad Town. Is that what you want to hear?"[197] Before the men finally seal their blood oath — both a figurative and literal pact — Malone must don "civilian clothes,"[198] necessarily discarding the uniform of his previous identifying group. Sean Connery, who won an Academy Award for Best Supporting Actor for his portrayal of Malone, suggested they move the pledge scene from station house to church, consequently stressing "his character's almost priestly supervision (grisly though his catechism is) of Ness...."[199] The church also supports Malone's vaguely biblical platitudes; by the story's end Ness, too, having forsaken his notion of lawfulness, appropriates such diction: "Evil Flee where no man Pursueth,"[200] he offers in a deleted line. To the convicted Capone, Ness both completes the crime lord's boxing metaphor and echoes Malone from the grave: "Never stop fighting 'til the fight is done. Here endeth the lesson."[201] Kael contends that the purpose of the Old Testament language is "preparation and justification for attacking the mobsters with the only means at hand. . . . [Ness is] carrying out Biblical law."[202] Mamet, she continues, "gives you revenge — an eye for an eye — and makes it seem just and righteous."[203] The resolution agrees with traditional Western subversion, where the ambiguity of the hero's position is glossed by giving a "sense of moral significance and order to violence."[204]

Ness is a slow learner, in need of constant shoves from both Malone and his wife to resist quitting. For example, after the initial raid debacle Mamet has Ness write a letter of resignation that only a surprise visit by the murdered girl's mother causes him to reconsider. Ironically, Malone's first rule of behavior for Ness is almost verbatim the advice Mike offers Ford in House of Games. "You can trust nobody,"[205] the cop warns. Indeed, Malone has more than a bit of the con artist and rogue in him, as when he "murders" a corpse to terrify a witness into testifying. Ness pulls a similar con at the end of the film, bluffing against a judge's likely taking of graft, and wins. There's no doubt where Ness acquired his knowledge of human nature:

> MALONE: Now: who can you trust?
> NESS: I can trust nobody.
> MALONE (nods, satisfied): That is the sorry truth.[206]

"Are you my 'tutor'. . . "[207] Ness inquires during their frontier stakeout. "Yes, sir, that I am,"[208] is the reply. The simple lessons Malone teaches concern survival — trust no one and shoot to kill. "If you got to fire, hold low and squeeze, and PUT YOUR MAN DOWN, 'cause he'd do the same to you."[209] Malone's motivation, aside from hatred of Capone and the "dagos" who have ruined his town, is never clarified. He drinks in his apartment, proving his agreement that Prohibition is a sham, an irony which pervades the story. Once he agrees to help Ness, the older man seems to come alive with the vibrancy of male action and in the company of his young and spirited followers; at the same time, he moves always closely to death, preoccupied with the inevitable, imminent end of his own life. Some part of a domestic impulse survives in Malone; at Ness' first visit, for example, he is served tea. Malone's apartment is ornate, cluttered with a lifetime's knickknacks, and undoubtedly including memories of a woman. The shotgun waiting in the gramophone epitomizes the paradox of cultivation and primitivism which defines the enigma, oppositions which finally cannot be reconciled.

Ness begins to learn his lessons. Although his first kill disturbs him, he quickly acclimates to an environment of survival. In the script's unfilmed racetrack scene, Ness shoots three men and chastises Stone's hesitation; his words echo Malone's credo: "If you get *in* to it, you do not stop until one of you is dead."[210] Death is the central, unalterable precept of Ness' newly acquired ethic. A climactic train chase is another example of remorseless killing. Due to late budget constraints, director Brian De Palma replaced the scene with an improvised staircase homage to Eisenstein's *Potemkin* — but here, as well, neither man hesitates to kill; vengeance is required for Malone's murder.[211] Ness is drawn deeply into a circle of blood, his culpability assured when he violates the hero's code of grace and throws Nitti, ironically, from the roof of the Hall of Justice. The elegance and control of killing, a "supreme mark of differentiation between the hero and the savage,"[212] is lost. This act of primitive violence forces Ness to confront his own corruption, and in the unlikely and striking setting of a judge's chambers he confesses:

> Your Honor. The *truth* of the case is that the man Capone is a killer and he will go free. There is only one way to *deal* with such men and that is *hunt them down*. I have . . . I have forsworn myself, I have . . . broken every law that I swore to defend, I have become what I beheld, and I am content that I have done right.[213]

The law courts of civilization prove themselves untrustworthy: both judge and jury have been bought by Capone. Ness, having fully accepted Malone's frontier justice, essentially *forces* indictment upon the court, using exploitation not unlike, perhaps, Capone's own muscling intimidation. Capone is found guilty not for murder, but for tax evasion, demonstrating where the government's, thus the law's, true concerns lie — with financial transgression.

Ness is able to return to a domestic routine which, although relinquished during the expulsion of Capone, will henceforth define him. The sparkling vision of Chicago engulfing Ness at the film's end is in contrast to the many compromises, and the great loss, attendant upon the "victory" of law and order. The repeal of Prohibition and the audience's historical foresight at continued violence, corruption, and organized criminality in America do indeed cloud the cheery conventions of the conclusion. Evil has not been defeated, not even satisfactorily identified and defined, has at best been momentarily inconvenienced. Ness leaves the world of men and action for a domestic fate which seems bland and deadening. Progress, as ideal, is dubious. Ness' most consistent and questionable virtue has been his loyalty to "Law": "So the more blatantly incorrect or foolish the content of a creed," writes Mamet, "the more useful it is as a test of loyalty. . . ."[214]

The previous comment originally referred to acting theory, and, similarly, Ness' band of Untouchables share many qualities with a theatre company. As a group they are unified in a single purpose, then shaken apart once that goal is achieved. Mamet considers the filling of roles in a society hastening its own decay: ". . . the necessity of the moment will create the expert, the reasonable man, the brash bully, the clown, and so on."[215] As Ness humbly comments, ". . . oh . . . I just happened to be there when the wheel went round."[216] *The Untouchables* anticipates the "roundness" of *Speed-the-Plow;* holes of annihilation are plugged by remnants of American dreams—rightness, law, community.

Terrence Rafferty sees in Mamet's screenplay a separation of "(contemporary) consciousness from the characters'. Whatever suspicions the Untouchables may have about the value of their mission, the moral ambiguity never seems to affect their behavior. . . ."[217] The film is finally a eulogy to elements of genre formulae and traditional American myth as cogent storytelling devices. Mamet's call to today's actor and artist could be his wish of purity for the lawman:

> This act, an act of self-effacement, of deference, of respect, creates order. It is the opposite of the act of corruption, which creates fear. . . . The man or woman in a position of authority who forgoes the inappropriate desire to control will stand . . . as an *example* of strength. . .[218]

*The Untouchables'* ostensibly simple story is actually an elaborate and sad metaphor of failed personal behavior. Eliot Ness may walk in blood, but his *attempt* to act honorably and correctly is a lesson in character for a society unable to prevent its end. "We are part of the process, the world is decaying rather rapidly, and there is *nothing* we can do about it,"[219] warns Mamet. "Apocalypse," adds Bigsby, "becomes a natural consequence of historical process."[220] Beneath its gloss of celebration, *The Untouchables* may contain a bleaker message than even *The Verdict's* dark journey of redemption. Mamet exposes, while indulging, motives of social ritual: the rejoicing in aggression, racism, and vengeance of a country enamored by its own mythic, thus imaginary, origins.

# We're No Angels

Mamet's screenplay for the 1989 *We're No Angels,* directed by Neil Jordan, shows remains of *The Untouchables'* Western trappings: outlaws in a border town, ruthless bounty hunters, a town whore with a generous heart awaiting revival. Moreover, the film is an odd mixture of widely played comedy and suspense in the mistaken identity vein, with touches of sadistic violence. Ansen's response is typical of critics' puzzled responses: "...you leave this comedy scratching your head at the nutty incongruity of the endeavor."[221] The broad dreamscape of a new land protected by a river alerts us to the film's metaphoric intentions.

Mamet's story bears no more than a shadow of resemblance to the 1954 Humphrey Bogart vehicle directed by Michael Curtiz and based on the play by Albert Husson. Both films posit the essential goodness of escaped convicts and explore feelings of entrapment in an insular community; here the similarities end, with the earlier film proposing none of Mamet's harshness toward the penal system or the society which spawned it and none of the metaphysical complexities.

Mamet writes, "'Is God dead?' and 'Why are there no real movies anymore?' are pretty much the same question. They both mean that our symbols and our myths have failed us...."[222] The writer's essays abound with discussion of America's lack of a nurturing spiritual community—"we have foresworn our rejuvenating rituals"[223] seems a typical sentiment—and the association between God and cinema is no casual or specious one. As *Speed-the-Plow* suggests, the paucity of modern beliefs is answered, primarily, by the cheap product of venal entertainment hucksters. *We're No Angels* and its spiritual concerns reflect significantly on many of Mamet's persistent themes: fraternal institutions, student-teacher dynamics, theatricality and role-playing, the taking and offering of trust. The film is set in 1935, a few years after *The Untouchables,* and in a sense shows the result of the merciless Old Testament "justice" the earlier film upholds; in *We're No Angels,* Mamet abandons the theme of justice, both legal and poetic, which pervades so much of his film work, abandons the notion at last, perhaps, as hopeless. In an extension of his characters' earlier calls for help, he offers an unabashed story of faith and, most of all, the necessity of grace. Simple and generous actions become, more than Aristotelian creation of character, the path of the soul's rejuvenation. Mamet offers this explanation in the essay "Some Lessons from Television":

> Our own time has quite understandably sickened of The Material, and needs to deal with things of The Spirit.
>
> So we must, simply, lay aside our boring and fruitless pursuit of the superficial and dedicate ourselves to Action, which is to say to *Will* as the expression, as it is, of the Spirit.[224]

The film begins in an unspecified penitentiary; in the Dantean depths of its work mines and on surreally steep and Kafkaesque steps, the prison unmistakeably identifies itself as hell. *"Camera reveals the various levels of the mine, a blur of steam, smoke, spurting gas jets, the prisoners, covered in dust, working like moles against the rock face. Guards with dogs pace the walkways above."*[225] Convicts are reduced to animals, watched over as by the heads of Cerberus. The Warden, ruler here, appears *"with a riding crop ... through a cloud of steam..."*[226] He advocates punishment indistinguishable from the original crime: "This man has killed, and he *will* be killed"[227]; little room is left for justice, none at all for compassion. In his rendering of the coming execution he is a gory raconteur of the nightmare: "... then his soul will be in that New Place. I leave you to conjecture where that place will be."[228]

It is difficult to imagine a worse hell than that contructed by the Warden here on earth, which extends beyond mere physical torture: "I want no demonstrations. I want no *comments,* I have no doubts that your thoughts will be troubled. Keep them to yourselves."[229] In a Mametic context, the punishment of forced silence essentially denies an individual his greatest weapon and tool. The unforgiven soul's enduring of silence is a curse perhaps equivalent, spiritually, to the body's subterranean destruction.

Once alone, convicts Ned and Jim lie in their bunks discussing, according to the limits of their knowledge, metaphysics. The scene recalls a similar tableau from *Edmond.* Ned and Jim, however, are innocents compared to that play's destructive protagonist. Jim, especially, seems incapable of any crime to warrant his sentence, an appearance strengthened by the wonderfully ingenuous performance of Sean Penn. Ned, as played by Robert De Niro, is all cynical posture over goodness. The film offers no hint of their crimes, only their punishment, thus indicting the paramount *in*justice of a system wholly designed to chastise, to inflict pain, and to kill. Jim quickly shows himself to be a willing student—questioning, repititous, confused; Ned is the nihilist—bitter, resistant to the teacher role his cellmate attempts to cast him in.

JIM *(voice-over)*: Can you believe it, can you believe it, Neddy...?

. . .

NED: I can believe most anything. My problem is I just don't care.

. . .

JIM: That, that's the end of it? That, that he goes in that room...

NED: ...and he goes in that room and they light him up and that's the end of it and there's no eternal life for his soul and the cruelty of the world ... izzat the thing? Izzat your problem this fine evening...?

JIM: Yes...

NED: You wanna talk to the chaplain.

JIM: Well, I'm talking to you...

NED: I'm busy. I've got my mind on higher things.

*Ned pulls down the pinup girl poster and looks at it.*[230]

Ned's callous rejection of rudimentary religious debate shows the men's distance from a life where personal choice or belief can have any influence against the hand of the master. Jim is childlike in his innocence; when chained by the guard, he begs, "Just tell me what it *is,* just tell me what it *is.*..."[231] He asks, in short, for some explanation of his presence there, justification for being treated like an animal without soul or meaning. His tendency to ask and repeat questions is a primitive attempt for some program of behavior to engender meaning. As they prepare to watch convict Bob's supposed execution, amid the blackness of faltering lights Ned reneges sufficiently to offer Jim one teacherly answer, *sotto voce*: "Life is a hellhole, pally."[232]

As if in response to Ned's comment, the Warden appears again. They were heard talking during his earlier exegesis: the punishment? — whipping with the riding crop. He chooses Jim to be beaten first, in this inverted hell *because* of the man's innocence and confusion, rather than his guilt. The Warden offers a dark glimpse of his true agenda, which has nothing to do with justice. A bloated, satanic face bellows, "You *swine,* you want order? *I'll* give you order: *I'll* give you order! You want a *lesson*...? Is that what you want...!"[233] Throughout the film, Jim's search is for answers to displace the Warden's lessons of pain, fear, and death. It remains unanswered what mammoth, horrifying concern secured the Warden his authority, but he is sure in his position. The Warden is, perhaps, the most purely evil character in all of Mamet. He employs the same sadistic, destructive approach once he enters the town; any illusion of his serving the public will is eradicated.

WARDEN: Every house. Clear it out, send the *dogs* in ... smoke 'em out...

SHERIFF: Well, people *live* here.
WARDEN: I don't give a goddamn, they can live here when those men are dead.

. . .

SHERIFF: We have a populace.
WARDEN: You don't have a populace, Sheriff. When I'm gone, you have a populace. All you have now is a bunch of suspects.[234]

With his demonic hounds and a morally unobstructed goal of retribution, he is like an Old Testament patriarch gone beserk. Evil, once birthed, spawns and nourishes itself, without reference to order, values, or originally good intentions *behind* its initiation. To Mamet, this is corruption of a higher order than the typical economic criminality found in his work: "Political corruption in the pursuit of money is limited by the location and the amount of the money; political corruption in pursuit of a personal vision of the public good is limited by nothing at all, and ends in murder and chaos, as it did in Nazi Germany...."[235] Possibly the seed of the Warden is already evident in the final murderous actions of Eliot Ness—the step beyond appropriating the villain's methods is perhaps becoming the villain oneself? In either case, the Warden is a nearly allegorical representation of punishment and vengeance—arbitrary and brutal, without respect, forgiveness, or a trace of belief in human goodness.

As the ritual of Bob's electrocution proceeds, the prison priest mumbles banalities of hope and afterlife blackly ironic to those behind bars and soon to die without repentance. "And there is none shut up or left, and He shall say where are their gods, their rock, in whom they trusted...?"[236] The scripture echoes Jim's own questions of faith, but the pain of his beating dims its applicability. In short, grace cannot penetrate the coal-black walls, painted in blood, that the Warden has constructed for his hell. The only "crime" Jim and Ned are seen to commit—other than later stealing clothes to disguise themselves—is their inadvertent escape, at gunpoint, with Bob. Bob is a murderer, unrelenting and pitiless in violence. He indeed resembles a beast—both the Warden's charge and partial creation.

The three men escape into a *"snowstorm raging outside against the face of the mountain,"* where Bob, before abandoning them, pushes Jim and Ned into *"a bottomless drop."*[237] The jump itself is an act of faith founded on desperation. The white storm—a force other than and greater than, the Warden's dark resources—enables the men to escape. Moreover, like the sincere request for help which in Mamet often

Jim (Sean Penn) and Ned (Robert De Niro) effect their prison escape across a bleak terrain in *We're No Angels*. **Photo by Takashi Seida.**

assures assistance, so the vulnerability of Jim and Ned, shackled together, creates a mutual dependence within which is the key to their survival. "*Ned* and *Jim, chained together, fall in deep snow....Ned tries to drag Jim up*"; Jim's cry for help is deleted from the film: "Oh, my God ... oh, my God..."[238] Jim frequently, unconsciously, calls upon God, and in the story's context the colloquial reference is reinvested with theological significance. Semantically, he reveals an inherent affinity with the Church. The script is also loaded with a conspicuous usage of "hell" as an expletive. These seemingly casual but continual insertions reinforce the film's salvation-damnation tension.

Upon first seeing a poster of the Weeping Virgin, Jim recites the printed scripture, obviously considering its relevance to his own life: "'Do not neglect to show hospitality to strangers, for thereby some have entertained angels unawares. Hebrews thirteen: one.'"[239] Ironically, this initial biblical encounter is an advertisement appropriating a miracle as a tourist attraction for business: "*Patronize the local Brandon merchants. When in Brandon visit the famous shrine of St. Ann, the Weeping Virgin.*'"[240] This is typical of the skeptical regard the border town community holds toward the monastery "dumb show,"[241] as a shopkeeper refers to its vows. Jim, however, soon reveals his Catholic heritage; as he attempts to cross the border, his hand grips a Weeping

Virgin key chain, and he spontaneously reverts to childhood habits: "...Hail Mary, full of grace..."[242] Ned is most effective as mentor while the men are shackled, reminding Jim of the roles they are playing, for their lives, and of their reciprocal dependency: "But there's two of us here, 'n' I'm counting on you, so you buck up, Jimmy, 'n' you act like a priest."[243] The men continually fail to cross the border, which is symbolically correct for the story; they may not reach a new place until unburdened both physically *and* spiritually. Father Levesque delivers them to the Madonna with this explanation: "That's why I took you back from the border.... I knew how much you wanted to be here"[244]; although comically ironic on the surface, Levesque's comments are prophetic and speak to the necessity of the men's trials. "You'll find some cassocks in here,"[245] he informs them, and Jim and Ned, anxious for the sanctuary, don priestly garments. Mamet writes that to assume the fashion of a group expresses a "wish to co-opt the experience — the tragedy, the joy, the nobility — of that group being emulated,"[246] thus suggesting the convicts' latent desires of affiliation.

Jim is asked to say the prayer over his first meal with the priests, foreshadowing his later joining of their brotherhood. Although he has much to learn, in his simplicity and unalloyed goodness he also has a valuable gift to impart; his role of priest is both teacher and student. In this way he is comparable to Gino in *Things Change*. Jim's ignorance of codes and rituals of behavior, like Gino's of the Mafia's, is interpreted as an unorthodox yet refreshing example of earnestness and sincerity. As in any Mamet work, in *We're No Angels* language and its difficulties are crucial. Jim and Ned respond to the group's Latin incantations with incoherent mumbling. The Bible Jim anticipates as *"his salvation"*[247] for the blessing is also in Latin, reiterating to the young man a history of scholarship and thought closed to him. He is saved by the poster advertisement, which he paraphrases roughly: "You know what? Let's just say something *appropriate. Here's* a good grace: Be nice to strangers, because sometimes *you're* a stranger too."[248] While Ned's concerns ostensibly remain physical escape from the country, Jim searches for the release of the spirit. His greatest problem is lack of direction; he samples whatever alternative ideas are offered him, for example a Colt firearms pamphlet taken from a shopkeeper. The pamphlet, concealed within a Latin prayer book, preaches the Warden's Old Testament law of retribution; the prayer book contains pacifistic views Jim cannot read, but which have already begun to envelope the primitive, the violent, the fearful.

Jim (Sean Penn) and Ned (Robert De Niro) adapt to the roles as Fathers Brown and Riley in *We're No Angels*. Photo by Takashi Seida.

Jim develops a rapport with a "Young Monk" who asks him to participate in the lottery. Jim's response again recalls Gino's resignation toward a world he cannot change: "What's the prize? Hey, don't bother. Well, no, I never won anything."[249] The prize, the right to deliver an annual sermon before the Procession of the Shrine, is perhaps the most valuable Jim could win, an act of personal interrogation which will result in his rebirth. Another staple theme, gambling, here assumes spiritual proportions; Mamet's interpretation of a particular kind of card player is analogous to the film's participants in the lottery: "...you may find that your real objective at the game is something else: you may be trying to prove yourself beloved of God."[250] This accurately summarizes the goal of the procession lottery, in which "the hand of God itself"[251] chooses the speaker. The Young Monk admires the work of Jim, *as* Father Brown, and he equally respects Jim's friendly and frank responses. Each seems to sense in the other a longing and a simple kindness unobscured by orthodox complexities. The church represents a historical tradition, a profession vaguely evocative of, if not like, the long-standing craft of the confidence man and his secrets of the pyramids: "'Love the stranger, for you yourself were stranger in the Land of Egypt,' and you use the word a 'sacrament,'"[252] notes the monk. Jim responds with legitimate interest in the monastery's practices: "What do you do?"[253]

Ned removes Jim's leg irons, and freedom from these physical burdens is the most Ned, as mentor, can effect. Jim's burdens of spirit remain, his desperation for beliefs sufficient to enable passage to a new and better place:

> JIM: Hell, whaddaya, whaddaya, Neddy. We're not going back. Bob, *Bobby* got across...
> NED: We don't know that he got across.
> JIM: We got to believe that, Ned. We got to.
> NED: We do?
> JIM: Yeah.
> NED: Why?
> *Beat.*
> JIM: Because if we don't, what will we believe...?[254]

Ned presumes the cutting of the shackles is the complete act necessary for passage. He has had to steal metal clippers from a fiery blacksmith shop; that is, symbolically, he returns to a hell like that he despised to ensure his rescue. While cornered there, he overhears a probable fate:

> SHERIFF *(offscreen)*: Y'ask me, though, I think it'd be a lot less problem shoot to kill.
> BLACKSMITH *(offscreen)*: Uh-huh...
> SHERIFF *(offscreen)*: I think that's the Bible, isn't it...? They killed and they shall be killed...?[255]

These are the faceless tormentors who reach Ned. Such priestly violence was the code of *The Untouchables'* Malone and more immediately is the biblically twisted, diabolic will of the Warden.

Only by moving into a confession box in the monastery chapel is Ned finally safe to remove the physical burden of evil. At the same time, unknown to him, the seeds of his spiritual regeneration are sown. The Deputy announces his infidelity, and Ned is forced to participate in a rough confession. He reveals his own Catholic background as he *"tries to remember the form etc."*[256] As is customary in Mamet, a direct appeal for help is not refused: "I can't, Father, I can't help myself. *You* have to help me."[257] Ironically, the Deputy requires a direct physical intervention by the priest, which would ordinarily be highly unusual but is perhaps the only assistance Ned can offer. By responding to the request for him to speak to the town whore, Ned displays a regretful generosity, but his reward for such service is to meet the woman who will ultimately, reluctantly, orchestrate his deliverance.

*We're No Angels* develops an extended analogy between the cloistered life of the monastery and an isolated prison cell. The cardinal difference, of course, is the monks' *choice* of such a life — of light, ascendency, hope; while the prison's rituals denigrate and destroy, the monastery's seem to be those of rejuvenation. In such different environments, the implications of similar rules become radically opposed. The enforced silence of prison is a mental torture, denying opposition and personal will; the monastery's Rule of Silence, however, becomes a habit of contemplation, a turning away from the exploitative possibilities of speech. In the script, Jim interrogates his new friend:

> JIM: Uh-huh, and, is that no talking stuff, is that *hard*. . .?
> YOUNG MONK: Actually, no, I think it's quite refreshing. . .
> *Jim nods.*[258]

Employing the rhetoric of con man and crook, Jim informs Ned he has decided to "check into the *deal* here . . . three squares and a cot."[259] The ascetic life offers Jim an opportunity to pursue elusive answers and to quiet fear born of the prison's beatings. The choice is assisted by his winning of the lottery, "awarded by the machinery of *chance*. . . ."[260]; that is, Jim is the chosen one to speak at the Shrine of St. Ann. More than having undergone a great personal change, Jim is, ironically, perhaps the best suited of them all to deliver the sermon, which epitomizes his best qualities: it is touching, simple, simultaneously naïve and lost, all revealing Jim to be, in his fashion, a superior priest. His message is one founded upon necessity. The scene is pivotal: he recites the Colt pamphlet as far as it will serve him, then is left alone with questions and unfinished thoughts. He abandons, as he moves beyond it, the code of violence and revenge, and with new courage he looks upon the emptiness of life. The law of the gun can only exacerbate the world's pain, not solace or heal. Jim finds, finally, not conclusive proof of divine providence, but a simple realization of the power and grace of belief: "All I know, something *might* give you comfort . . . maybe you *deserve* it . . . it *comforts* you to believe in God, you *do* it."[261]

The monastery also represents another manifestation, perhaps the apotheosis, of Mamet's male communities, free not only of obscurities of speech but of sexual tensions. Mamet's own words imply a close association between male and religious pursuits:

It's good to be in an environment where one is understood, where one is not judged, where one is not expected to perform — because there is room in Male Society for the novice and the expert. . . .

Is this male companionship about the quest for grace? Yes, it is. But not the quest for a mythical grace, or for its specious limitations. This joy of male companionship is a quest for and can be an experience of *true* grace, and transcendent of the rational and, so, more approximate the real nature of the world.[262]

The circumstances of the monastery — its male sharing, its opportunities for learning and ritual, its contemplative silence — offer Jim a legitimate chance for a new life, whether or not God and miracles exist. In belief, in sharing, hope and rejuvenation await. As Levesque remarks to Ned concerning the Weeping Virgin: "That's the wonderful thing about what you have written, you and your friend. . . . That we never forget that it's simply a hole in the roof."[263]

Ned must undergo a different trial than Jim, to suit different needs. In place of Jim's hurt bewilderment, Ned rages, albeit comically, against his world's unreasonableness. His initial conception of a new world is predictably limited, a vague reversal of power: "I'm gonna do it all, pal. . . . And then I'm gonna do it again — and I'm gonna get two the best of everything — and anybody muck with me is going down."[264] The attitude is reminiscent of De Niro's confident, spiteful, nearly omnipotent Capone; Ned is, before his conversion, a hopeful petty crook, but lacking the essential corruptness for success. Instead, from the beginning — studying the poster pinup in his cell as if it were a beatific figure, watching the whore Molly change clothes before a window — Ned's concerns are of the flesh. What Mamet's characters traditionally lack, writes Bigsby, "is any definable sense of values beyond the material, any clear conception of need unrelated to immediate physical urgencies."[265] But like Jim, Ned finally seeks higher assistance:

NED: Sometimes you just need *help*.
FATHER LEVESQUE: Yes.
NED: . . . and there *is* no help.
FATHER LEVESQUE: Did you ask *her*?
NED: I suppose I *did*.
FATHER LEVESQUE: For what?
NED: For help to get from one place to another.[266]

The script contains much skepticism toward true miracles, but nevertheless each sincere request for help *seems* to be met by divine, mystical generosity. Often, of course, the solution arrives in a manner radically different from the speaker's intention. Ned's move to a new place, for example, is most significantly a move toward peace, away from lust toward *union* with a woman. Molly and Ned express to each other desire to change, and although hers is cloaked in the bitter business of selling her body and his in desperation to escape, still their eventual mutual dependence assures success together.

For Molly, the act of faith which begins her salvation — ironically, initiated by Jim's sermon — is the giving of her mute girl to Ned for the shrine's Procession of the Afflicted. This demonstrates a hesitant trust in Ned, honest wish for change, and acknowledgement of the *possibility* of miracles. For Ned's part, he must make a selfless act. By diving into raging water after Molly's child, he both puts the girl's life ahead of his own and surrenders himself to the will of nature, a power beyond him. The water, moreover, functions as a purifying baptismal sacrament.

> The wall of water. The figures of Ned and the Little Girl are dragged through the foam. They plunge into the fury below. . . . The foaming reservoir. Ned, struggling in the current, going under. The Madonna floats by him. He grabs it, floats with it, pulling the Little Girl with him.[267]

By "submerging" personal resistance to faith and placing the life of the child first, Ned is granted the Madonna as a raft. Like much of the film, the rescue seems arbitrary, accidental, yet with a slight inexplicable mystery. In *The Shawl,* confidence games and mystical powers are obscurely united; here the Madonna, before plummeting into water, is conspicuously wrapped in a shawl, which Levesque opens to reveal that the *"area around the heart and that area on the shawl are covered in blood."*[268] Although the miracle is quickly dispelled by the emergence of Bob, wounded and hiding, still the evocative potency of the bleeding Virgin, wrapped in a shawl, contains all the power of a personally efficacious folk religion, where a worshipper may touch and see directly, where an explanation of miracles is seldom convincing.

The consequence of Ned's act is the "miracle" of the child speaking, unfortunately of the men's secret. That "convict" is misheard as "convert" is comical and appropriate, as by this point both men are indeed converted. This is the act of contrition and confession necessary before Ned and Jim pursue new lives. Final assurance of their freedom is the discovery of the corpses of Fathers Brown and Riley, to serve as scapegoats for the men's pasts and, most importantly, to satisfy the Warden's Old Testament lust for blood: "There is no escape from fate, gentlemen. As it is written, so shall it be done. Thus men pursue a life of crime. They sought death and shame, and they have received it."[269] Only once fear of capture is gone and the bridge is open before him can Jim freely choose a monastic life. Ned essentially replaces his lost companion with Molly and her girl; his response to Molly's amazement at his recent actions is a last reminder of the necessity of belief:

> MOLLY: You worked a miracle, is that the truth?
> NED: Hey, believe what you *wanna* believe...
>                 . . .
> MOLLY: It *moved* me, I'm thinking about, I'll take holy order.
> NED: Holy orders.
> MOLLY: Yeah.
> NED: You're sure that's what you want to do...?
> MOLLY: Can you think of a better idea...?
> NED: A better idea ... Yeah. Maybe I can ... maybe I can.[270]

Thus, Ned's libidinous hostility is reborn as traditional familial affection, which the three will explore in a new land. The script stresses that Jim *"retreats toward the American side,"*[271] while Ned and Molly *"walk farther into Canada."*[272] One is reminded of Mamet's continual concern with immigration, an open policy of which would "give us humility before God."[273] Here the story is inverted—America has become, rather than a haven, a prison to escape. In his review of *We're No Angels,* Travers makes the following comparison:

> Mamet's theme of redemption—that two crooks can supply the inspiration religion cannot—is sweet but slight.... In Mamet's recent play, the Hollywood satire *Speed-the-Plow,* a secretary played by Penn's former wife, Madonna, tried to persuade a studio hotshot to make a serious film instead of a prison buddy picture. *Angels* sounds a lot like that film. A Mamet in joke?[274]

Further, the star of *Speed-the-Plow's* proposed trash film, Doug Brown, is repeated in *Father* Brown, a name Jim recalls with difficulty. At one point, Ned and Jim overlap: "I think *you're* Brown."[275] Perhaps within *We're No Angels* is indeed the post-apocalTyptic vision anticipated in the amoral negotiations of Mamet's play. The prison/hell seems recognizable as a doomsday prognosis of *The Bridge;* if so,

Mamet's screenplay offers two alternatives of escape from the torture the country has become, in a film which conflates sadistic entertainment and revelatory prophecy. Jim chooses the cloistered life, the company of men under patronage of the Virgin, in silent denunciation of the Warden's hatred. Ned escapes with his newly acquired family to a virgin land. The alternatives, then, are either spiritual retreat or physical departure.

*Speed-the-Plow* anticipates both actions. Moreover, Ned's elemental trial by water is related in Mamet's short story "The Bridge": "The river kept rising, and he was filled with great remorse. All of a sudden the hot water from the river came up in a rush and, at once, the lake beyond became a wall of cool and saving water. . . ."[276] And from *Speed-the-Plow* is an echo of Ned's miracle:

> He puts his hand on the child's chest . . . if *ever* in his life he had the power, any power. . . He says: years later: it did not occur to him then that this was happiness. That the thing he lacked, he says, was *courage*. What does the tramp say? "All fears are one fear. Just the fear of death. And we accept it, then we are at peace."[277]

*The Bridge*'s gospel of a world aflame is realized in *We're No Angels'* subterranean prison and in the fear of two men who escape it. Karen's explanation could be those very feelings the convicts cannot articulate:

> A life lived in fear, and he says, It Says In The Book, it doesn't have to *be* so. . . . And you *can't* join a convent, or "cut off your hair," or, or, or, you see, this is our pain, I think, we *can't* embrace Jesus. *He,* you see, and he says, "I know. And you don't have to be afraid." And I realized: I haven't *breathed*. How long? In *years*. From, I don't know. From terror, perhaps ever. . . . And he says that, that these are the Dark Ages.[278]

And these, perhaps, are finally and centrally the lessons of *We're No Angels*: realization of nothingness, reconciliation with personal mortality, the necessity of belief and generous actions. The film, psychologically, is the casting off of childhood and imposed self-loathing for the assumption of humility and a *desire* to nurture and share.

Mamet's cleverness is his creation of a script in which the most compelling theme transforms earlier concerns—gambling, speech, male relations—in a light of spiritual relevance, the same social concerns Bobby Gould explains "Won't Make A Good Movie."[279] Mamet welds a blighted landscape to buddy picture, prison-break thriller, border town Western; he creates, in essence, the film *Speed-the-Plow*'s operators lack the courage and resources to accomplish, the "stories people need to see. To make them less afraid. It says in *spite* of our transgressions — that we could do something. Which would bring us alive. So that we needn't feel ashamed."[280] Vaguely, wishfully, Jim announces to Ned: ". . . I'm gonna do something *important*. . . . I figure you're only alive so long, you might as well *do* something with yourself."[281] Perhaps nowhere else do con man and instructor, entertainer and esthete, come together so completely in a single Mamet work. The writer professes identification with criminals, but neither do the metaphysical overtones of his profession escape him:

> If you are going to work in the true theater, that job is a great job in this time of final decay; that job is to bring to your fellows, through the medium of your understanding and skill, the possibility of communion with what is essential in us all: that we are born to die, that we strive and fail, that we live in ignorance of why we were placed here, and, that, in the midst of this we need to love and be loved, but we are afraid.[282]

Theatre, like so many lives, "is about longing and the desire for answers. . . ."[283] Mamet feels as much priest and prophet as he does criminal outcast; the nature of his vocation seems finally religious, but including a necessary and ideally beneficial confidence game of belief.

# CHAPTER V

# *Homicide*
## Dark Conclusions

Three-quarters through *Homicide,* Mamet's third film as writer/
director, Detective Robert Gold commits to the harrowing night which
will leave him devastated and without alliances. He issues the Mametic
cry for help, inverted as a deeper need *to* help. "What you're doing
tonight. Let me help. Please. (*Beat.*) I'm begging you."[1] Such a request
requires and receives an answer. Gold finally is willing, even eager, to
submit to a darkness that has continually surrounded him, to *act*
regardless of consequences. As reward, the "Dark Woman" listens to
his café confession — "They said I was a pussy, because I was a Jew"[2] — of
a lifetime's repression and ethnic self-hatred. Gold is assigned an act
of contrition, not verbal or intellectual but physical, a demand to begin
to answer the conflicts of loyalties which suffocate him.

He takes lock pick and briefcase bomb, removes his badge. An irrevocable shift in alliances "from his uniform to his heritage"[3] has taken
place. He forces entry into Andersen's model train store. Inside, he is
surrounded by miniature representations of American tradition, har-
mony, and peace. His view holds for a moment on a display of police
officers in a small town setting. The figures are idealized, yet also speci-
mens under glass. Raised arms promise protection for the innocent and
also recall a Nazi salute. The toys represent a utopic America, unsoiled,
untarnished, full of hope and helpfulness; meanwhile, they subvert
this dream. Gold approaches a door which reads "Stock Room: Keep
Out." Throughout the film he has disregarded warnings of demarcated
areas. What he finds in the forbidden space is the cancer beneath
the toys' deceitful placidity: Nazi uniforms — suggesting police uniforms — and photos of genocide hung as if trophies of accomplishment.

141

A prominent Swastika hangs as if in a shrine, while beneath waits an antiquated printing machine, functional, lurid, twisted in black steel like an obscure torture instrument. Indeed it inflicts torture, in the form of a palpable hatred sufficient to destroy a country from within. *"CRIME IS CAUSED BY THE GHETTO, THE GHETTO IS CAUSED BY THE JEWS!"*[4] fliers attest. Gold finds behind the door a library of lies, a terrifying embodiment of evil. His hand traces over pamphlets. He lifts a copy of *The American Christian Sentinel.* Ironies invade his naïveté. He returns to the storefront, heaves a model train through glass protecting an idealized American town. He sets the bomb and crosses the street as the shop explodes into flame, a miniature holocaust of his own making.

Such is the most emotionally charged sequence, the true climax, of Mamet's *Homicide.* The cogency of Gold's conversion from decorated officer to Zionist terrorist—that is, from one protecting the illusion of a sparkling America to one revealing its hypocritic underbelly—is dependent on the shock of the unadulterated racial hatred he exposes. *Homicide* is a relentlessly bleak film, Mamet's darkest work physically, philosophically, psychologically. The descent of its protagonist recalls both *Edmond* and *The Verdict,* but finally the story doesn't extend even the slight hope of those works.

Much of the film's action comprises exploration of physical darkness. In the opening sequence, an F.B.I. SWAT team bursts into a black (in both respects) tenement apartment. They are armed, ready to either administer or receive death, penetrating the dark with frantic flashlights which suggest both a myopia of violence and a great opacity that will not be penetrated. In a screenplay draft, the criminal Randolph is a representation of this blackness, of an unalterable racial separation symbolizing deep division in the human psyche: "You'll never get me, *I cannot be killed.* I curse you all. You try to kill me? I cannot be killed. *I curse all who come after me!!!"*[5] The violence he represents is primordial, discerned only in the shimmerings of indirect light. Likewise, Gold undertakes much of his police activity in the dark. Trying to determine whether a sniper may be shooting at the Klein family, he climbs to an adjoining roof, ignores another "Keep Out" sign, and steps into unremitting nighttime. This indicates a search more significant than routine police work. Gold, as detective, peers into darkness, rounds blind corners, and continually leaps into the unknown. Even when working in daylight, the cops stalk into dim rooms, guns drawn, through cramped, empty interiority. In an unmistakable action, Gold, late at night, crosses the boundary into Klein's candy store, searching for answers not only to an old woman's murder, but to his own existence. If a toy store may reveal unanticipated malevolence, so too in this incongruous setting Gold may find an old woman's supposed treasure and its attendant meanings. *"A large sticker:* CRIME SCENE. DO NOT ENTER. *Gold's hand comes into the frame with his flashlight, rips the sticker."*[6] He descends to the basement — having earlier dispatched its gate-guarding hound — and searches debris. A cop overhead asks, "You all right down there, Detective?"[7] and ruminates whether the presence of a "rich Jew lady" might indeed cause violence in such a ghetto, a philosophy unconsciously, frighteningly akin to the neo–Nazi fliers.

Mamet says *Homicide* superficially concerns "a fellow trying to find out where he belongs. . . ." "He's an assimilated American Jew and he's also a policeman, so to which society does he belong?" More basically, Gold is "a mythic character trying to find out where and how to belong in the world."[8] *Homicide* doesn't initially appear as convoluted or clever as Mamet's earlier films. The plot, in which physical action on the urban battlefield mirrors a spiritual struggle, is immediately evident in its dual function. Caryn James notes that Mamet "uses a pop genre to delve into these volatile, serious issues." Beyond being merely a "buddy-cop-murder-mystery," the film presents a "harsh, revisionist view of America as a land of ethnic hatred."[9] Owen Glieberman feels *Homicide* is "a clever package" and "comes on as more of a down-and-dirty *movie* than Mamet's previous two films. . . . Beneath its seamy, violent surface, *Homicide* turns out to be a somber meditation. . . ."[10] Ansen agrees the film is Mamet's "most visually fluid," but elaborates that "it shares with his other films a relish for the kind of old-fashioned, rat-tat-tat plotting that entraps its hero (and the audience) in its steel claws."[11] Mamet supports both apparent and cloaked interpretations. He acknowledges the story is "about belonging" and is "based on my experience and the experience of a lot of my friends who grew up not feeling sufficiently Jewish or American. . . . It's a problem of reconciliation and self-worth"[12]; he also notes his enjoyment in making an action film: "I've always believed in good, old-fashioned American movie-making where there is suspense and resolution. *Homicide* is ultimately a cop movie, so I wanted to be true to the genre. . . ."[13] Nevertheless, the film's cynicism, especially in its ending, caused reviewers difficulty. Although Gold is indeed trapped, essentially "conned" by impossible circumstances, his damnation seems inevitable, ordained finally by neither professional hustler nor malignant deity, but simply by the corrosive nature of unalterable cosmic forces.

The deputy mayor's assistant, Patterson (Louis Murray), turns away from Robert Gold (Joe Mantegna), raising racial and political tensions; Tim Sullivan (William H. Macy) sits between his partner and trouble in *Homicide*.

Every significant Mametic theme is represented in *Homicide,* and each is given a new, frequently darker, interpretation in the context of Bobby Gold's self-destruction. Gold shares traits with previous protagonists, his situation with previous settings. He is introduced as a loyal and decorated cop. Police work is the "source of his loyalty, his pride, his identity as a man."[14] The job brings men together in a gritty and familial interdependency. "You're like my family, Tim," Gold admits to his partner; the response is a matter-of-fact, "Bob ... I *am* your family..."[15] In the script draft, Gold's partner gushes, "Cause I love you, Babe. I love you.... Closer than a brother, Baby."[16] Like other Mamet men, Gold has no family besides his male peer group. Like the salesmen and hustlers preceding them—the values in *Homicide* deviate alarmingly little—the police share a sense of group history, effectiveness, and romanticism. "Gimme couple serious Irish cops," says one detective, echoing a group sentiment, *"cigars* in their mouths, go out there..."[17] They pride themselves on a street toughness missing from the F.B.I.'s aloofness and excess and, perhaps naïvely, separate themselves from the politics of City Hall. Gold, writes Corliss, "thinks of himself as traditional cops do: in his heart he's Irish."[18] Problems arise when the good cop realizes conflicting currents of Judaic blood.

Certainly Gold is a recognizable Mamet "hero," although his particular dilemma and resolution ring telling changes on such expectations. In an earlier draft, Gold's name is Robert Ross, associating him
with both Richard Roma and his unseen namesake "R. Ross" in *Speed-
the-Plow.* The altered name, however, forces a comparison to
Robert—i.e. Bobby—*Gould,* who undergoes a comparable, if less
devastating, quest for meaning and identity. Variously, Gold reminds
one of all these characters, as well as both Mike *and* Ford from *House
of Games.* Early in *Homicide,* he is a curious mixture of tentativeness
and cocksure aggression. In his first scene, a tense meeting between city
cops and the deputy assistant mayor and his assistant Patterson (both
black),[19] Gold criticizes the FBI and boasts of the police's ability to
crack a volatile racial manhunt. Patterson is combative, bigoted, sim-
mering with violence and accusations. Yet only when he calls Gold a
"kike" is the detective shocked; Gold backs away, muttering obscenities
and slurs, while his partner (whose name the film changes from Senna
to Sullivan) defends his partner's reputation. Originally, Gold/Ross
himself explodes in response, yet the film's reversal of lines is more convincing. Gold's vulnerability, which a lifetime of bravado has attempted to conceal, is his Jewishness. Mamet discusses the process of
such denial: "We Reform Jews would be so stalwart, so American, so
non– Jewish, in fact, as to Play the Game. . . . We celebrated our
autonomy, our separateness from God and from our forefathers, and
so, of course, we were afraid."[20] Such a result explains Bob Gold.

Sullivan, in assuming his partner's defense, seems not so much
offended by the implied belittling of the Jewish race as by the reminder
of Gold as part of that cultue, which thereby revokes his membership
in the Irish clan of policemen. Sullivan may call Gold a "kike" with im-
punity, as he "loves" him and has granted honorary Irish heritage. In
the draft, the detectives "kid" Gold about being a "fucken *Christ
killer*";[21] Sullivan/Senna later remarks they have "*Jews* up the *wazoos*
today. . . ."[22] Small wonder, surrounded by such family warmth, Gold
is confused within his defensive constructs and eagerly susceptible to
pressures brought upon him by militant Zionists, a clandestine faction
understanding of his own covert motives.

Early on, Gold *is* an effective cop—confident, assured, experienced, easily recognizable as the informed half of Mamet's typical mentor-
protegé dynamic. He and Sullivan accidentally come across the murder
in Klein's candy store—the beginning of continual, inextricable overlapping of two racially charged cases involving Gold—and while Sullivan

is anxious to leave, Gold, as is his wont, cannot resist a cry for help, this time from a pair of scared rookies. A patrolman stutters, "Give me a hand, man, just, just, just..."[23] Gold coolly assumes control — clarifying, explaining, ordering: "You cordon off the fucken area, nobody in, nobody out, you wait 'til your sergeant shows up, I was never here. Where's your partner?"[24] He rescues the second man, issues further instructions — including correct advice that someone "hanging 'round could be the *guy,* ya understand, the ... *killer*..."[25] — and, in *Homicide's* unsettling habit, is penalized for his helpfulness by being pulled off the nationally prominent Randolph manhunt and instead having to "babysit" the candy store. A black captain commands: "You got the case. You caught the case. Do your job."[26] The price of decency is admonishment, reprimand, and penalty. Ms. Klein, granddaughter of the murdered woman, tells Gold, "We need your help, Detective"; he responds, "And I swear to you that I will give it to you."[27] Where often in Mamet's work a direct and sincere request for help is invariably answered with generosity, again *Homicide* is pessimistic. A pattern emerges where Gold insists upon helping, whether such assistance is requested or not, and invariably is made to regret his involvement.

Early in the film, to offer aid is shown to cause both physical and psychological injury. Gold is verbally assaulted by the assistant Patterson for his offer to bring Randolph in; soon afterward Gold is attacked by a prisoner. Referred to in the script as the Grounder, the latter is a sort of theological inquisitor, a murderer and philosopher: "Perhaps I could tell you the nature of Evil.... Would you like to know how to solve the problem of evil?" Gold responds, "No, man, cause if I did, then I'd be out of a Job..."[28] During the Grounder's attack (an attempt to steal a weapon for suicide) Gold's gun strap is torn, a reiterated motif in the film; Gold attempts to retain his gun even as his identity as police detective slips away, leaving him unarmed during a final, symbolic encounter with Randolph. The strap, in the interim, becomes entangled in his pocket with evidence from the Klein case, just as two identities, cop and Jew, wrestle for dominance. Gold sustains a head wound during his scuffle with the Grounder; from then on he is in pain, often woozy, "marked" by his encounter with evil. Where in the past Mamet presented acts of charity as crucial to grace, it is typical of *Homicide* that Gold suffers for his assistance. Corliss refers to the movie as "Mamet's dandy morality play, where bad things not only happen to good people, they are caused by them."[29] Sullivan's offhand response to Gold's wound tells of the operating theology: "Well, that's

Detective Bobby Gold (Joe Mantegna) and his partner Tim Sullivan (William H. Macy) stake out the tenement of Randolph's mother in *Homicide*.

what you get for Being Born,"[30] a guilt-by-birth association Gold secretly believes.

As Gold's response to the Grounder indicates, the careers of the detectives — thus the perpetuation of their group — are like those of the con men, gangsters, and thieves before them in Mamet, dependent on evil, specifically on the existence and healthy continuation of crime. In the world of *Homicide,* there is little chance the police will lessen suffering and victimization. In this America, writes James, "there is plenty of evil to go around."[31] In a profession predicated on violence, the men remain playful, enjoy a recognizable banter and wit, and perceive their job as both performance and play. Gold and Sullivan are frequently self-conscious of their *roles* as detectives. Early on, they agree a situation needs "Some of that 'police' work that people talk about."[32] Sullivan later pulls Gold out of musings on the candy story by suggesting they "play some cops and robbers, we'll bust this Big Criminal. We'll swagger around..."[33] In the draft, Gold invites a shoemaker to "play 'policeman'"[34] with him. Existential questions are answered with routines of job and office, as Gold explains in the draft: "No such *thing*'s a mystery.... This is police work."[35] Corliss argues that *Homicide* preaches a "truism of urban survival: You're what you do (cop work) more than what you are (a Jew)."[36] Ironically, the men's

professional view of themselves is always either cryptically cynical—
Gold confesses to Randolph's mother, "we're the garbage men"[37]—or
among themselves full of mocking derision for traditional ideals of the
officer in society. Gold answers the press with a sardonic cliché of service: "Our 'plan'? Our 'plan' is to serve and protect. . . ."[38] Like Stone's
introduction in *The Untouchables,* when asked of his allegiance and intentions Gold slips into anachronistic jargon.[39] The police's function in
*Homicide* is not to serve the innocent—who are they?—but to
perpetrate their livelihood through a symbiotic relationship with crime.
They exist not as embodiments of a peaceful America upholding community, but as testimony to anarchy and proliferating violence, a profession offering haven for the nihilism, profanity, and anger of Mamet's
male society.

Along with denigrating self-consciousness and mockery of their
roles—and since such roles define the men, questions of personal worth
and the value of right and law-abiding actions is cast into doubt—are
references to play and gamesmanship such as constitute other ostensibly serious and deadly professions in Mamet. On the first page of the
script an F.B.I. gunman is described only as a *"man in a baseball cap."*[40]
Referring to the rendezvous to apprehend Randolph, a dangerous
setup where fatalities are likely, Sullivan's metaphor is the Mametic
poker game: "You bring the Chips, I'll bring the Cards."[41] This allu-
sion to *House of Games'* activities is appropriate; the cops are attempting to con the fugitive with a false passport and a betraying mother.
City government, too, seems inculcated in performance and play, is
"producer" of the cops' drama: "City wants to pay to put a *show* on,
put on a show," rationalizes Gold.[42] His role in the show is as
benevolent half of a traditional "good cop–bad cop" burlesque. In a
deleted scene where detectives interrogate Sims for his brother-in-law
Randolph's location, Gold admonishes his colleague's harshness: "Back
off. Back off, Charlie. Leave the kid alone." Olcott, playing his own
part with a convincing cruelty indistinguishable from reality, responds,
"Fuck you, I ain't leav'n him *nothing*. . ."[43] Gold is the pacifying, ar-
bitrating influence, extracting trust through kindly earnestness. But as
he leaves the room, a simple direction exposes the artificiality and true
agenda of such behavior: Gold *"exchanges a look with Olcott. They
both nod."*[44] Their scam is rendered all the worse by the implication
of its being enacted by "public servants," men with a Machiavellian
justification lacking sympathy. Physical threats seem honest by comparison to their betrayals of trust.

[GOLD]: Kid's gonna topple.

. . .

JAMES: You got the touch, Bobby.
[GOLD]: Uh-huh.
JAMES: Y'always did.[45]

Perhaps the most distinguishing characteristic of Robert Gold as a Mamet protagonist, aside from the ubiquitous presence of Joe Mantegna, is the verbal facility he brings to his role of "hostage negotiator," of trust-inducing manipulator. He is the designated speaker of his group, recognized likewise by criminals (Sims) and citizenry (the mother). "His reputation as a cop," writes J. Hoberman, "is based on his (crypto–Jewish) linguistic skill . . . but that's only a trick for the goyim."[46] Gold's self-defining power of language is stressed particularly early in the film, when the ability is most stable and persuasive. In the script draft, Sullivan explains his partner's importance in their process: "We get the broth-in-law, Sims, we sic the Mouthpiece . . . on him, turn him around, give his brother up. . . . Who could charm a bird off a Fig Tree."[47] Sullivan protests when "downtown" forces transfer Gold to the candy store case. "We're goin' in, Mutt and Jeff, and we need Bobby. We need 'The Orator.'"[48] Sims recognizes Gold as "the *talkin'* man,"[49] implying their past encounters. Gold is recognizably, conspicuously Mametic in this regard. He sits down to talk like a skilled craftsman going to work. As usual, Mantegna's performance is powerful, convincing in both Gold's early braggadocio and the deterioration of this façade into hesitation, doubt, and fear. John Powers agrees that Mamet's repetitive, theatrical dialogue works most effectively and unobtrusively "whenever Bobby's doing the talking. Joe Mantegna slips into Mamet's lines like a surgeon into his gloves."[50] Yet again style and content form a seamless whole: Mantegna is the most fluid and persuasive of Mamet's actors; Gold is the chosen, accomplished speaker of the cops' "lines."

Gold is implicated further by the purpose and result of his velvety speech. He succeeds in coercing Sims into betraying Randolph and with almost equal ease convinces the mother to give the police her son. The implication in both cases is destruction of the family. Olcott instructs Sims of his compromising situation: "You don't give him up, you're goin' inside, you know *you're* going. . ."[51] Ruin one's own life, ruin one's brother-in-law's — for Sims the choice is unavoidable. Mantegna's overview of *Homicide*'s compassionless world applies at every level: "It seems to come down to being *alone* as opposed to that old saying, we're all in this together. In other words, what's first and foremost is that you have to do what's right for you."[52] This holds equally true for victim and bully. As the most accomplished speaker, Gold is thereby spokesman for his group and the group's purpose. Again language is power, and again it is put to terrible use. In eradicating the family it charts a death Mamet has lamented throughout his work. Doubly terrifying is that this seems the singular purpose of men whose job it is not to "serve and protect," but to manipulate, brutalize, and debase, to preserve a filmic desert Ansen refers to as "Mametland, that gritty, aggressive, masculine universe that looks like reality but sounds like the theater, where every pungent insult and staccato phrase is savored by the actors like a holy wafer."[53] The *characters* proceed as if on an unquestioned, unquestionable crusade of punishment. Because Gold is a law officer, rather than thief, salesman, or confidence artist, he is the least sympathetic protagonist of the Mamet-Mantegna collaborations.

Gold's "finest" moment of persuasion comes in a tenement apartment when he convinces an old woman to surrender her son, promising help, promising with twisted syntax "to bring him down alive."[54] When the detectives' aggression fails, Gold, to the continued marvel of his colleagues, assumes his part. He removes his tie — recalling the symbolic ties in *Things Change,* now law enforcement rather than crime — and loosens his collar to imply expansion, opening of generosity and understanding. Gold is a rhetorician in the tradition of Ricky Roma, and he is a passionate performer. He inverts the mother's beliefs to the extent that to *not* turn in Randolph would be betrayal:

> You think I don't know that? I know that. Looking for something to love. You *got* something to love. You got your boys. That's something. Look in my eyes. *(Beat)* I want to save your son. Before God. I want to save your boy. *(Beat)* Will you help me?[55]

Gold is a speaker worthy of his predecessors. His "sympathy" touches the mother's sole remaining value, confuses right and wrong, duty and need, invokes the name of a higher force, and in a pleading tone both vow and confession ends with a Mametic cry for help which cannot be resisted.

However, who is helping whom? Since Gold's primary need is *to* help, wherein he *is* helped, his assistance throughout the film is problematized, subverted. In the scene with the mother his monologue is interrupted at its tearful climax by intrusion, via telephone, of "the Yids," a pattern repeated with increasing frequency as the story proceeds, loyalty superceding loyalty. The question is not whether Gold is insincere during his performances — often the words ring with bitter truth — but whether sincerity is important compared to intention. Gold's goals ostensibly are his partner's goals: to uncover the hidden, to capture or kill the pursued. One senses that, sadly, taking Gold's advice may be the mother's best chance to prolong her son's life; however, he proves woefully untrustworthy. Later, the old woman's hateful, defeated eyes pass over Gold as a cruiser takes her slowly from the place where her son will soon die. Such is the consequence of trust; *she* is responsible, sharing a burden of guilt with Gold, who is singled out as the cause of her tragedy: "You the one. I'm going to *do* it, but I'm goin' to do it with *you*."[56] Gold fails as the chosen one, and as the script suggests the result of his failure is inescapable: "I swear it. The fires of hell on my head should I fail ... I'll take him in."[57] Gold invokes for himself a rhetoric of the questing hero he cannot equal in action.

Powers notes that Gold, like most Mamet protagonists, "uses daily routine to ward off the demons of self-knowledge."[58] Such artificial habits in a largely meaningless life identifies Gold, like the others, as philosopher. He initially lacks the self-awareness of, perhaps, Mike in *House of Games,* but his early con jobs of speech, particularly with the old woman, match Mike's challenging of Ford's reality, which soothes and leads toward trust, belief, risk. Less intentionally than Mike, but ironically with more completeness, he causes his "mark" to lose everything ventured. After Gold is called away from the mother, he arrives at the Kleins' with an attitude of defensiveness markedly lacking patience or charity — an attitude similar to Mike's peevishness once Ford has found him out. With a rushed, hyper-reasonability, with truncated sentences and even Mike's degrading use of quotation marks, Gold attempts to pacify a suspicious, hostile audience: "Look. You, you're under a lot of stress today, your 'tragedy,' I'm sorry for you. What happened to your mother. I'm going to station a man on the roof. You keep away from this side of the house. Okay?"[59] In the context of a grandmother having just been murdered, Gold's tone, while not as disparaging as Mike's "You got 'Stung,' and you're 'Hurt,'" is even more appalling. The detective evokes little sympathy during his descent in the film, from acquaintances or from audience, due to his own lack of compassion.

Curiously, Gold is as susceptible to language as he is dangerous with it. His loyalties are challenged by all around him, with a related question of his ability to do his job uncompromised. The nature and purpose of his job, of course, is cyclically determined by loyalties. Gold is easily shaken by the Klein family. After overhearing his vitriolic anti–Semitic tirade on the telephone, the grieving granddaughter, Ms. Klein, chastises Gold for his antagonism: "Do you hate yourself that much? [*Beat*] Do you belong nowhere. . . ?"[60] This last question seems to reverberate in Gold's muddled, injured head for the remainder of the film. Powers notes that the scornful question "becomes another kind of homicide: It shatters Bobby's rickety self-image."[61] What *are* one's loyalties? From every corner Gold is accused, suspected, a cop himself interrogated. The sway of language reinforces itself in symbols and by words cloaked in mystery. Most prominently, the term "Grofaz," found on a scrap of paper on the dark rooftop, exerts a hypnotic, totemic power over Gold. Mamet also stresses Gold's ignorance of Hebrew and Yiddish. The secret language, the tongue of heritage and identity present in such films as *Things Change,* is here incomprehensible to Gold, merely complicating his already cloudy alliances.

Unknown words are mere sound and symbol, and *Homicide* mixes physical images with its foreign languages. "Grofaz" itself is a sign of sorts, the explication of which becomes an obsession for Gold. The term literally wraps around the torn gun holster of lost retributive restraint. Among other prominent symbols is the gold Magen David on the corpse of Mrs. Klein.[62] At seeing the star, Gold *"fingers the bruise on his head. Beat. He looks down at the woman again."*[63] An enigmatic connection is sensed, a ghost exhumed. The scene foreshadows Gold's confrontation with the young Hassidic "Scholar" who compares this star to Gold's prominently worn gold detective star. "The pentagram cannot be deconstructed,"[64] reasons the man, and is a symbol of the earth and five senses which proves Gold's tie to the physical, the base, the spiritually limited and foresworn. In popular folklore, moreover, the pentagram marks one as a beast. The man also reiterates, during his exegesis on representative symbols, the significance of Gold's lingual ignorance: "You say you're a Jew and you can't read Hebrew. What *are* you then. . . ?"[65] In this library setting Gold explores the seeming clue of GROFAZ as an acronym for Hitler, a misleading trust in facts—on which empiricism his job is founded—greatly responsible for leading him deeper into the Jewish mystery of identity and determining his later actions.

Entranced by the power of signs, by arcane—to him—meanings,

by a growing paranoia of interrelatedness, Gold delivers himself for manipulation. The psychologist become patient, at this stage he is more similar to Ford than to Mike in *House of Games.* Anxiously, still on the pretext of a proper police investigation, Gold propels himself into unknown, unguessed mysteries of a militant Zionist subculture.

> CHAUFFEUR: How did you get this address? What are you doing here?
> BENJAMIN: Why are you here?
> GOLD: I need help. I want to know why she was killed.[66]

Gold's questions connote a concern beyond superficial procedure, a concern for the heritage on which his life depends. The sincere request for help receives an answer: a door opens, illuminating the night. Typical for *Homicide,* however, the light is partial, disguising a more dangerous deception; rather than purifying, light complicates and further obscures. Like Ford, Gold approaches by choice, compelled by personal necessity, the unknown rituals of a familial sub-society; as with Ford, the giving of trust is a mistake.

The Zionist faction euphemistically identifies itself as the "Society for Comparative Linguistics."[67] The script draft has the chauffeur ironically ask Gold, "You interested in the study of languages?"[68] Gold *is* interested; these unknown symbols may hold answers. The chauffeur reminds one of Silver from *Things Change;* burly Ricky Jay performs both parts, and both are powerful, articulate to the point of contrivance, and use speech to conceal, rather than reveal, a long tradition, a society with dual allegiances to word and gun. Gold steps from lonely darkness into a bright, relaxed, sharing male world that stuns and further confuses him. In Mamet's essay "The Decoration of Jewish Houses," the author considers what it means to be "racially" Jewish: "It meant that, among ourselves, we shared the wonderful, the warm, and the comforting codes, language, jokes, and attitudes which make up the consolations of strangers in a strange land."[69] Such comforts Gold lacks. The cost of application to such an organization, to a family, is recognition of his heritage *through* betrayal of police vows. Accusations are repeated:

> GOLD: . . . I am a sworn Police Officer, I . . .
> BENJAMIN: WHERE ARE YOUR LOYALTIES?[70]

The chauffeur responds reminiscently of Mike to Ford, delineating culpability: "You sought us out. I won't lie to you. We could use you."[71] Like a good confidence man, the chauffeur warns Gold of the danger impending on their continued association; like Ford, Gold ignores the warning, interpreted *merely* as candor.

The film makes an important alteration to the script draft. In the earlier story, Gold finds not only a confessor and compassionate ear in the figure of the Dark Woman/Chava, but also a lover. This would heighten a comparison to *House of Games,* where intercourse is crucial to Ford's involvement. The first time Gold and the woman meet, in the Klein house, she acts as his translator to a point, then stops. In the script draft she also washes Gold's face—ergo, his wound—after he returns from the roof. At first he *"flinches away from her"*[72] then responds to her offer of "Let me help you."[73] Later, she again succors him:

> *Beat. She moves toward him. She touches his forehead where it is bandaged. He recoils slightly, she touches it again. She touches his face very softly:*
> Would you like to make love to someone who looks like you?
>
> . . .
>
> [GOLD]: Yes. I would.[74]

The couple have intercourse in a car on a deserted street; afterwards, Gold lounges against the car, smokes a cigarette, and awaits the continuation of an irrevocable evening. The situation is comparable, except for shifts in gender, to the hotel tryst in *House of Games.* This original development also locates *Homicide's* structure, and Gold's dilemma, in conspicuous proximity to *Speed-the-Plow.* Even without sexual consummation, the comparison is telling. Sullivan/Fox is the pragmatic, profane male companion, suspicious of Gold/Gould's conversion, doubting anything beyond his cynical sphere of influence:

> What does it mean?
> Don't mean nothing. Some broad got killed.[75]

In the script draft, even Gold announces that "No such *thing*'s a mystery. *Women* are a mystery."[76] Clearly, Gold's struggle is analogous to Bobby Gould's: an attractive, mystical woman and a male partner in derision vie for his soul. Mamet's comments in "Women" seem applicable to either film or play:

> The difficulty, of course, is one *wants* something from women: notice, sex, solace, compassion, forgiveness; and that many times one

wants it sufficiently desperately that it clouds one's perception of what *they* want. And, in negotiations, it is never a good idea to lose sight of what your opponent wants.[77]

Just as Gould initially fails to recognize Karen's agenda with a proper "male" interpretation, Gold too surrenders to the Dark Woman/Chava's solace.

On one level, the tragedy of *Homicide*'s conclusion is Gold's failure to expose the woman until too late. Gould is allowed to return to a status quo of male power; but Gold is not. This identifies not only the utter bleakness of the film's world, but defines it as tragic rather than comic. Mamet's own classically influenced definition of the tragic protagonist seems perfectly descriptive of Gold and his fate: "He becomes, in one moment, the perfection of the Tragic Form: he gains self-knowledge at the same moment that his state is transformed from King to Beggar—like Oedipus Rex, like Lear, like any nation which has grown old."[78] The inclusion of an entire land in such a thesis is revealing, but first consider Gold: his ruination distinguishes *Homicide* from most Mamet works, where an element of redemptive possibility persists even in blackest scenarios. The film doesn't merely reflect typical concerns, but deals with questions of identity and spiritual trust in a manner that earlier work considered in indirect, representative forms, be it through con games, mafia structures, or national ideologies. Like the central, amorphous confessor in Mamet—psychic, con man, priest, salesman—the Dark Woman pulls Gold in with seductive syntax, leads him in a struggle for recognition of secrets:

> [CHAVA]: . . . What?
> [GOLD]: The way you spoke to each other.
> [CHAVA]: The way we spoke to each other tonight. And you saw what?
>    *(Beat)* What?
> [GOLD]: That you would die for each other. *(Beat)* Be . . .
> [CHAVA]: . . . yes . . .
> [GOLD]: . . . because . . . because of your . . . "race."
> [CHAVA]: You can say the word.
> [GOLD]: Because you're Jews. *(Beat)*
> [CHAVA]: That's right.
> [GOLD]: I . . . uh . . . you know . . . you know . . .
> [CHAVA]: No, but you can tell me . . . [79]

The woman is both inquisitor and therapist, while Gold performs as patient/confessor. Like his Mametic antecedents, namely Gould, he loses masculine bravado, instead stammering, faltering, struggling with unknown things, ideals, silences, and pauses. The woman, as archetypal figure, relieves the man of linguistic power and touches his need for meaning.

Much of Gold and the woman's conversations, both in tone and content, echo *Speed-the-Plow*'s discussions of *The Bridge*. Gold's need is virtually indistinguishable from Gould's. Cop, like film producer, strives to embrace an unlikely idealism:

> . . . sent to "Repair the World." All right. Fine. *I'll* do that. *I'll* fight for something. Listen, you, your people, looked at me. You said, "*He's* a Candidate . . . He's a loose cannon." It's true. Looking for something to . . .[80]

As in *Speed-the-Plow*, the script has Gold's conversion following coitus with a seductress. Such redundancy may be one reason Mamet altered the story. Gold's conversion is more compelling when caused by factors unrelated to sex. More significant issues of acceptance, release, compassion, and trust all remain intact and more focused by the absence of intercourse, which distracts from the story's heart. Gold's emptiness and self-loathing are the catalysts, assisted by but not dependent upon a woman—a story fresher, more moving, and finally more convincing. Nevertheless, critics questioned Gold's rapid conversion to saboteur: "But can we believe in Bobby's new, questioning spirit?"[81] wrote one reviewer; another argued that "Gold's transformation seems willed by artistic fiat."[82] Ironically, these echo a complaint leveled against *Speed-the-Plow*, the implausibility of Gould's rapid change; the alteration in *Homicide*'s plot to a less traditional cause must have been partially to avoid such resistance. Gold *does* convert rapidly once the single night that comprises the second half of the film has begun, and the audience is asked to believe this as consequence of a lifetime's denial. Travers offers a more generous and perhaps fairer interpretation of the film's concentrated action: "Gold's swift transition from cop to terrorist is hard to swallow, but its suddenness is integral to a man whose sense of duty is inextricably linked to violence."[83] Certainly the woman's presence, as confidant, *as* bridge, remains imperative to the film.

Chava's betrayal of Gold is devastating to him. With determined trust, Gold demands involvement with the terrorists. He blows up the train store, destroying not only previously unacknowledged bigotry and hatred but also the myth of a peaceful, virtuous, domestic America.

Bobby Gold (Joe Mantegna) confesses to Chava, the "Dark Woman" (Natalija
Nogulich), in *Homicide*.

Afterwards, the couple return to the all-night diner which serves as
Gold's confession booth and as their ersatz criminal hideaway. Here,
the detective's world effectively ends. One critic notes that the "complicated series of betrayals that climax the film are as deftly managed
as anything in *House of Games*...."[84] The chauffeur appears, again
demands Gold violate evidence and, at the detective's continued
refusal, produces snapshots of Gold in front of the exploding train
shop. In this case, the request for help may not be denied. Mantegna
plays the scene with beautiful subtlety. Gold looks up, acknowledging
betrayal but only gradually calculating the evening's cost. Two strangers
before him speak in a tongue he cannot decipher. When he resists, the
chauffeur hits him in the stomach; they leave him alone, staggered
against the bar. Gold pulls out Randolph's fake passport, sees the time
and location of the missed stakeout, and fully realizes the collapse of
his life. "My God," he whispers to no one but himself.

Betrayal, in *Homicide,* is mutual, reciprocal, and vindictive. As
Gold has been destroyed, so he destroys. He arrives at the erupting
crime scene in time to see Randolph's mother being driven away; she
has been made to betray her own son; she is finished. Gold has betrayed
Sullivan for a new and false partnership. He rushes through the hellish,

apocalyptic flames of an exploding police cruiser, a second holocaust of his own making, in time for Sullivan to die in his arms. There will be no return to the momentarily denied world of law and male companionship. Travers considers Gold's defeat: "In trying to trade one identity for another, he winds up in limbo, a permanent outsider. The film's climax places Gold in a bloody police shootout that is shattering in its desolation."[85] Mantegna elaborates that Gold, in trying to decide between loyalties, fails at both: "Gold says, 'Okay, if I can't be a good cop, I'm going to try to be a good Jew.' In the end, he winds up being neither."[86]

*Homicide* is a film without compassion or forgiveness; the entire society's motive seems a deep-seated ethnic hatred which inescapably ends in violent death. The bigotry which simmers in the background of other Mamet scripts—*The Postman Always Rings Twice, The Verdict,* especially in the idealized spectacle of *The Untouchables*—finds full force in a film where Mamet at last deals, albeit ambiguously, with his own heritage. After Sullivan's death, Gold screams at the unseen Randolph: "You shot my partner, you fucking nigger ... I'm going to kill you."[87] Gold, who has striven relentlessly for a sustaining family, to be Mamet's "team player," finds himself instead "cast in a traditional Jewish role he hadn't counted on, the eternal outsider."[88] Hoberman sees in Gold "an unhappy version of the abstract, essential Jew" evoked at the conclusion of Philip Roth's *The Counterlife,* further contending that in *Homicide* the "fantasies of Jews that haunt the gentile mind return to spook the Jews as well. The fact is, the Jews ... seem Other to Mamet, Gold, and even themselves."[89] Gold races alone into the bowels of the building which lead him to Randolph; his recklessness suggests not anger so much as willingness, indeed readiness, to die. This penultimate sequence is terrifying in its darkness of setting and tone, its resonance of death, imprisonment, and dungeon-like torture. Gold plunges into the black tomb. In Randolph he sees a representation of evil inextricable from his own bigotry, alienation, and guilt. After at last losing his gun, Gold arms himself with a convenient chain, a fated chain of unrelievable burdens. He stalks, as from the beginning, an indeterminate figure of shadows, steps unsteadily over a shifting floor. Of coal shale? Stones? The sounds evoke piles of bone, worthless human remains. "That's death calling, baby," taunts Randolph, "For you and for me."[90] If the Grounder is allegorical, teasing with explanations of evil, then Randolph is that evil in action. In the script draft, the black man's grandiose speech at the end echoes the opening scene: "I kilt

you *buddies* and I will kill *you,* I'll kill *all* of you, *you* cannot stop me.
*Nothing* can stop me. Nothing can stop me for I'll kill you *all. . . "*[91]
Randolph shoots Gold suddenly, pulling the trigger with precision and
shocking nonchalance.

Throughout the scene, Gold effects complete, almost divine
knowledge. He recognizes his burdens by the chain and accepts them.
He is strangely calm in acceptance, in the final minutes he shares with
Randolph, and suggests an authority which doesn't require a gun:

> RANDOLPH: Where's your gun, maan. . .? Motherfuckers, got lucky,
>     put me away, hour I'd of been an *airplane long gone* out of here.
> [GOLD]: No. You weren't going nowhere.
> RANDOLPH: Fuck you, you know, Baby Jim. . .?
> [GOLD]: I know everything. I know it all.
> RANDOLPH: Where's your gun?
> [GOLD]: I don't have one.[92]

Randolph, though barbaric and little more than an animal, elicits surprising pity. He is unredeemed, unredeemable, and without method
of escape. It is Gold, in this scene, who is unsympathetic. Having
resigned himself to damnation and death, to his own *essential* worthlessness, his weapon now is not the gun, but knowledge of betrayal,
knowledge sufficient to strip Randolph of a last dream—a narrowly
denied new life—and last hope—a mother's love. "It's all a piece of
shit," explains Gold. "I killed my partner. And your momma turned
you in, man."[93] In one bitter, terrible sentence, Gold announces the
charade of loyalties, an end of meaningful life and action, and delimits
his horrible omniscience. Betrayal is, his behavior testifies, all one can
or need know. "So we, like the heroes of tragedy," writes Mamet, those
who try to "appropriate . . . the attributes of God . . . must and will
and do suffer."[94] Gold undertakes the spiritual destruction of Randolph with a sadistic and masochistic glee, his torn body prostrate like
an unacknowledged sacrifice. While the setting—a black man and
white man together in isolated, circumscribed darkness, suffering their
and the race's sins—recalls *Edmond, Homicide* denies that play's final
possibility of at least the potentiality for union, meaning, and conti-
nuance. The only sharing between Gold and Randolph is a failed communion of pain. The police break in and fill Randolph with bullets; the
murderer, in turn murdered, offers in his final words not only an evocation of the almighty which echoes Gold's moment of betrayal, but also
a pitiful plea for help: "God . . . God . . . Help me. . ."[95] Although in

the script draft Gold *"pulls himself over to Randolph"* and *"cradles his head on his lap,"*[96] the film lacks such sympathetic recognition. Randolph dies alone, untouched by any kindness; the two men form a bloody, fatalistic tableau in the wavering of police flashlights.

Mamet's treatment of the individual invariably has social, and frequently national, significance. Just as his definition of tragic form includes the nation, so too *Homicide's* conclusion has relevance to specifically American themes in earlier works. This country, itself once haven and escape, has rather become the nightmare. Even the options of *We're No Angels,* of either spiritual or physical withdrawal, are revoked. One cannot remain immune to the far-reaching evil of this community, where the "hero's" climactic wish is to ravage and destroy. The passport necessary for escape is issued only *"for the purposes of . . . entrapment."*[97] The fate of Robert Gold reflects the degenerating events being undergone by American society. Mamet writes in his essay "Liberty":

> "Are we not," we ask, "the same good-hearted good-willed," in effect "lovable people we have always been? Are we not still beloved of God?" And as we ask we are brought low by humiliation after inevitable humiliation. These blows are inevitable because, as per the laws of tragedy, our story is not yet complete. We are undergoing reversal of our situation, but we are far from recognizing it.[98]

*Homicide* is the enactment of such a doomed fate. Mamet's recent efforts to locate grace, meaning, or alternative to apocalypse have rendered, at best, enigmatic results; his reversed attempt, however—life *without* hope—is convincing.

*Homicide* is so stark partly because it includes little of Mamet's trademark humor—jokes, always at their foundation, despairing. The comedy in this film is cosmic and ironic, a Job-like stripping of Gold far past his saturation point for suffering. He is denied the release of death; in the film's final sequence, he limps through the station house aided by a cane. His injuries are debilitating. The scene stresses irreparable separation from the police fraternity; his dress is civilian, and the interaction is uncomfortable and stressed. Gold learns for certain what he already knows, that he is no longer a homicide detective. Powers contends that *Homicide* is less about ethnicity than the broader issue of "people's desire for a sense of belonging, their way of battling isolation with paranoid fantasies that help them make sense of the madness around them."[99] As in Mamet's best work, subject and style are inseparable even if, as Powers contends, such unity is partly un-conscious: "Ironically, Mamet's own artistic stance smacks of paranoia — he's a control freak, bent on making everything fit his overall concep-tion."[100] By the end, Gold has lost even the fantasies which might sus-tain him. Mrs. Klein's killer — a casual, unrepentant black boy — has confessed. There has been no conspiracy, only a desire for hidden trea-sures, again revealing inherent ethnic tension and reinforcing two types: the black juvenile delinquent and the frugal old Jewish woman. "I told you why they killed her, man," a boy guilelessly repeats. "She had that *fortune* in her basement. . ."[101] This is *Homicide*'s humor.

The final joke against ex–Detective Robert Gold, in a malevolent universe where "good intentions curdle into disasters,"[102] is the revela-tion of "Grofazt" as a brand name for pigeon feed. Gold's information throughout has been incomplete; in his need to make connections, to be accepted and respected at both job and in performance of duty, he has collaborated in an elaborate paranoid fantasy of Nazism and Jewish persecution. Or *is* it fantasy? Are "Grofazt" and GROFAZ connected? The information arrives unexpectedly, without elaboration. The ap-pearance of the scrap of paper on the roof reinforces the world's ar-bitrariness, meaninglessness, and either lack of mystery or lack of abil-ity to define the mystery adequately. Still, the mere reappearance of the term is ominous, paradoxically evidence of unproveable intercon-nectedness, all with underlying Nazi cruelty.

The Grounder earlier promises Gold an explanation of evil, and the script draft fulfills this commitment with a silent communication at the end. The scene, although obscure, signifies the necessity of con-tinued pursuit of one's heritage and the unacceptability of shrugging responsibilities. In the film, this transaction is limited to a nod; the Grounder is uncommunicative. Gold is allowed no guidance. The Grounder's role in the film is, finally and appropriately, unsettling. The *possibility* of explicable causes, of any redemption, is denied. James corroborates this view: "When the man who offered to explain evil walks by at the end of *Homicide,* he is silent. Mr. Mamet has already shown the nature of evil and transformed a cop movie into a disturbing statement about American life."[103] Gold has learned, the reviewer continues, that "only a slap-happy fool believes in the myth of the melting pot."[104]

The script draft's final directions are also altered on film: *"In the background, the Grounder, in chains being led away by his guards. [Gold] walks to and past the camera. Fade out."*[105] Gold, like the

Grounder, fails in his pursuit of death and, like the other, for awhile must bear his chains. The film is consistently rendered even bleaker than its script draft, denying solace, contact, or forgiveness. Gold is last seen not moving beyond the framework of the camera, but *un*moving, silent, barred from former office. By all appearances, it is hard to imagine him ever again moving. Rather, one suspects his fade-out will be rapid. When searching *Homicide* for hopeful elements, there is little encouragement except perhaps the medium of film itself—"...a momentary and beautiful aberration of a technological society in the last stages of decay,"[106] declares Mamet. Film intrinsically prophesies, according to Mamet, the end of our life on the planet:

> Our confusion with the accelerated world created the need of and the fact of the first new art form in fifty thousand years, the movies.
> The movies stand between the past and the future, between human history and human extinction. They come into being at the beginning of the last stage of the Industrial Revolution, which is to say at the beginning of the End of the World.[107]

Mamet's allegiance to the art form which now occupies the majority of his attention is conclusive; it is a grim vision, however, which charts film's most valuable effect as record of man's inevitable self-destruction. *Homicide* is such a story of a species' race for annihiliation—lost, forelorn, imprisoned, without grace or compassion, an ending to con games and betrayals and language. As its title alludes, the film delineates a thankful, rather than mourned, obsolescence.

# CHAPTER VI

# Another Furious Season:

## *Glengarry Glen Ross,*
## *Hoffa,* Ad Infinitum

If during the beginning months of 1992 David Mamet's voice was uncharacteristically silent, the second half of the year was compensated by an explosion of material. Turner Network Television's Screenworks series debuted with an adaptation of *The Water Engine* in August. This production was the beginning of a remarkable season for Mamet. The author's first full-length play in nearly four years, *Oleanna,* opened under his direction Off Broadway at the Orpheum Theatre (following its original staging in Cambridge, Massachusetts, a year earlier); James Foley directed a stunning cast in the film version of *Glengarry Glen Ross;* and *Hoffa,* a big-budget production of Mamet's original screenplay, opened on Christmas Day. *American Theatre* cited Mamet as an "Editor's Choice" and noted, in addition to the above works, six productions of Mamet plays across the country during the forthcoming theatrical season.[1] *The Cabin,* a collection of prose reminiscences, was published in November.[2]

TNT Screenworks apparently considered *The Water Engine* a piece of authentic Americana. The film was directed by Steven Schachter, who originally brought the play to the stage, and based on a revised script by Mamet. Its most remarkable feature is a large and outstanding cast which includes virtually every recognizable Mamet player and a cameo by the author. As Charles and Rita Lang, William H. Macy and Patti LuPone reprise their roles from previous productions. John Mahoney is especially effective as the darkly avuncular patent officer Gross. Mamet tailors and refines the role of Oberman to suit Joe Mantegna, whose stylized performance is delivered through a clipped German

Carol (Rebecca Pidgeon) addresses her professor, John (William H. Macy), in *Oleanna*. Photo by Brigitte Lacombe.

accent. The lawyer represents those vague "concerns" of unnamed hierarchies of industry; the menace in his advice italicizes the limitations of realizing any personal ideal of success: "I swear to you, our offer is in your own best interests. Mr. Lang, I swear to you, you're in danger, and those who deal *with* you are in danger. You think I like conducting business in darkness?"[3] Macy, as the naïve inventor up against forces well beyond him, is touchingly convincing in his pride for a creation impossible to realize in the public sphere of profit: "I made it. . . . I saw it work."[4] The primary disappointment of the TNT production is the necessary elimination of stagecraft, which is arguably *The Water Engine*'s primary enjoyment. Layers of theatrical artifice — the ironic effect of presenting Lang's story through an on-stage radio production, the concurrent stories and voices unrestrained by the screen's temporal and spatial demands — self-consciously comment upon an otherwise flat, though bleak, story. The film's last scene is contemporary, visually panning across the voice-over's romantic notion of "torn and filthy manuscripts misfiled in second-hand bookstores"[5]; the tableau returns much of the story's poignancy, if not entirely the cryptic artifice of *The Water Engine* as mythologized past.

*Oleanna*, Mamet's controversial play of sexual harassment between a professor and his student featuring Macy and Rebecca Pidgeon, is expectedly provocative and topical. Critics agree the play is some sort of response to the Clarence Thomas hearings, and most remark upon its archetypal exploration of animosity between genders: ". . . the male fear of castration and the female fear of male force and rape."[6] Arthur Holmberg's lengthy review of *Oleanna* locates the play in a familiar Mametic territory "in which misunderstanding piled on misunderstanding builds a labyrinth of ambiguity."[7] Both professor and student — the defining Mamet relationship, endlessly inverted — whether or not they are willfully deceptive, portray incompatible views of "truth" and in doing so reveal their own manipulative agendas. The entire institution of higher education is "a house of cards, subject to linguistic instabilities."[8] Rich contends that *Oleanna* "is likely to provoke more arguments than any play this year"[9] and brings into question any possibility of meaningful discourse between men and women; Kroll remarks that "cunning logic"[10] is the source of the work's power. Mamet defends his unclarified alliances: "I write plays, not political propaganda. . . . We are living through a time of deep transition, so everyone is unsettled."[11] The play is, like *Speed-the-Plow*, notably *un*cinematic; on a sparse, interior battleground two characters enact their drama. Also like the previous play, and its recent coda *Bobby Gould in Hell*, the male struggles to maintain his identity, his defenses, his essence. While *Oleanna* shares concerns with Mamet's films, it also benefits from the director's cinematic experience with technique: "Filming *Homicide*, I learned the traditional bang-bang-bang way is wrong. It's too fast. Do it like a slow dance. . . . Be gentle with the violence. Then it terrifies."[12]

**Shelley Levene (Jack Lemmon) works to initiate a deal in the long night of** *Glengarry Glen Ross.* **Photo by Andy Schwartz.**

William H. Macy has emerged as a star to rival Mantegna on Mamet's dramatic horizon. The actor appears only in modest roles in *House of Games* and *Things Change,* but gives a vivacious, memorable turn as the partner Sullivan in *Homicide.* A hardened, cynical, and authentic Irish cop, Sullivan dies, possibly, as a consequence of his unrewarded trust in Gold. This tension is accountable partly to the difference in the actors. Macy's voice is generally softer than Mantegna's, the demeanor vaguely startled. His pale complexion and thin blond hair support such a delivery, suggesting him as a foil to his swarthy companion. Such an opposition is effective in both *Homicide* and TNT's *The Water Engine,* adding an additional elusive but germane complexity to Mamet's ensemble projects.

A separate but equally powerful ensemble, headed by Al Pacino and Jack Lemmon, populates the film version of *Glengarry Glen Ross.* Mamet's screenplay keeps the conventional second act largely intact, and it plays well on screen. Unfortunately, the virtuoso first act, flawless but inescapably "stagy," is dismantled and reconstructed for filmic presentation. Kauffmann commends the author's "sensitivity to form. . . . Mamet obviously wanted to reshape the work, to gather it back into himself and give it a new manifestation."[13] The Foley-Mamet film is notably darker than its antecedent; it lacks the play's humor and sympathetic portrayals. The film's halves represent day and night, and the first segment is especially somber, malicious, and as stormy as the rain which saturates every exterior. Director of photography Juan Ruiz Anchia's lush lighting is memorable; rich blues, reds, and greens flood the early scenes, surreally illuminating locales, designating the salesmen as alternately lurid or demonic. The long night constituting *Glengarry Glen Ross'* first half seems damned and unending. According to Kroll, it is "Mamet's vision of an American hell, a mutual trap for the chiselers and the chiseled."[14] Similarly, Corliss examines the work's revision: "The play was zippy black comedy about predators in twilight; the film is a photo-essay, shot in morgue closeup...."[15]

Foley's stylistic choices merely elaborate the persistent malice of Mamet's screenplay, the latter achieved primarily through the addition of Blake, a pressuring '90s sales consultant whose venom infects the film with virulent bitterness. In a single scene he elaborates his cruel equation of sales efficiency as manhood, as virtue, as character:

> You can't close shit, you *are* shit.
>
> . . .
>
> Fuck you, that's my name. You drove a Hyundai here tonight, and I drove here in an $80,000 BMW, that's *my* name.
>
> . . .
>
> You can't play in a man's game, you can't close them, go home and tell your wife.
>
> . . .
>
> They're sitting out there waiting to give you their money. Are you going to take it? Are you *man* enough to take it?
>
> . . .
>
> Nice guy? I don't give a shit. Good father? Fuck you, go home and play with your kids.
>
> . . .
>
> It takes brass balls to sell real estate.[16]

Blake's early presence radically shifts the story's tone and momentum, heightening the invective of subsequent exchanges. The salesmen, indignant but overwhelmed by his presentation, cannot help but accept its decimating ethic. Aaronow confesses to Roma, the salesman/priest: "I'm fucked on the board. I can't, I can't ... I can't close them.... I'm no fucking good."[17] During his brief triumph, Levene announces, employing Blake's analogy, "I am back. I got my balls back."[18] The film also establishes Levene, rather than Roma, as its central character

during the first half. Several new scenes develop his slipping skills and
the background priority of a daughter in the hospital. Roma, except for
an introductory moment, does not have a scene until forty minutes into
the film, although he dominates the second/daylight segment. Jack
Lemmon, as Levene, attempted to perform against the pathos inherent
in his character's situation. "I did everything I could to make this guy
a shit. . . . I played it as bitter as I could. If he got a chance, he'd screw
you. It's part of business."[19] Indeed, Levene's ingratiating warmth is invariably undercut by instantaneous shifts into excoriating profanity and
petty cruelties. Despite his efforts, Levene seems to dissolve before our
eyes; in cars, in a phone booth, indistinct through glass, he is washed
away by the night's storm. Corliss suggests that the audience is as prone
as the salesmen to the seductive rhythms and rituals of predatory
language. "We watch these zoo creatures and realize that we too are in
the cage."[20]

If there is a hint of anachronism surrounding Mamet's real estate
hucksters, the force of change is even more apparent in his rendering
of Jimmy Hoffa. Virtually all of Mamet's signature motifs are displayed
in *Hoffa*. The protagonist is a fluent and profane speaker in the Mametic
vein and is a mentor, educator, and self-conscious performer. His
message is empowerment through unity; that is, he preaches the
supreme lesson of the necessity of being a team player: ". . .*I* ain't
afraid to get my hands dirty, I ain't afraid to gettem *bloody,* baby, I
ain't afraid of *any* motherfucking thing, and you know why? Cause I'm
part of a *brotherhood.* . . ."[21] Within the fraternity awaits strength, a
continual idea in Mamet's search for a sufficient community. As one of
Hoffa's many supporters pridefully announces: "Weathered the storm,
yes. And Been Part of the Family."[22] A man alone has little chance
against the grinding machinery of commerce, capitalism, and bureau-
cracy:

> You want to live your life that way? What kind of fucken pussy are you,
> some guy in Duluth gone tell you who goes in the cab. Who's *driving*
> this truck? WHO'S DRIVING THIS MOTHERFUCKING TRUCK . . . hey,
> hey, hey, look slanty at me all you want to, Dago, you wan pull the rig
> over, and fight it out, fine, we'll do that, you ain't *gone* to do that, you
> drive, listen to me. Ye-ah yeah yeah yeah yeah yeah, listen to what I'm
> fucken telling you. *Listen* to me:[23]

Hoffa is easily identified as saleman, as hustler, as rhetorician whose
utopian vision both inflames and intoxicates.

Unwitting client James Lingk (Jonathan Pryce) lowers his head penitently before the unfolding sales prowess of Ricky Roma (Al Pacino) in *Glengarry Glen Ross.* Photo by Andy Schwartz.

*Hoffa,* like *The Untouchables,* subverts the American Dream with an unrealized ideal of progress, fairness, and true democratic equity. Hoffa opposes the traditional myth of "growing up" to be president of the country: "Fuck that. *Someday,* I'm gonna be the President, the Fucken *Teamsters.* . ."[24] Indeed, the government is menacingly antagonistic to the values of the Brotherhood: "SQUARE OFF WITH THE *WHITE HOUSE?* Then they don't Square Off with *Me*!!!"[25] Hoffa's protégé Ciaro refers to his leader as the "Little Guy," a title ironized by its capitalization and the larger than life figure Hoffa represents. *Hoffa's* further ironies involve the behavior and character of its hero: the man is a loud and profane bully, an advocate of extortion and violence. In fact, Hoffa's methods consistently effect a justice outside the framework of law, government, or the press. He is, in his manner and tone, akin to Mamet's Capone, an angry and racist crime lord, a "Don" who will not be denied or revoked.[26] Nevertheless, he is the sympathetic center of the story, and his problematic sermon of unity seems necessary and appealing. Not surprisingly, Hoffa is finally betrayed by his own people. To conjure even such a tarnished hero, Mamet must return to the past. The "present" of *Hoffa's* flashback frame is 1975, date of the labor leader's probable murder. As Mamet did with *The Untouchables,* the

Jimmy Hoffa (Jack Nicholson), supported by "brother" Bobby Ciaro (Danny DeVito), performs for the press in *Hoffa*. Photo by Francois Duhamel.

author has fashioned *Hoffa* as nostalgia; however, the story is closer to the present and to that degree bleaker and more unsettling. Capone's bullying bluster welded to Malone's Old Testament justice account for Hoffa's effectiveness, then even this troubling conflation is swept under by the unnamed agencies of corrupted power.

# Notes

## Chapter I: *House of Games*

1. David Mamet, *On Directing Film* (New York: Viking, 1991), pp. 28–29.
2. Ibid, p. 23.
3. Mamet, *House of Games* (New York: Grove, 1987), p. viii.
4. Mamet, *Film,* p. 20.
5. Ibid, p. 11.
6. Ibid, p. 64.
7. Ibid, p. 27.
8. Ibid, p. 69. However, William E. Lenz points out important differences between a willing audience, such as, to employ his examples, those marveling at the illusions of P. T. Barnum's American Museum or readers of Johnson Jones Hooper's Simon Suggs stories, and unwitting characters, fictional or not, within a confidence game. "The tension and uncertainty experienced by Barnum's and Hooper's audiences is of a different order than that felt by Simon Suggs's victims; the audience consciously and deliberately seeks out the experience and consents to it, while the victims of the confidence man are unwilling and unknowing participants in his performance. And of course at any moment Barnum's spectator can leave the American Museum just as Hooper's reader can put down *Simon Suggs,* whereas the fictional Simon Suggs inhabits a restricted, self-enclosed realm that has no clear exit and is self-referential" (Lenz, *Fast Talk & Flush Times,* [Columbia: U of Missouri P, 1985], p. 28).
9. Stanley Kauffmann, "Tangled Web," *New Republic* 16 Nov. 1987, p. 22. Again, Lenz's excellent study of the confidence man in American literature, *Fast Talk & Flush Times* shows the similarity of *House of Games'* effect on audience to that of *The Confidence-Man* on Melville's readership: "The reader is led to suspect every character's motives, to doubt every conventional appearance, to question the authority or reliability of the narrator, and to mistrust his own complacent patterns of response" (124). Melville's novel is, after all, the seminal work by which all other serious artistic treatments of confidence games must be measured, and Mamet achieves in his film, by substantially different means, a nonetheless comparable indeterminacy.

10. Ibid.

11. David Denby, "What's in a Game," *New York* 19 Oct. 1987, p. 101.

12. Dave Kehr, "*House of Games* Stylishly Meshes Stage, Film," *Chicago Tribune* 16 Oct. 1987, p. 7A.

13. Peter Travers, "Screen," *People* 16 Nov. 1987, p. 14.

14. Tom O'Brien, "Obsession & Memory," *Commonweal* 4 Dec. 1987, p. 704.

15. Vincent Canby, "Mamet Makes a Debut with *House of Games*," *New York Times* 11 Oct. 1987, p. 94.

16. Mamet, *Film*, p. 2.

17. Ibid, p. 51.

18. Ibid, p. 32.

19. Ibid, p. 70.

20. Canby, p. 94.

21. Kehr, p. 7A.

22. Mamet, *Film*, p. 85.

23. Todd London, "Chicago Impromptu," *American Theatre* July/Aug. 1990, p. 14.

24. T. E. Kalem, "Curtain Call," *Time* 31 Oct. 1977, p. 94.

25. Richard Eder, "David Mamet's New Realism," *New York Times Magazine* 12 Mar. 1978, p. 45.

26. Jack Kroll, "The Muzak Man," *Newsweek* 28 Feb. 1977, p. 79.

27. In Jean Vallely, "David Mamet Makes a Play for Hollywood," *Rolling Stone* 3 Apr. 1980, p. 46.

28. In Esther Harriott, "Interview with David Mamet," *American Voices: Contemporary Playwrights in Essays and Interviews* (Jefferson, NC: McFarland, 1988), p. 89.

29. In Henry I. Schvey, "Celebrating the Capacity for Self-Knowledge," *New Theatre Quarterly* 4.13 (Feb. 1988), p. 95.

30. Mamet, *Film*, p. 72.

31. Ibid, p. 72.

32. Mamet, *Games*, p. vi.

33. Ibid, p. vii.

34. Mamet, *Film*, p. 95.

35. Ibid, p. 71.

36. Ibid, p. 73.

37. Molly Haskel, "Psycho Therapy," *Vogue* Sept. 1987, p. 140.

38. Mamet, *Games*, p. 37.

39. Haskel, p. 140. Moreover, perhaps Mamet intends "Ford" as an inversion of "Freud"?

40. Alfie Kohn, "Therapy Gone Awry," *Psychology Today* Apr. 1988, p. 64.

41. Mamet, *Games*, p. 10.

42. Mamet, *Film*, p. 13.

43. Ibid, p. 12.

44. Mamet, *Games*, p. 10.

45. Mamet, *Film*, p. 7.

46. Mamet, *Games*, p. 11.

47. Mamet, *Film*, p. 28.

48. Kauffmann, p. 22.
49. Mamet, *Games,* p. 11.
50. Ibid, p. 11.
51. Richard Schickel, "Con Jobs," *Time* 19 Oct. 1987, p. 76.
52. O'Brien, p. 704.
53. Anne Dean, *David Mamet: Language as Dramatic Action* (Madison, NJ: Fairleigh Dickinson UP, 1990), p. 47.
54. Ibid, p. 46.
55. Ned Polsky, *Hustlers, Beats, and Others* (1967; Chicago: U of Chicago P, 1985), p. 21.
56. Mamet, "Pool Halls," *Writing in Restaurants* (New York: Viking, 1986), pp. 88–90.
57. Ibid, p. 91.
58. Mamet, *Games,* p. 12.
59. Ibid, p. 13.
60. Ibid, p. 14.
61. Ibid, p. 15.
62. Kroll, "The Profane Poetry of David Mamet," *Newsweek* 19 Oct. 1987, p. 85.
63. Mamet, *Glengarry Glen Ross* (New York: Grove, 1984), p. 46.
64. Gene Siskel, "Mamet at 40," *Chicago Tribune* 11 Oct. 1987, sec. 13, p. 8.
65. Denby, p. 101.
66. Kehr, p. 7A.
67. Kroll, "Profane Poetry. . . ," p. 85.
68. Mamet, *Games,* p. 62.
69. Denby, p. 101.
70. Ibid, p. 101.
71. Mamet, *Games,* p. 25.
72. Kehr, p. 7A.
73. Mamet, *Games,* p. 26.
74. In Matthew C. Roudané, "An Interview with David Mamet," *Studies in American Drama, 1945–Present* 1, 1986, p. 79.
75. Mamet, *A Life in the Theatre* (New York: Grove, 1978), p. 18.
76. Ibid, p. 35.
77. Pascale Hubert-Leibler, "Dominance and Anguish: The Teacher-Student Relationship in the Plays of David Mamet," *Modern Drama* 31.4 (Dec. 1988), p. 558.
78. Polsky, pp. 63–64.
79. Ibid, p. 81.
80. Mamet, *Games* p. 30.
81. Ibid, p. 31.
82. Ibid, p. 31.
83. Ibid, p. 31.
84. Ibid, p. 25.
85. Ibid, p. 25.
86. Mamet, *American Buffalo* (New York: Grove, 1977), p. 54.
87. Ibid, p. 55.

88. Mamet, *Games,* p. 25.
89. In Roudané, p. 75.
90. Polsky, p. 94. Anyone needing further proof of the remarkable authenticity of Mamet's hustlers should consult David W. Maurer's fascinating study *The American Confidence Man* (Springfield, IL: Charles C. Thomas, 1974). Nearly every page contains remarkable and familiar accounts which attest to Mamet's expertise in creating Mike and his followers. "Hence the insideman . . . must have a vast knowledge of human nature, a dignified and impressive manner, and a perfect sense of showmanship. His story must take effect naturally" (131). Maurer discusses the themes of fraternity, performance, specialization, and honor, offering numerous actual examples. Law and business are also considered: "If confidence men operate outside the law, it must be remembered that they are not much further outside than many of our pillars of society who go under names less sinister. They only carry to an ultimate and very logical conclusion certain trends which are often inherent in various forms of legitimate business" (152). Another intriguing text is Erving Goffman's *Frame Analysis* (1974; Boston: Northeastern U P, 1986); the author's lengthy discussion of layers of experience and interpretation has obvious applications to *House of Games* as both story and film. "In sum, observers actively project their frames of reference into the world immediately around them, and one fails to see their so doing only because events ordinarily confirm these projections, causing the assumptions to disappear into the smooth flow of activity" (39).
91. In Siskel, p. 6.
92. Ibid, p. 6..
93. Mamet, *Games,* p. 27.
94. Ibid, p. 28.
95. Kehr, p. 7A.
96. Canby, p. 94.
97. Schickel, p. 76.
98. Mamet, *Games,* p. 29.
99. Ibid, p. 30.
100. Ibid, p. 34.
101. Ibid, p. 37.
102. Mamet, *Glengarry,* pp. 48, 49, 51.
103. Dean, p. 47.
104. Mamet, *Games,* p. 37.
105. Ibid, p. 38.
106. Ibid, p. 40.
107. Ibid, p. 41.
108. Ibid, p. 41.
109. Ibid, pp. 42–43.
110. Ibid, p. 43.
111. William F. Van Wert, "Psychoanalysis and Con Games: *House of Games,*" *Film Quarterly* 43.4 (Summer 1990), p. 7.
112. Mamet, *Film,* p. 31.
113. Mamet, *Games,* p. 55.
114. Ibid, p. 56.
115. Ibid, p. 58.

116. Ibid, p. 60.
117. Mamet, *Film,* p. 50.
118. Mamet, *Games,* p. 61.
119. Ibid, p. 62.
120. Ibid, p. 61.
121. Ibid, p. 62.
122. Van Wert, p. 6.
123. Mamet, *Games,* p. 41.
124. Ibid, p. 10.
125. Mamet, *Sexual Perversity in Chicago,* in *Sexual Perversity in Chicago and The Duck Variations: Two Plays* (New York: Grove, 1978), p. 12.
126. Dean, p. 66.
127. Mamet, *Games,* p. 64.
128. Ibid, p. 65.
129. Ibid, p. 65.
130. Van Wert, p. 7.
131. Van Wert, p. 8. While Van Wert's argument is provocative, it contains some damaging errors, pointed out in a caustic response by James Hyder in "Controversy & Correspondence," *Film Quarterly* 44.3 (Spring 1991). Hyder acccuses Van Wert of "seeking to intimidate his readers under the pretext of enlightening them to deeper realities which only he has seen" (62); Van Wert rebuts that the brilliance of *House of Games* lies in Mamet's "invitation to co-construct, to play with our own voyeurism, suspicions, doubts, to think and rethink, read and remember backwards into the film" (63).
132. Mamet, *Games,* p. 67.
133. Ibid, p. 66.
134. Ibid, p. 67.
135. Ibid, p. 68.
136. Ibid, p. 70.
137. Ibid, p. 70.
138. O'Brien, p. 704.
139. Kohn, p. 65.
140. Mamet, *Games,* p. 70.
141. Ibid, p. 71.
142. Ibid, p. 72.
143. Ibid, p. 72.
144. In Dean, p. 64.
145. Mickey Spillane, *I, The Jury,* 1947, in *Five Complete Mike Hammer Novels* (New York: Avenel, 1987), p. 136.
146. Haskel, p. 147.

# Chapter II: Recent Plays in Context

1. Gay Brewer and Leslie Kane, "Bibliography," *David Mamet: A Casebook* (Leslie Kane, editor; New York: Garland, 1991); 271–298.
2. In Schvey, "Celebrating...," p. 95.
3. Mamet, "Preface," *Writing in Restaurants* (New York: Viking, 1986), p. viii.

4. Ibid, p. viii.

5. Mamet, "Notes on *The Cherry Orchard,*" *Writing in Restaurants* (New York: Viking, 1986), p. 125.

6. C. W. E. Bigsby, *David Mamet* (London: Methuen, 1985), p. 25.

7. In Richard Christiansen, "*Vanya* Revisited," *Chicago Tribune* 29 Apr. 1990, sec. 13, p. 12.

8. In Schvey, "Celebrating...," p. 90.

9. Ibid, p. 91.

*The Shawl*

10. Mamet, *The Shawl,* in *The Shawl and Prairie du Chien: Two Plays* (New York: Grove, 1985), p. 22.

11. Bob Daily, "Mamet on the Make," *Chicago* May 1988, p. 138.

12. In Samuel G. Freedman, "Theater Returns to Lincoln Center," *New York Times* 21 Dec. 1985, p. L15.

13. Ibid, p. L15.

14. Schvey, "The Plays of David Mamet: Games of Manipulation and Power," *New Theatre Quarterly* 4.13 (Feb. 1988), p. 77.

15. Philip C. Kolin, "Revealing Illusions in David Mamet's *The Shawl,*" *Notes on Contemporary Literature* 16.2 (Mar. 1986), p. 9.

16. Bigsby, p. 128.

17. Robert Brustein, *New Republic* 10 Feb. 1986, p. 28.

18. Mamet, *Glengarry,* p. 47.

19. Mamet, *Shawl,* p. 5.

20. Ibid, p. 4.

21. Mamet, *Glengarry,* p. 50.

22. In Schvey, "Celebrating...," p. 93.

23. Kolin, p. 10.

24. Mamet, *Shawl,* p. 24.

25. Ibid, p. 12.

26. Ibid, p. 7.

27. Ibid, p. 9.

28. Ibid, p. 5.

29. Ibid, p. 10

30. Mamet, *Games,* p. 41.

31. Mamet, *Shawl,* p. 20.

32. Ibid, p. 13.

33. Ibid, pp. 16–17.

34. Ibid, p. 3.

35. Ibid, p. 47.

36. Christiansen, "Mamet's *Shawl* Plays Perfectly in New Theater," *Chicago Tribune* 24 Apr. 1985, sec. 2, p. 5.

37. Douglas Watt, quoted in Sid Smith, "Mamet Plays Strike Out with Critics," *Chicago Tribune* 27 Dec. 1985, sec. 5, p. 3.

38. Freedman, "The Gritty Eloquence of David Mamet," *New York Times Magazine* 21 Apr. 1985, p. 32.

39. In Schvey, "Celebrating...," p. 90.

40. Ibid, p. 90.
41. Dennis Carroll, *David Mamet* (Houndmills, England: Macmillan, 1987), p. 112.
42. Ibid, p. 115.
43. Mamet, *A Life in the Theatre* (New York: Grove, 1978), p. 12.
44. Mamet, "A Tradition of the Theater as Art," *Writing in Restaurants* (New York: Viking, 1986), p. 20.
45. In Schvey, "Celebrating...," p. 94. *A Life in the Theatre* also contains comic instances of homosexual innuendo. Perhaps something in the performer's life, with its evanescent identity, its hypersensitivity to fellow actors, explains a revised sexual orientation. As in *Edmond,* homosexuality in *The Shawl* seems a natural variation on the community of men, integrating romantic and masculine need.
46. Kolin, p. 9.
47. Mamet, *Shawl,* p. 26.
48. Ibid, p. 26.
49. Ibid, p. 22.
50. Mamet, *Games,* p. 69.
51. Mamet, *Shawl,* p. 49.
52. Carroll, p. 112.
53. In Schvey, "Celebrating...," p. 91.
54. Mamet, *Shawl,* p. 19.
55. Ibid, p. 27.
56. Ibid, p. 20.
57. Mamet, "Preface," p. viii.
58. Ibid, p. vii.
59. Carroll, p. 117.
60. Christiansen, "*Shawl...*," p. 5.
61. Mamet, *Shawl,* p. 33.
62. Ibid, p. 35.
63. Mamet, "A National Dream-Life," *Writing in Restaurants* (New York: Viking, 1986), p. 8.
64. Mamet, *Shawl,* p. 39.
65. Ibid, pp. 38–39.
66. Ibid, p. 44.
67. Ibid, p. 45.
68. Schvey, "Games...," p. 78.
69. Kolin, p. 10.
70. Ibid, p. 10.
71. Ibid, p. 10.
72. Freedman, "Gritty...," p. 46.
73. Mamet, *Shawl,* p. 50.
74. Ibid, p. 50.
75. Mamet, *Games,* p. 41.
76. Mamet, *Shawl,* p. 52.
77. Mamet, "Stanislavsky and the American Bicentennial," *Writing in Restaurants* (New York: Viking, 1986), p. 28.
78. Carroll, p. 116.

79. Dean, p. 65.
80. In Schvey, "Celebrating...," p. 92.
81. Ibid, p. 93.

*The Spanish Prisoner, Prairie du Chien,* and *Vint*

82. Christiansen, "*Shawl*...," p. 5.
83. Mamet, "National Dream-Life," pp. 8–9.
84. Mamet, *The Spanish Prisoner,* in *Goldberg Street: Short Plays and Monologues* (New York: Grove, 1985), p. 22.
85. Ibid, p. 25.
86. Mamet, *Games,* p. 34.
87. Mamet, *Prisoner,* p. 27.
88. Ibid, p. 28.
89. Ibid, p. 27.
90. Ibid, p. 28.
91. Carroll, p. 144.
92. Brustein, p. 26.
93. In Dean, p. 176.
94. Carroll, p. 128.
95. Mamet, *Prairie du Chien,* in *The Shawl and Prairie du Chien: Two Plays* (New York: Grove, 1985), p. 59.
96. Ibid, p. 81.
97. Mamet, "Radio Drama," *Writing in Restaurants* (New York: Viking, 1986), p. 14.
98. Bruno Bettelheim, *The Uses of Enchantment* (New York: Vintage, 1977), p. 60.
99. Mamet, *Dark Pony,* in *Reunion, Dark Pony, The Sanctity of Marriage: Three Plays* (New York: French, 1982), p. 40.
100. Bettelheim, pp. 5, 6.
101. Bigsby, p. 24.
102. Mamet, *Prairie,* p. 71.
103. Ibid, p. 84.
104. Mamet, *Games,* p. 19.
105. Mamet, *Vint,* in *Orchards* (New York: Broadway Play Publishing, 1987), p. 20.
106. Ibid, p. 21.
107. Ibid, p. 22.
108. Ibid, pp. 22–23.
109. Mamet, "Things I Have Learned Playing Poker on the Hill," *Writing in Restaurants* (New York: Viking, 1986), pp. 93, 96.
110. Ibid, p. 97.

*Speed-the-Plow*

111. Frank Rich, "Mamet's Dark View of Hollywood as a Heaven for the Virtueless," *New York Times* 4 May 1988, p. C17.

112. Jonathan Lieberson, "The Prophet of Broadway," *New York Review* 21 July 1988, p. 4.

113. In Christiansen, "The 'Plow' Boy," *Chicago Tribune* 19 Feb. 1989, sec. 13, p. 18.

114. Christiansen, "Mamet's Madonna," *Chicago Tribune* 4 May 1988, sec. 5, p. 3.

115. In David Savran, "David Mamet," *In Their Own Words* (New York: Theatre Communications Group, 1988), p. 144.

116. Kroll, "The Terrors of Tinseltown," *Newsweek* 16 May 1988, p. 83.

117. Mamet, *Speed-the-Plow* (New York: Grove, 1988), p. 31.

118. Christiansen, "'Plow'...," p. 18.

119. Mamet, *Plow,* p. 29.

120. Ibid, p. 15.

121. Ibid, p. 42.

122. Ibid, p. 16.

123. Ibid, p. 25.

124. Mamet, *Buffalo,* p. 8.

125. Christiansen, "...Madonna," p. 3.

126. David Blum, "Pal Joey," *New York* 2 May 1988, p. 46.

127. Ibid, p. 46.

128. William A. Henry III, "Madonna Comes to Broadway," *Time* 16 May 1988, p. 99.

129. Mamet, *Plow,* p. 3.

130. Ibid, p. 7.

131. Ibid, p. 14.

132. Ibid, p. 19.

133. Ibid, p. 33.

134. Ibid, p. 37.

135. Ross is once referred to as merely "Richard R" (p. 7)—a deified Richard Roma?

136. Mamet, *Plow,* p. 18.

137. Ibid, p. 31.

138. Ibid, p. 22.

139. Ibid, p. 19.

140. Ibid, p. 32.

141. Ibid, p. 40.

142. Ibid, p. 40.

143. Ibid, p. 41.

144. Ibid, p. 42.

145. Ibid, p. 43.

146. Ibid, p. 50.

147. Ibid, p. 37.

148. Ibid, p. 53.

149. Ibid, p. 70.

150. Edith Oliver, "Mamet at the Movies," *New Yorker* 16 May 1988, p. 95.

151. Kroll, "...Tinseltown," p. 83.

152. Rich, p. C17.

153. Mamet, *Plow,* p. 58.

154. In Henry, p. 99.

155. Mamet, *Plow*, p. 60.

156. Ibid, p. 69.

157. Ibid, p. 66.

158. Rich, p. C17.

159. Mamet, *Plow,* p. 69.

160. Ibid, p. 70.

161. Henry, p. 99.

162. Mel Gussow, "Mamet's Hollywood Is a School for Scoundrels," *New York Times* 15 May 1988, sec. 2, p. 55.

163. Mamet, *Plow,* p. 49.

164. Ibid, p. 57.

165. Brustein, "The Last Refuge for Scoundrels," *New Republic* 6 June 1988, p. 30.

166. Moira Hodgson, "Theater," *The Nation* 18 June 1988, p. 875.

167. Walter Kerr, "Verbal Witchcraft Produces Magical Responses Out Front," *New York Times* 12 June 1988, sec. 2, p. 22.

168. John Simon, *"Word Power,"* *New York* 16 May 1988, p. 106.

169. Rich, p. C17.

170. William L. Petersen, quoted in Sid Smith, "The 'Plow' and the Stars: A Family Reunion," *Chicago Tribune* 19 Feb. 1989, sec. 13, p. 19.

171. Rich, p. C17.

172. Kevin Kelly, "Good Mamet, Passable Madonna," *Boston Globe* 4 May 1988, p. 79.

173. Brustein, "Refuge ..," p. 30.

174. Kelly, p. 79.

175. Simon, p. 106.

176. Mamet, *Plow,* p. 68.

177. Henry, p. 99.

178. Mamet, *Plow,* p. 74.

179. Ibid, p. 74.

180. Ibid, p. 74.

181. Ibid, p. 72.

182. Ibid, p. 76.

183. Ibid, p. 76.

184. Ibid, p. 71.

185. Ibid, p. 77.

186. Brustein, "Refuge...," p. 29.

187. Mamet, *Plow,* p. 22.

188. Ibid, p. 69.

189. Ibid, p. 70.

190. Ibid, p. 3.

191. Ibid, p. 73.

192. Ibid, p. 16.

193. Ibid, p. 76.

194. Brustein, "Refuge...," p. 29.

195. Mamet, *Plow,* p. 81.

196. Ibid, p. 81.
197. Ibid, p. 82.
198. Ibid, p. 78.
199. Ibid, p. 82.
200. Gussow, p. H5.
201. Henry, p. 99.
202. Ibid, p. 99.
203. Rich, p. C17.
204. In Christiansen, "'Plow'...," p. 18.

## Chapter III: *Things Change*

1. In "David Mamet: Biography," press kit, Columbia Pictures, 1988, p. 1.
2. David Ansen, "An Offer You Can't Refuse: Mamet's Little Treat," *Newsweek* 31 Oct. 1988, p. 72.
3. In "...Mamet...," p.1
4. Daily, p. 105.
5. Ibid, p. 105.
6. Ibid, p. 106.
7. "*Things Change*: Production Information," press kit, Columbia Pictures, 1988, p. 7.
8. Ibid, p. 5.
9. Ibid, p. 4.
10. Ibid, p. 5.
11. Daily, p. 104.
12. Ibid, p. 106.
13. In Glenn Lovell, "David Mamet Keeps His Multifaceted Career Speeding Along," *Chicago Tribune* 28 Oct. 1988, sec. 7, pp. D-E.
14. Daily, p. 137.
15. Mamet and Shel Silverstein, *Things Change* (New York: Grove, 1988), p. 56.
16. Lovell, p. 7E.
17. Ibid, p. 7E.
18. Daily, p. 139.
19. In Lovell, p. 7E.
20. Ibid, p. 7E.
21. In Daily, p. 141.
22. Ibid, p. 141.
23. This paradox of the crime lord is best represented in Mamet by his rendering of Al Capone in *The Untouchables*.
24. In Daily, p. 137.
25. Ibid, p. 137.
26. Ibid, p. 140.
27. In Lovell, p. 7D.
28. Kehr, "In *Things Change*, Mamet Alters Rules of Comedy," *Chicago Tribune* 21 Oct. 1988, sec. 7, p. A.

29. Ibid, p. A.
30. Ansen, p. 72.
31. Travers, "Screen," *People* 24 Oct. 1988, pp. 17–18.
32. Pauline Kael, "The Current Cinema: Unreal," *New Yorker,* 14 Nov. 1988, p. 128.
33. Ibid, p. 129.
34. Kauffmann, "One Weekend," *New Republic* 7 Nov. 1988, p. 27.
35. Mamet, *Change,* p. 4.
36. Ibid, p. 5.
37. Ibid, p. 6.
38. Ibid, p. 6.
39. Mamet, "The Clothes Have All the Lines," *Mirabella* Feb. 1991, p. 112.
40. Mamet, *Change,* p. 7.
41. Ibid, p. 8.
42. Ibid, p. 8.
43. Mamet, *Change,* film only.
44. Richard Corliss, "Shaggy Don Story," *Time* 24 Oct. 1988, p. 103.
45. In "Don Ameche: Biography," press kit, Columbia, 1988, p. 1.
46. Mamet, *Change,* p. 10.
47. Ibid, p. 10.
48. Ibid, p. 11.
49. Ibid, p. 11.
50. Ibid, film only.
51. Ibid, p. 12.
52. Ibid, p. 13.
53. In "Joe Mantegna: Biography," press kit, Columbia Pictures, 1988, p. 1.
54. Mamet, *Change,* p. 14.
55. Bigsby, p. 99.
56. Mamet, *Change*, p. 15.
57. Ibid, p. 15.
58. Ibid, p. 16.
59. Ibid, p. 16.
60. Ibid, p. 17.
61. Ibid, p. 17.
62. Ibid, p. 19.
63. Denby, "Small Change," *New York,* 7 Nov. 1988, p. 102.
64. Kehr, ". . .Rules of Comedy," p. 7A.
65. Mamet, *Change,* p. 21.
66. Ibid, p. 22.
67. Ibid, p. 22.
68. Ibid, p. 24.
69. Ibid, p. 24.
70. Ibid, p. 24.
71. Denby, ". . .Change," p. 102.
72. Kehr, ". . .Rules of Comedy," p. 7A.
73. Mamet, *Change,* p. 25.

74. Mamet, "...All the Lines," p. 112.
75. Mamet, *Change*, p. 26.
76. Ibid, p. 27.
77. Ibid, p. 28.
78. Ibid, p. 29.
79. Ibid, p. 31.
80. Ibid, p. 32.
81. Ibid, p. 33.
82. Ibid, p. 34.
83. Ibid, p. 35.
84. Ibid, p. 37.
85. Ibid, p. 39.
86. Ibid, p. 40.
87. Ibid, p. 41.
88. Ibid, p. 42.
89. Contrast the women to *American Buffalo*'s absentees Ruth and Grace. Hersh Zeifman notes that the earlier play "is thus *literally* ruthless and graceless" (Zeifman, "Phallus in Wonderland: Machismo and Business in David Mamet's *American Buffalo* and *Glengarry Glen Ross*, in *David Mamet: A Casebook* [Leslie Kane, Editor; New York: Garland, 1992], p. 129).
90. Mamet, *Change*, p. 43.
91. Ibid, p. 43.
92. Ibid, p. 43.
93. Ibid, p. 44.
94. Ibid, film only.
95. Ibid, film and p. 44.
96. Ibid, p. 45.
97. Ibid, p. 46.
98. Ibid, p. 48.
99. Jerzy Kosinski, *Being There* (New York: Bantam, 1972), p. 55.
100. Mamet, *Change*, p. 49.
101. Ibid, p. 50.
102. Ibid, p. 50.
103. Ibid, p. 51.
104. Ibid, p. 51.
105. Ibid, p. 51.
106. Ibid, p. 52.
107. Ibid, p. 53.
108. Ibid, p. 56.
109. In "...Production Information," p. 15.
110. Mamet, *Change*, p. 57.
111. Ibid, p. 57.
112. Ibid, p. 57.
113. Ibid, p. 58.
114. Ibid, p. 58.
115. Ibid, p. 59.
116. Kosinski, p. 55.
117. Mamet, *Change*, p. 60.

118. In "...Ameche...," pp. 1–2.
119. Mamet, *Change,* p. 60.
120. Ibid, p. 61.
121. Ibid, p. 62.
122. Ibid, p. 63.
123. Ibid, p. 73.
124. Ibid, p. 73.
125. Ibid, p. 75.
126. Ibid, p. 75.
127. Ibid, p. 76.
128. Ibid, p. 77.
129. Ibid, p. 78.
130. Ibid, p. 78.
131. Ibid, p. 79.
132. Ibid, p. 80.
133. Ibid, film only.
134. Ibid, p. 81.
135. Ibid, p. 81.
136. Ibid, pp. 81–82.
137. Ibid, p. 82.
138. Ibid, p. 83.
139. Ibid, p. 84.
140. Ibid, p. 85.
141. Ibid, p. 89.
142. Ibid, p. 89.
143. Ibid, p. 90.
144. Ibid, p. 91.
145. Ibid, p. 91.
146. Denby, "...Change," p. 102.
147. Mamet, *Change,* p. 92.
148. Ibid, p. 93.
149. Ibid, p. 93.
150. Ibid, p. 93.
151. Ibid, p. 93.
152. In "...Mantegna...," p. 1.
153. In "...Ameche...," p. 1.
154. Mamet, *Change,* p. 93.
155. Ibid, p. 94.
156. Ibid, p. 19.
157. Ibid, p. 95.
158. Ibid, p. 95.
159. Ibid, p. 95.
160. Ibid, p. 96.
161. Ansen, p. 72.
162. Kehr, "...Rules of Comedy," p. 7M.

# Chapter IV: The Screenplays

## The Postman Always Rings Twice

1. Mamet, *Directing,* p. xiv.
2. Ibid, p. xv.
3. In Vallely, p. 46.
4. In Dan Yakir, "The Postman's Words," *Film Comment* Mar./Apr. 1981, p. 22.
5. In Vallely, p. 46.
6. Mamet, *Directing,* pp. 104–105.
7. Ibid, p. 77.
8. Ibid, p. 72.
9. Ibid, p. 61.
10. Ibid, p. 62.
11. In Yakir, p. 22.
12. Mamet, *Directing,* p. 4.
13. In Yakir, p. 21.
14. In Vallely, p. 46.
15. In Yakir, p. 24.
16. Ibid, p. 24.
17. In David Thomson, "Raising Cain," *Film Comment* Mar./Apr. 1981, p. 30.
18. Ibid, p. 25.
19. Diane Jacobs, "Murder in the Dark," *Horizon* Apr. 1981, p. 71.
20. Mamet, *Directing,* p. 20.
21. In Vallely, p. 44.
22. In Yakir, p. 21.
23. Ibid, p. 21.
24. Ibid, p. 21.
25. Kauffmann, "Still Ringing," *New Republic* 11 Apr. 1981, p. 27.
26. Robert Hatch, "Films," *The Nation* 4 Apr. 1981, p. 413.
27. Jacobs, p. 71.
28. Denby, "Return to Sender," *New York* 30 Mar. 1981, p. 39.
29. Ibid, p. 39.
30. Mamet, *Edmond,* in *The Woods, Lakeboat, Edmond: Three Plays* (New York: Grove, 1981), p. 273.
31. Mamet, *The Postman Always Rings Twice,* unpublished screenplay, 1980, p. 88.
32. Mamet, *Edmond,* p. 297.
33. Corliss, "The Post-Mark of Cain," *Time* 23 Mar. 1981, p. 62.
34. Mamet, *Lakeboat,* in *The Woods, Lakeboat, Edmond: Three Plays* (New York: Grove, 1981), p. 161.
35. James M. Cain, *The Postman Always Rings Twice* (1934; New York: Vintage, 1978), p. 15.
36. Mamet, *Postman,* p. 1.
37. Ibid, pp. 30–31.
38. Corliss, "...Cain," p. 62.

39. Yakir, "'The Postman' Rings Six Times," *Film Comment* Mar./Apr. 1981, p. 19.

40. In Yakir, "...Words," p. 21.

41. Hatch, p. 413.

42. Mamet, *Directing,* p. 12.

43. Mamet, *Postman,* p. 21A.

44. Cain, p. 119.

45. Ibid, p. 120.

46. Mamet, *Postman,* p. 21.

47. In Yakir, "...Words," p. 21.

48. Ibid, p. 22.

49. Mamet, *Postman,* p. 14.

50. Jacobs, p. 71.

51. Ibid, p. 71.

52. Carroll, p. 67.

53. Colin L. Westerbeck, Jr., "Razing Cain," *Commonweal* 22 May 1981, p. 306.

54. Mamet, *Postman,* p. 112.

55. Michael Sragow, "Movies." *Rolling Stone* 30 Apr. 1981, p. 38.

56. Mamet, *Postman,* p. 14.

### *The Verdict*

57. Kroll, "Newman Vs. 'The System,'" *Newsweek* 6 Dec. 1982, p. 151.

58. Carroll, p. 91.

59. Ibid, p. 106.

60. Dean, pp. 37–38.

61. Ibid, p. 38.

62. Mamet, *Directing,* p. 28.

63. Kael, "The Current Cinema: The Cool and the Dead," *New Yorker* 10 Jan. 1983, p. 91.

64. Carroll, pp. 96–97.

65. Denby, "Rough Justice," *New York* 20 Dec. 1982, p. 62.

66. Kroll, "Newman...," p. 151.

67. Kael, "...Dead," p. 92.

68. Mamet, *Directing,* p. 43.

69. Mamet, *The Verdict,* unpublished screenplay, 1981, p. 30.

70. Mamet said of his *Postman* creation, "One of my favorite characters is Katz, the crooked lawyer. He's basically all made-up on my part, which is also why I like him" (in Yakir, "...Words," 23).

71. Barry Reed, *The Verdict* (New York: Simon and Schuster, 1980), p. 25.

72. Kenneth R. Hey, "Films." *USA Today* Mar. 1983. p. 69.

73. Dean, p. 46.

74. Mamet, *Verdict,* p. 2.

75. Hatch, "Films," *The Nation* 18 Dec. 1982, p. 668.

76. Mamet, *Verdict,* p. 3.

77. Ibid, p. 10.

78. Ibid, p. 48.

79. Kael, "...Dead," p. 92.

80. Mamet, *Verdict*, p. 6.

81. In fact, a comparably habitual con occurs at the beginning of *Postman*—Frank Chambers waits in the diner's men's room until a free breakfast is assured.

82. Mamet, *Verdict*, p. 51 (script only).

83. Ibid, p. 96.

84. Mamet, *Directing*, p. 13.

85. Mamet, *Verdict*, p. 37.

86. Ibid, p. 23.

87. Denby, "...Justice," p. 62.

88. Mamet, *Verdict*, p. 31.

89. Ibid, p. 105.

90. Ibid, p. 77.

91. Carroll, p. 94.

92. Mamet, *Verdict*, p. 13.

93. Ibid, p. 25.

94. Ibid, p. 27.

95. Ibid, p. 28.

96. Ibid, p. 29. In *Things Change*, Jerry displays a similar incredulity toward Gino, whose faith will ultimately save them: "Are you *nuts*? Are you *nuts*?"(94).

97. Ibid, p. 30.

98. Reed, p. 9. The Church clearly represents another "team" which demands loyalty and performance from its members.

99. Mamet, *Verdict*, p. 35.

100. Reed, p. 69.

101. Mamet, *Verdict*, p. 44, 69.

102. Ibid, p. 45.

103. Reed, p. 35.

104. Ibid, p. 145.

105. Ibid, p. 149.

106. Mamet, *Verdict*, p. 61.

107. Mamet, *Directing*, p. 71.

108. Reed, p. 101.

109. Mamet, *Verdict*, p. 41.

110. Ibid, p. 43.

111. Ibid, p. 89.

112. Ibid, p. 120.

113. Ibid, p. 119.

114. Mamet, *Buffalo*, p. 103.

115. Mamet, *Verdict*, p. 120.

116. Hatch, Dec. 1982, p. 666.

117. Carroll, p. 96.

118. Kael, "...Dead," p. 92.

## The Untouchables

119. In Tom Mathews, "The Mob at the Movies," *Newsweek* 22 June 1987, p. 64.
120. Mamet, *The Untouchables,* unpublished screenplay, 1986, p. 28.
121. Mamet, "Chicago," *Writing in Restaurants* (New York: Viking, 1986), pp. 70–71.
122. In Lovell, p. 7E.
123. Mamet, *Untouchables,* p. 63.
124. Ibid, p. 20.
125. In Corliss, "Shooting Up the Box Office," *Time* 22 June 1987, p. 78.
126. Mamet, "On Paul Ickovic's Photographs," *Writing in Restaurants* (New York: Viking, 1986), p. 73.
127. Mamet, "Some Freaks," *Some Freaks* (New York: Viking, 1989), p. 5.
128. John G. Cawelti, *The Six-Gun Mystique* (2nd ed.; Bowling Green, OH: Popular Press, 1984), p. 100.
129. Ibid, p. 11.
130. Ibid, p. 79.
131. Ibid, p. 12.
132. Ibid, p. 13.
133. Kauffmann, "The Bad Old Days," *New Republic* 22 June 1987, p. 27.
134. Mamet, *Directing,* p. 17.
135. Denby, "Big Caesar," *New York* 8 June 1987, p. 68.
136. Mamet, "Concerning *The Water Engine,*" *Writing in Restaurants* (New York: Viking, 1986), pp. 107–109.
137. Ibid, p. 109.
138. Mamet, *The Water Engine,* in *The Water Engine and Mr. Happiness: Two Plays* (1977; New York: French, 1983), p. 11.
139. Ibid, p. 11.
140. Mamet, *Untouchables,* p. 9.
141. Mamet, *Water Engine,* p. 29.
142. Mamet, *Untouchables,* p. 43.
143. Schickel, "In the American Grain," *Time* 8 June 1987, p. 83.
144. Mamet, *Directing,* p. 6.
145. Cawelti, pp. 107–108.
146. Mamet, *Directing,* p. 7.
147. Cawelti, p. 102.
148. Mamet, *Water Engine,* p. 55.
149. Ibid, p. 48.
150. Bigsby, p. 92.
151. Mamet, *Water Engine,* p. 55.
152. Mamet, *Untouchables,* p. 9.
153. Mamet, "Stanislavky and the Bearer Bonds," *Some Freaks* (New York: Viking, 1989), p. 72.
154. Mamet, *Untouchables,* p. 119.
155. Ibid, p. 119.

156. Ibid, p. 1.
157. Ibid, p. 1.
158. Mamet, "Oscars," *Writing in Restaurants* (New York: Viking, 1986), pp. 82–83.
159. Mamet, *Untouchables*, p. 2.
160. Ibid, p. 41.
161. Ibid, p. 2.
162. Mamet, "Corruption," *Some Freaks* (New York: Viking, 1989), p. 98.
163. Kael, "The Current Cinema: Broad Strokes," *New Yorker* 29 June 1987, p. 70.
164. Mamet, *Untouchables*, p. 38.
165. Ibid, p. 39.
166. Cawelti, p. 88.
167. Mamet, *Untouchables*, p. 64.
168. Ibid, p. 64.
169. Mamet, "A Speech for Michael Dukakis," *Some Freaks* (New York: Viking, 1989), p. 115.
170. Corliss, "Shooting...," p. 79.
171. Mamet, *Untouchables*, p. 68.
172. Cawelti, p. 75.
173. Mamet, *Untouchables*, p. 78.
174. Ibid, p. 83.
175. Ibid, p. 58.
176. Cawelti, p. 98.
177. Ibid, p. 99.
178. Mamet, *Untouchables*, p. 32.
179. Ibid, p. 54.
180. Ibid, p. 97.
181. Ibid, p. 31.
182. Mamet, "Practical Pistol Competition," *Some Freaks* (New York: Viking, 1989), p. 153.
183. Mamet, *Untouchables*, p. 93.
184. Ibid, p. 96.
185. Ibid, p. 74.
186. Ibid, p. 112.
187. Mamet, "Liberty," *Some Freaks* (New York: Viking, 1989), p. 106.
188. Cawelti, p. 53.
189. Ibid, p. 90. Cawelti goes on to discuss such masculine groups in the context of Leslie Fiedler's argument of their persistent presence in American literature.
190. Ibid, p. 91.
191. Ibid, p. 76.
192. Mamet, "In the Company of Men," *Some Freaks* (New York: Viking, 1989), p. 90–91.
193. Mamet, "Memorial Day, Cabot, Vermont," *Some Freaks* (New York: Viking, 1989), p. 50.
194. Mamet, *Untouchables*, p. 7.
195. Ibid, p. 20.

196. Ibid, p. 25.
197. Ibid, p. 25.
198. Ibid, p. 27.
199. Fred Schruers, "Movies: *The Untouchables,*" *Rolling Stone* 26 Mar. 1987, p. 50.
200. Mamet, *Untouchables,* p. 115.
201. Ibid, p. 116.
202. Kael, "Broad...," p. 72.
203. Ibid, p. 72.
204. Cawelti, p. 88.
205. Mamet, *Untouchables,* p. 29.
206. Ibid, p. 29.
207. Ibid, p. 53.
208. Ibid, p. 54.
209. Ibid, p. 55.
210. Ibid, p. 91.
211. As in *Things Change*'s murder, Malone is killed at the corner of Racine, juxtaposing contemporary urban violence against the calm and restraint of French classicism. Malone's platitudes also remind one of Jean Racine's predilection for Greek and Roman legends and his common theme of good versus evil.
212. Cawelti, p. 87.
213. Mamet, *Untouchables,* p. 114.
214. Mamet, "...Bearer Bonds," p. 75.
215. Mamet, "Decay: Some Thoughts for Actors," *Writing in Restaurants* (New York: Viking, 1986), p. 115.
216. Mamet, *Untouchables,* p. 119.
217. Terrence Rafferty, "Films," *The Nation* 27 June 1987, p. 901.
218. Mamet, "Corruption," pp. 95, 97.
219. Mamet, "Decay...," p. 114.
220. Bigsby, p. 81.

## We're No Angels

221. Ansen, "It's a Puzzlement," *Newsweek* 25 Dec. 1989, p. 74.
222. Mamet, "Some Thoughts on Writing in Restaurants," *Writing in Restaurants* (New York: Viking, 1986), p. 35.
223. Mamet, "Oscars," p. 81.
224. Mamet, "Some Lessons from Television," *Some Freaks* (New York: Viking, 1989), p. 64.
225. Mamet, *We're No Angels* (New York: Grove Weidenfeld, 1990), p. 3.
226. Ibid, p. 3.
227. Ibid, p. 3.
228. Ibid, p. 4.
229. Ibid, p.4.
230. Ibid, pp. 5–6.
231. Ibid, p. 6.

232. Ibid, p. 7.
233. Ibid, p. 8.
234. Ibid, pp. 70–71.
235. Mamet, "Corruption," p. 93.
236. Mamet, *Angels*, p. 9.
237. Ibid, p. 11.
238. Ibid, p. 11.
239. Ibid, p. 13.
240. Ibid, p. 13.
241. Ibid, p. 23.
242. Ibid, p. 29.
243. Ibid, p. 29.
244. Ibid, p. 37.
245. Ibid, p. 38.
246. Mamet, "Decadence," *Writing in Restaurants* (New York: Viking, 1986), p. 58.
247. Mamet, *Angels*, p. 42.
248. Ibid, p. 42.
249. Ibid, p. 45.
250. Mamet, "Things I Learned...," p. 94.
251. Mamet, *Angels*, p. 104.
252. Ibid, p. 56.
253. Ibid, p. 56.
254. Ibid, pp. 74–75.
255. Ibid, p. 46.
256. Ibid, p. 48.
257. Ibid, p. 49.
258. Ibid, p. 85.
259. Ibid, pp. 86–87.
260. Ibid, p. 104.
261. Ibid, p. 108.
262. Mamet, "...Company of Men," pp. 88, 90.
263. Mamet, *Angels*, p. 76.
264. Ibid, p. 19.
265. Bigsby, p. 49,
266. Mamet, *Angels*, pp. 77–78.
267. Ibid, pp. 116–117.
268. Ibid, p. 113.
269. Ibid, p. 127.
270. Ibid, pp. 128–129.
271. Ibid, p. 129.
272. Ibid, p. 131.
273. Mamet, "Liberty," p. 108.
274. Travers, "Holiday Hits and Misses," *Rolling Stone* 11 Jan. 1990, p. 30.
275. Mamet, *Angels*, p. 41.
276. Mamet, "The Bridge," *Granta* 16 (Summer 1985), p. 168.
277. Mamet, *Plow*, p. 47.

278. Ibid, p. 49.
279. Ibid, p. 53.
280. Ibid, pp. 59–60.
281. Mamet, *Angels,* p. 62.
282. Mamet, "Decay...," pp. 116–117.
283. Mamet, "Realism," *Writing in Restaurants* (New York: Viking, 1986), p. 133.

## Chapter V: *Homicide*

1. Mamet, *Homicide* (New York: Grove Weidenfeld, 1992), p. 102.
2. Ibid, p. 103.
3. Travers, *"Homicide,"* *Rolling Stone* 31 Oct. 1991, p. 99.
4. Mamet, *Homicide,* p.75.
5. Mamet, *Homicide,* unpublished draft, 1989, p. 2.
6. Mamet, *Homicide,* p. 70.
7. Ibid, p. 72.
8. In Eliza Bergman Krause, et al., *"Premiere's* Ultimate Fall Preview: *Homicide,"* *Premiere* Oct. 1991, p. 82.
9. Caryn James, *"Homicide:* The Victims Abound," *New York Times* 20 Oct. 1991, p. H17.
10. Owen Glieberman, "Ethnic Tension," *Entertainment Weekly* 25 Oct. 1991, p. 56.
11. Ansen, "Dark Nights of the Soul," *Newsweek* 14 Oct. 1991, p. 70.
12. In "Production Notes," press kit for *Homicide* from Clein and White Marketing/Triumph Pictures, 1991, p. 5.
13. Ibid, p. 5.
14. Glieberman, p. 59.
15. Mamet, *Homicide,* p. 80.
16. Mamet, draft, p. 82.
17. Mamet, *Homicide,* p. 13.
18. Corliss, "Dead End on Sesame Street," *Time* 21 Oct. 1991, p. 101.
19. *"Homicide* retails a generic asphalt jungle in which African American officers run the police department, and black cops routinely blame white victims of senseless violence" (J. Hoberman, "Rootless," *Village Voice* 15 Oct. 1991, p. 61).
20. Mamet, "A Plain Brown Wrapper," *Some Freaks* (New York: Viking, 1989), pp. 17–18.
21. Mamet, draft, p. 11.
22. Ibid, p. 43.
23. Mamet, *Homocide,* p. 26.
24. Mamet, draft, p. 26. The order is slightly altered in the published screenplay.
25. Mamet, *Homicide,* p. 31.
26. Ibid, p. 35.
27. Mamet, draft, p. 36.
28. Mamet, *Homicide,* p. 30.

29. Corliss, "Dead End...," p. 101.

30. Mamet, draft p. 23.

31. James, p. H17.

32. Mamet, *Homicide,* p. 23.

33. Ibid, p. 80.

34. Mamet, draft p. 87.

35. Ibid, p. 13.

36. Corliss, "Dead End...," p. 101.

37. Mamet, *Homicide,* p. 49.

38. Ibid, p. 15.

39. In the script of *Homicide* the press are frequently present, as either reporters or newspaper headlines, reminiscent of their use in *The Untouchables* and *The Water Engine.* In the former, however, media are relegated to the background, their influence over events implied rather than explicit. The detectives are still affected, indirectly, by political pressures of public opinion filtering from "downtown."

40. Mamet, *Homicide,* p. 3.

41. Mamet, draft, p. 82.

42. Ibid, p. 61.

43. Ibid, p. 40.

44. Ibid, p. 42.

45. Ibid, p. 42. For clarity, and where appropriate, characters' film names are substituted in brackets for their earlier incarnations. The primary changes are Gold/Ross, Sullivan/Senna, and Chava/Dark Woman.

46. Hoberman, p. 61.

47. Mamet, draft, p. 14.

48. Mamet, *Homicide,* p. 40.

49. Ibid, p. 38.

50. John Powers, "Murder, He Wrote," *New York* 21 Oct. 1991, p. 94.

51. Mamet, draft, p. 34.

52. In Kane, "Mantegna Acting Mamet," *American Theatre* Sept. 1991, p. 25.

53. Ansen, "Dark Nights...," p. 70.

54. Mamet, *Homicide,* p. 49.

55. Ibid, p. 49.

56. Ibid, p. 76.

57. Mamet, draft, p. 79.

58. Powers, p. 94.

59. Mamet, *Homicide,* p. 55.

60. Ibid, p. 63.

61. Powers, p. 94.

62. Moreover, in the draft the corpse's hand points *"at a large book on a low shelf ... Travels in Egypt"* (28). The fascination with ancient mysteries, common in Mamet, begins for Robert Gold.

63. Mamet, *Homicide,* p. 31.

64. Ibid, p. 90.

65. Ibid, p. 91.

66. Ibid, p. 96.

67. Mamet, draft, p. 93.
68. Ibid, p. 94.
69. Mamet, "The Decoration of Jewish Houses," *Some Freaks* (New York: Viking, 1989), p. 8.
70. Mamet, *Homicide,* p. 101.
71. Mamet, draft, p. 100.
72. Ibid, p. 61.
73. Ibid, p. 62.
74. Ibid, p. 104.
75. Mamet, *Homicide,* film only.
76. Mamet, draft, p. 13.
77. Mamet, "Women," *Some Freaks* (New York: Viking, 1989), p. 22.
78. Mamet, "Liberty," p. 105.
79. Mamet, draft, p. 102.
80. Ibid, p. 107.
81. Glieberman, p. 59.
82. Ansen, "Dark Nights...," p. 70.
83. Travers, *"Homicide,"* p. 99.
84. Hoberman, p. 61.
85. Travers, *"Homicide,"* p. 99.
86. In Susanna Sonnenberg, "Joe Cool," *Premiere* Oct. 1991, p. 70.
87. Mamet, *Homicide,* p. 117.
88. Ansen, "Dark Nights...," p. 70.
89. Hoberman, p. 61.
90. Mamet, *Homicide,* p. 119.
91. Mamet, draft, p. 119.
92. Ibid, p. 121.
93. Mamet, *Homicide,* p. 122.
94. Mamet, "Liberty," p. 107.
95. Mamet, *Homicide,* p. 123.
96. Mamet, draft, p.124.
97. Ibid, p. 83.
98. Mamet, "Liberty," p. 107.
99. Powers, p. 95.
100. Ibid, p. 95.
101. Mamet, *Homicide,* p. 125.
102. Powers, p. 95.
103. James, p. H17.
104. Ibid, p. H17.
105. Mamet, draft, p. 132.
106. Mamet, "Encased by Technology," *Some Freaks* (New York: Viking, 1989), p. 164.
107. Ibid, p. 161.

## Chapter VI: *Another Furious Season*

1. Catherine Sheehy, "Editors' Choice: Mamet Dammit," *American Theatre* Oct. 1992, p. 53.

2. *The Cabin* (New York: Turtle Bay Books, 1992) contains recollections of childhood abuse and isolation which lend further credence to the theory of Mamet's thematic and theatrical searches for a surrogate family.

3. Mamet, *Engine,* film only, slightly altered from the play.

4. Ibid, p. 54.

5. Ibid, p. 60.

6. Arthur Holmberg, "The Language of Misunderstanding," *American Theatre,* Oct. 1992, p. 95.

7. Ibid, p. 94.

8. Ibid, p. 95.

9. Rich, "Mamet's New Play Detonates the Fury of Sexual Harassment," *New York Times* Oct. 26, 1992, p. B1.

10. Kroll, "A Tough Lesson in Sexual Harassment," *Newsweek* Nov. 9, 1992, p. 73.

11. In Holmberg, p. 94.

12. Ibid, pp. 94–95.

13. Kauffmann, "Deaths of Salesmen," *The New Republic* Oct. 26, 1992, p. 30.

14. Kroll, "Heels, Heroes and Salesmen," *The New Republic* Oct. 26, 1992, p. 73.

15. Corliss, "Sweating Out Loud," *Time* Oct. 12, 1991, p. 84.

16. Mamet, *Glengarry,* film only.

17. Ibid, film only, slightly altered from the play.

18. Ibid.

19. In Sean Mitchell, "A Slice of Lemmon," *Premiere* Nov. 1992, p. 106.

20. Corliss, "Sweating...," p. 84.

21. Mamet, *Hoffa,* unpublished screenplay, 1991, p. 27.

22. Ibid, p. 73.

23. Ibid, pp. 3–4.

24. Ibid, p. 28.

25. Ibid, p. 87.

26. The resources of Hoffa's organization occasionally recall the Corleone family. For example, Ciaro's delivery of a human phallus and testicles to an adversary echoes *The Godfather's* famous horse head scene. The teamsters make the man an offer he can't refuse.

# Filmography

*"About Last Night..."* Directed by Edward Zwick. Screenplay by Tim Kazurinsky and Denise DeClue, based loosely on the play *Sexual Perversity in Chicago* by David Mamet. With Demi Moore, Rob Lowe, and James Belushi. Tri-Star, 1986.

*Ace in the Hole.* Screenplay by David Mamet, 1990. Paramount.

*Black Widow.* Directed by Bob Rafelson. Screenplay by Ronald Bass. With Debra Winger, Theresa Russell, and a cameo appearance by David Mamet. Twentieth Century–Fox, 1987.

*Deerslayer.* Screenplay by David Mamet, 1990. Paramount.

*Edmond.* Screenplay by David Mamet, based on his play. To be directed by Gregory Mosher.

*Glengarry Glen Ross.* Directed by James Foley. Screenplay by David Mamet, based on his play. With Al Pacino, Jack Lemmon, Ed Harris, and Alan Arkin. New Line, 1992.

*High and Low.* Screenplay by David Mamet, 1990. Universal.

*Hoffa.* Directed by Danny DeVito. Screenplay by David Mamet. With Jack Nicholson and Danny DeVito. Twentieth Century–Fox, 1992.

*Homicide.* Written and directed by David Mamet. With Joe Mantegna and William H. Macy. Triumph, 1991.

*House of Games.* Written and directed by David Mamet, based on a story by David Mamet and Jonathan Katz. With Joe Mantegna and Lindsay Crouse. Orion, 1987.

*Malcolm X.* Screenplay by David Mamet. Warner Bros. Unreleased.

*The Postman Always Rings Twice.* Directed by Bob Rafelson. Screenplay by David Mamet, based on the novel by James M. Cain. With Jack Nicholson and Jessica Lange. Paramount, 1981.

*Things Change.* Directed by David Mamet. Screenplay by David Mamet and Shel Silverstein. With Joe Mantegna and Don Ameche. Columbia, 1988.

*The Untouchables.* Directed by Brian De Palma. Screenplay by David Mamet. With Kevin Costner, Sean Connery, and Robert De Niro. Paramount, 1985.

*The Verdict.* Directed by Sidney Lumet. Screenplay by David Mamet and

Sidney Lumet, based on the novel by Barry Reed. With Paul Newman, Jack Warden, and James Mason. Columbia, 1982.

*The Water Engine.* Directed by Stephen Schachter. Written by David Mamet, based on his play. With William H. Macy, Joe Mantegna, John Mahoney, and a cameo appearance by David Mamet. Turner Network Television, 1992.

*We're No Angels.* Directed by Neil Jordon. Screenplay by David Mamet. With Robert De Niro and Sean Penn. Paramount, 1989.

# Bibliography

Ansen, David. "An Offer You Can't Refuse: Mamet's Little Treat." *Newsweek* 31 Oct. 1988: 72.
_____. "Dark Nights of the Soul." *Newsweek* 14 Oct. 1991: 70.
_____. "It's a Puzzlement." *Newsweek* 25 Dec. 1989: 74.
Bettelheim, Bruno. *The Uses of Enchantment*. New York: Vintage, 1977.
Bigsby, C. W. E. *David Mamet*. London: Methuen, 1985.
Blum, David. "Pal Joey." *New York* 2 May 1988: 46–50.
Brewer, Gay, and Leslie Kane. "Bibliography." *David Mamet: A Casebook*. Ed. Leslie Kane. New York: Garland, 1991. 271–298.
Brustein, Robert. "The Last Refuge of Scoundrels." *New Republic* 6 June 1988: 29–31
_____. *New Republic* 10 Feb. 1986: 26+.
Cain, James M. *The Postman Always Rings Twice*. 1934. New York: Vintage, 1978.
Canby, Vincent. "Mamet Makes a Debut with *House of Games*." *New York Times* 11 Oct. 1987: 94.
Carroll, Dennis. *David Mamet*. Houndmills, England: Macmillan, 1987.
Cawelti, John G. *The Six-Gun Mystique*. 2nd ed. Bowling Green, OH: Popular Press, 1984.
Chekhov, Anton. *The Cherry Orchard*. Mamet adaptation of literal translation by Peter Nelles. New York: Grove, 1987.
_____. *The Three Sisters*. Mamet adaptation of literal translation by Vlada Chernomordik. New York: Grove Weidenfeld, 1990.
_____. *Uncle Vanya*. Mamet adaptation of literal translation by Vlada Chernomordik. New York: Grove, 1988.
Christiansen, Richard. "Mamet's Madonna." *Chicago Tribune* 4 May 1988, sec. 5:3
_____. "Mamet's *Shawl* Plays Perfectly in New Theater." *Chicago Tribune* 24 Apr. 1985, sec. 2:5.
_____. "The 'Plow' Boy." *Chicago Tribune* 19 Feb. 1989, sec. 13:18–20.
_____. "*Vanya* Revisited." *Chicago Tribune* 29 Apr. 1990, sec. 13:12.
Corliss, Richard. "Dead End on Sesame Street." *Time* 21 Oct. 1991: 101.
_____. "The Post-Mark of Cain." *Time* 23 Mar. 1981: 62+.

————. "Shaggy Don Story." *Time* 24 Oct. 1988: 103.

————. "Shooting Up the Box Office." *Time* 22 June 1987: 78–79.

————. "Sweating Out Loud." *Time* Oct. 12, 1992: 84.

Daily, Bob. "Mamet on the Make." *Chicago* May 1988: 104+.

Dean, Anne. *David Mamet: Language as Dramatic Action*. Madison, NJ: Fairleigh Dickinson UP, 1990.

Denby, David. "Big Caesar." *New York* 8 June 1987: 68–69.

————. "Return to Sender." *New York* 30 Mar. 1981: 39–41.

————. "Rough Justice," *New York* 20 Dec. 1982: 62+.

————. "Small Change." *New York* 7 Nov. 1988: 102.

————. "What's in a Game." *New York* 19 Oct. 1987: 101–102.

"Don Ameche: Biography." Press kit for *Things Change*. Columbia Pictures, 1988.

Eder, Richard. "David Mamet's New Realism." *New York Times Magazine* 12 Mar. 1978: 40–47.

Freedman, Samuel G. "The Gritty Eloquence of David Mamet." *New York Times Magazine* 21 Apr. 1985: 32+.

————. "Theater Returns to Lincoln Center." *New York Times* 21 Dec. 1985: L15.

Glieberman, Owen. "Ethnic Tension." *Entertainment Weekly* 25 Oct. 1991: 56+.

Goffman, Erving. *Frame Analysis*. 1974. Boston: Northeastern UP, 1986.

Gussow, Mel. "Mamet's Hollywood Is a School for Scoundrels." *New York Times* 15 May 1988, sec. 2: H5+.

Harriott, Esther. "Interview with David Mamet." *American Voices: Contemporary Playwrights in Essays and Interviews*. Jefferson, NC: McFarland, 1988. 77–97.

Haskel, Molly. "Psycho Therapy." *Vogue* Sept. 1987: 140+.

Hatch, Robert. "Films." *The Nation* 4 Apr. 1981: 412–413.

————. "Films." *The Nation* 18 Dec. 1982: 666+.

Henry, William A., III. "Madonna Comes to Broadway." *Time* 16 May 1988: 98–99.

Hey, Kenneth R. "Films." *USA Today* Mar. 1983: 68–69.

Hoberman, J. "Rootless." *Village Voice* 15 Oct. 1991: 61.

Hodgson, Moira. "Theater." *The Nation* 18 June 1988: 874–875.

Holmberg, Arthur. "The Language of Misunderstanding." *American Theatre* Oct. 1992: 94–95.

Hubert-Leibler, Pascale. "Dominance and Anguish: The Teacher-Student Relationship in the Plays of David Mamet." *Modern Drama* 31.4 (Dec. 1988): 557–570.

Hyder, James. "Controversy & Correspondence." *Film Quarterly* 44.3 (Spring 1991): 61–62.

Jacobs, Diane. "Murder in the Dark." *Horizon* Apr. 1981: 70–71.

James, Caryn. "*Homicide:* The Victims Abound." *New York Times* 20 Oct. 1991: H17.

"Joe Mantegna: Biography." Press kit for *Things Change*. Columbia Pictures, 1988.

Kael, Pauline. "The Current Cinema: Broad Strokes." *New Yorker* 29 June 1987: 70–72.

_____. "The Current Cinema: The Cool and the Dead." *New Yorker* 10 Jan. 1983: 90–92.

_____. "The Current Cinema: Unreal." *New Yorker* 14 Nov. 1988: 127–129.

Kalem, T. E. "Curtain Call." *Time* 31 Oct. 1977: 94.

Kane, Leslie, ed. *David Mamet: A Casebook*. New York: Garland, 1992.

_____. "Mantegna Acting Mamet." *American Theatre* Sept. 1991: 18+.

Kauffmann, Stanley. "The Bad Old Days." *New Republic* 22 June 1987: 26–27.

_____. "Deaths of Salesmen." *New Republic* Oct. 26, 1992: 30–31.

_____. "One Weekend." *New Republic* 7 Nov. 1988: 26–27.

_____. "Still Ringing." *New Republic* 11 Apr. 1981: 26–27.

_____. "Tangled Web." *New Republic* 16 Nov. 1987: 22–23.

Kehr, Dave. "*House of Games* Stylishly Meshes Stage, Film." *Chicago Tribune* 16 Oct. 1987: 7A

_____. "In *Things Change,* Mamet Alters Rules of Comedy." *Chicago Tribune* 21 Oct. 1988, sec. 7: A+.

Kelly, Kevin. "Good Mamet, Passable Madonna." *Boston Globe* 4 May 1988: 77+.

Kerr, Walter. "Verbal Witchcraft Produces Magical Responses Out Front." *New York Times* 12 June 1988, sec 2: 5+.

Kohn, Alfie. "Therapy Gone Awry." *Psychology Today* Apr. 1988: 64–65.

Kolin, Philip C. "Revealing Illusions in David Mamet's *The Shawl.*" *Notes on Contemporary Literature* 16.2 (Mar. 1986): 9–10.

Kosinski, Jerzy. *Being There*. New York: Bantam, 1972.

Krause, Eliza Bergman, et al. "*Premiere's* Ultimate Fall Preview: *Homicide.*" *Premiere* Oct. 1991:82.

Kroll, Jack. "The Muzak Man." *Newsweek* 28 Feb. 1977: 79.

_____. "Heels, Heroes and Hustlers." *Newsweek* Oct. 5, 1992: 73–74.

_____. "Newman Vs. 'The System.'" *Newsweek* 6 Dec. 1982: 151.

_____. "The Profane Poetry of David Mamet." *Newsweek* 19 Oct. 1987: 85.

_____. "The Terrors of Tinseltown." *Newsweek* 16 May 1988: 82–83.

_____. "A Tough Lesson in Sexual Harassment." *Newsweek* Nov. 9, 1992: 65.

Lenz, William E. *Fast Talk & Flush Times: The Confidence Man as a Literary Convention*. Columbia: U of Missouri P, 1985.

Lieberson, Jonathan. "The Prophet of Broadway." *New York Review* 21 July 1988: 3–6.

London, Todd. "Chicago Impromptu." *American Theatre* July/August 1990: 14+.

Lovell, Glenn. "David Mamet Keeps His Multifaceted Career Speeding Along." *Chicago Tribune* 28 Oct. 1988, sec. 7: D-E.

Mamet, David. *All Men Are Whores: An Inquiry*. In *Goldberg Street: Short Plays and Monologues*. New York: Grove, 1985. 183–199.

_____. *American Buffalo*. New York: Grove, 1977.

_____. *Bobby Gould in Hell*. In *Oh, Hell!: Two One-Act Plays*. David Mamet and Shel Silverstein. New York: French, 1991.

_____. "The Bridge." *Granta* 16 (Summer 1985): 167–173.

_____. *The Cabin*. New York: Turtle Bay Books, 1992.

(Mamet, David, *cont.*) "Chicago." *Writing in Restaurants.* New York: Viking, 1986. 69–72.

_____. "The Clothes Have All the Lines." *Mirabella* Feb. 1991: 112–113.

_____. "Concerning *The Water Engine.*" *Writing in Restaurants.* New York: Viking, 1986. 107–109.

_____. "Corruption." *Some Freaks.* New York: Viking, 1989. 92–98.

_____. *Dark Pony.* In *Reunion, Dark Pony, The Sanctity of Marriage: Three Plays.* New York: French, 1982.

_____. "Decadence." *Writing in Restaurants.* New York: Viking, 1986. 57–59.

_____. "Decay: Some Thoughts for Actors." *Writing in Restaurants.* New York: Viking, 1986. 110–117.

_____. "The Decoration of Jewish Houses." *Some Freaks.* New York: Viking, 1989. 7–14.

_____. *Edmond.* In *The Woods, Lakeboat, Edmond: Three Plays.* New York: Grove, 1981.

_____. "Encased by Technology." *Some Freaks.* New York: Viking, 1989. 158–164.

_____. *Glengarry Glen Ross.* New York: Grove, 1984.

_____. *Homicide.* Unpublished screenplay draft, 1989.

_____. *Homicide.* New York: Grove Weidenfeld, 1992.

_____. *House of Games.* New York: Grove, 1987.

_____. "In the Company of Men." *Some Freaks.* New York: Viking, 1989. 85–91.

_____. *Lakeboat.* In *The Woods, Lakeboat, Edmond: Three Plays.* New York: Grove, 1981.

_____. "Liberty." *Some Freaks.* New York: Viking, 1989. 104–108.

_____. *A Life in the Theatre.* New York: Grove, 1978.

_____. "Memorial Day, Cabot, Vermont." *Some Freaks.* New York: Viking, 1989. 45–50.

_____. "A National Dream-Life." *Writing in Restaurants.* New York: Viking, 1986. 8–11.

_____. "Notes on *The Cherry Orchard.*" *Writing in Restaurants.* New York: Viking, 1986. 118–125.

_____. *On Directing Film.* New York: Viking, 1991.

_____. "On Paul Ickovic's Photographs." *Writing in Restaurants.* New York: Viking, 1986. 73–74.

_____. "Oscars." *Writing in Restaurants.* New York: Viking, 1986. 80–86.

_____. "A Plain Brown Wrapper." *Some Freaks.* New York: Viking, 1989. 15–20.

_____. "Pool Halls." *Writing in Restaurants.* New York: Viking, 1986. 87–92.

_____. *The Postman Always Rings Twice.* Unpublished screenplay, 1980.

_____. "Practical Pistol Competition." *Some Freaks.* New York: Viking, 1989. 144–153.

_____. *Prairie du Chien.* In *The Shawl and Prairie du Chien: Two Plays.* New York: Grove, 1985.

_____. "Preface." *Writing in Restaurants.* New York: Viking, 1986. vii–viii.
_____. "Radio Drama." *Writing in Restaurants.* New York: Viking, 1986. 12–18.
_____. "Realism." *Writing in Restaurants.* New York: Viking, 1986. 130–134.
_____. *Sexual Perversity in Chicago.* In *Sexual Perversity in Chicago and The Duck Variations: Two Plays.* New York: Grove, 1978.
_____. *The Shawl.* In *The Shawl and Prairie du Chien: Two Plays.* New York: Grove, 1985.
_____. "Some Freaks." *Some Freaks.* New York: Viking, 1989. 1–6.
_____. *Some Freaks.* New York: Viking, 1989.
_____. "Some Lessons from Televison." *Some Freaks.* New York: Viking, 1989. 59–65.
_____. "Some Thoughts on Writing in Restaurants." *Writing in Restaurants.* New York: Viking, 1986. 34–38.
_____. *The Spanish Prisoner.* In *Goldberg Street: Short Plays and Monologues.* New York: Grove, 1985. 21–28.
_____. "A Speech for Michael Dukakis." *Some Freaks.* New York: Viking, 1989. 109–115.
_____. *Speed-the-Plow.* New York: Grove, 1988.
_____. "Stanislavsky and the American Bicentennial." *Writing in Restaurants.* New York: Viking, 1986. 28–30.
_____. "Stanislavsky and the Bearer Bonds." *Some Freaks.* New York: Viking, 1989. 69–77.
_____. "Things I Learned Playing Poker on the Hill." *Writing in Restaurants.* New York: Viking, 1986. 93–97.
_____. "A Tradition of the Theater as Art." *Writing in Restaurants.* New York: Viking, 1986. 19–23.
_____. *The Untouchables.* Unpublished screenplay, 1986.
_____. *The Verdict.* Unpublished screenplay, 1981.
_____. *Vint.* Adaptation of Chekhov story from Avrahm Yarmolinsky's translation. In *Orchards.* New York: Broadway Play Publishing, 1987. 15–24.
_____. *The Water Engine.* In *The Water Engine and Mr. Happiness: Two Plays.* New York: French, 1983.
_____. "Women." *Some Freaks.* New York: Viking, 1989. 21–26.
_____. *We're No Angels.* New York: Grove Weidenfeld, 1990.
_____. *The Woods.* In *The Woods, Edmond, Lakeboat: Three Plays.* New York: Grove, 1981.
_____. *Writing in Restaurants.* New York: Viking, 1986.
_____, and Shel Silverstein. *Things Change.* New York: Grove, 1988.
Mathews, Tom. "The Mob at the Movies." *Newsweek* 22 June 1987: 62+.
Maurer, David W. *The American Confidence Man.* Springfield, IL: Charles C. Thomas, 1974.
Melville, Herman. *The Confidence-Man: His Masquerade.* 1857. Ed. Hershel Parker. New York: W. W. Norton, 1971.
Mitchell, Sean. "A Slice of Lemmon." *Premiere* Nov. 1992: 102–109.
O'Brien, Tom. "Obsession & Memory." *Commonweal* 4 Dec. 1987: 703–704.

Oliver, Edith. "Mamet at the Movies." *New Yorker* 16 May 1988: 95.
Polsky, Ned. *Hustlers, Beats, and Others.* 1967. Chicago: U of Chicago P, 1985.
Powers, John. "Murder, He Wrote." *New York* 21 Oct. 1991: 94–95.
"Production Notes." Press kit for *Homicide.* Clein and White Marketing/
    Triumph Pictures, 1991.
Rafferty, Terrence. "Films." *The Nation* 27 June 1987: 900–902.
Reed, Barry. *The Verdict.* New York: Simon and Schuster, 1980.
Rich, Frank. "Mamet's Dark View of Hollywood as a Heaven for the Virtueless."
    *New York Times* 4 May 1988: C17.
————. "Mamet's New Play Detonates the Fury of Sexual Harassment."
    *New York Times* Oct. 26, 1992: B1+.
Roth, Philip. *The Counterlife.* New York: Farrar, Straus, Giroux, 1986.
Roudané, Matthew C. "An Interview with David Mamet." *Studies in American
    Drama, 1945–Present* 1 (1986): 73–81.
Savran, David. "David Mamet." *In Their Own Words.* New York: Theatre
    Communications Group, 1988. 132–144.
Schickel, Richard. "Con Jobs." *Time* 19 Oct. 1987: 76.
————. "In the American Grain." *Time* 8 June 1987: 83.
Schruers, Fred. "Movies: *The Untouchables.*" *Rolling Stone* 26 Mar. 1987.
    47–51.
Schvey, Henry I. "Celebrating the Capacity for Self-Knowledge." *New Theatre
    Quarterly* 4.13 (Feb. 1988): 89–96.
————. "The Plays of David Mamet: Games of Manipulation and Power."
    *New Theatre Quarterly* 4.13 (Feb. 1988): 77–89.
Sheehy, Catherine. "Editors' Choice: Mamet Dammit." *American Theatre*
    Oct. 1992: 53.
Simon, John. "Word Power." *New York* 16 May 1988: 106.
Siskel, Gene. "Mamet at 40." *Chicago Tribune* 11 Oct. 1987, sec. 13: 6+.
Smith, Sid. "Mamet Plays Strike Out with Critics." *Chicago Tribune* 27 Dec.
    1985, sec. 5:3.
————. "The 'Plow' and the Stars: A Family Reunion." *Chicago Tribune* 19
    Feb. 1989, sec. 13: 19.
Sonnenberg, Susanna. "Joe Cool." *Premiere* Oct. 1991: 68–72.
Spillane, Mickey. *I, The Jury.* 1947. In *Five Complete Mike Hammer Novels.*
    New York: Avenel, 1987.
Sragow, Michael. "Movies." *Rolling Stone* 30 Apr. 1981: 38+.
"*Things Change:* Production Information." Press kit. Columbia Pictures, 1988.
Thomson, David. "Raising Cain." *Film Comment* Mar./Apr. 1981: 25+.
Travers, Peter. "Holiday Hits and Misses." *Rolling Stone* 11 Jan. 1990: 30.
————. "*Homicide.*" Rolling Stone 31 Oct. 1991: 99.
————. "Screen." *People* 16 Nov. 1987: 1.
————. "Screen." *People* 24 Oct. 1988: 17–18.
Vallely, Jean. "David Mamet Makes a Play for Hollywood." *Rolling Stone* 3
    Apr. 1980: 44–46.
Van Wert, William F. "Controversy & Correspondence." *Film Quarterly* 44.3
    (Spring 1991): 62–63.
————. "Psychoanalysis and Con Games: *House of Games.*" *Film Quarterly*
    43.4 (Summer 1990): 2–10.

Westerbeck, Colin L., Jr. "Razing Cain: The Shock of Amorality." *Commonweal* 22 May 1981: 305–306.

Yakir, Dan. "*The Postman* Rings Six Times." *Film Comment* Mar./Apr. 1981: 18–20.

_____. "The Postman's Words." *Film Comment* Mar./Apr. 1981: 21–24.

Zeifman, Hersh. "Phallus in Wonderland: Machismo and Business in David Mamet's *American Buffalo* and *Glengarry Glen Ross*," in *David Mamet: A Casebook*. Ed. Leslie Kane. New York: Garland, 1992. 123–135.

# Index

"*About Last Night . . .*" 197
Academy Award 99, 123
*Ace in the Hole* 197
*All Men Are Whores* 95
Ameche, Don 68, 72, 79, 83, 84,
    89, 90, 197
*American Buffalo* 15, 22, 51, 52,
    85, 108, 183
*The American Confidence Man* 174
*American Theatre* 163
Anchia, Juan Ruiz 167
Ansen, David 63, 68, 90, 127,
    143, 150, 156, 158
Aristotle 8, 31, 45, 94
Arkin, Alan 197

Balaban, Bob 33
Barnum, P. T. 171
Bass, Ronald 197
*Being There* 81, 83
Belushi, James 197
Bettelheim, Bruno 47
Bigsby, C. W. E. 32, 36, 47, 73,
    116, 126, 136
*Black Widow* 197
Blum, David 52
*Bobby Gould in Hell* 165
Bogart, Humphrey 35, 127
*The Bridge* (novel) 57, 59, 60,
    138, 156
"The Bridge" (short story) 57, 139

Brown, Arvin 57
Brustein, Robert 36, 47, 56, 57,
    59, 60

*The Cabin* 163
Cain, James M. 5, 93–99, 197
Campbell, Joseph 100
Canby, Vincent 2, 4, 16
Carroll, Dennis 39, 40, 42, 44, 46,
    47, 99–102, 105, 109
Cawelti, John G. 111, 112, 114, 115,
    119, 120, 122, 124, 125, 190
Chekhov, Anton 31, 32, 48, 49, 56
*The Cherry Orchard* 31, 32
"Chicago" 110
Christiansen, Richard 38, 42, 50, 52
"The Clothes Have All the Lines"
    70, 76
"Concerning *The Water Engine*"
    113
*The Confidence-Man* 171
Connery, Sean 115, 123, 197
Cooper, Gary 123
Corliss, Richard 71, 72, 95, 96,
    119, 144, 146–148, 167, 168
"Corruption" 118, 130
Costner, Kevin 115, 197
*The Counterlife* 158
Crouse, Lindsay 12, 13, 22, 34, 35,
    37, 54, 55, 106, 197
Curtiz, Michael 127

Daily, Bob 34, 35, 64, 66, 67
*Dark Pony* 47
Dean, Anne 9, 18, 23, 44, 45, 100
"Decadence" 132
"Decay: Some Thoughts for Actors"
    126, 140
DeClue, Denise 197
"The Decoration of Jewish
    Houses" 153
*Deerslayer* 197
Denby, David 2, 11, 74, 75, 88,
    89, 94, 102, 105, 113
De Niro, Robert 121, 128, 131,
    133, 136, 197, 198
De Palma, Brian 112, 125, 197
Derrida, Jacques 24
DeVito, Danny 170, 197
Dirty Harry 112
Drago, Billy 121
Duhamel, Francois 170
Dukakis, Michael 119

Eastwood, Clint 112
Eder, Richard 5
*Edmond* 31, 94, 95, 100–102, 104,
    128, 142, 159, 177, 197
Eisenstein, Sergei 3, 4, 31, 92, 125
"Encased by Technology" 162

*Fast Talk & Flush Times* 171
Fiedler, Leslie 190
*Film noir* 7, 16, 98
Foley, James 163, 166, 167, 197
Fonda, Henry 66
Foucault, Michel 21, 24
*Frame Analysis* 174
Freedman, Samuel G. 38, 44
Freud, Sigmund 172

*Glengarry Glen Ross* 10, 15, 18,
    22, 29–31, 36, 49, 52, 57, 66,
    67, 112, (film) 166–169, 197

Glieberman, Owen 143, 144, 156
*The Godfather* 65, 196
Goffman, Erving 174
Grant, Cary 66
Gussow, Mel 55–57, 61

Harris, Ed 197
Haskel, Molly 7, 27, 28
Hatch, Robert 94, 96, 103, 109
Hausman, Mike 13, 22, 67
Henry, William A., III 49, 52, 55,
    58, 61
*The Hero with a Thousand Faces*
    100
Hey, Kenneth R. 103
*High and Low* 197
Hitchcock, Alfred 98
Hoberman, J. 149, 157, 158, 193
Hodgson, Moira 56
*Hoffa* 163, 168–170, 197
Holmberg, Arthur 165
*Homicide* 141–162, 165, 166, 193,
    197
Hooper, Johnson Jones 171
*House of Games* 1–28, 31, 34–38,
    42, 45, 48, 54, 55, 57, 63–68,
    71, 75, 80, 91, 93–96, 124, 145,
    148, 151, 153, 154, 157, 166, 171,
    174, 175, 197
Hubert-Leibler, Pascale 14
Huffman, Felicity 33
Husson, Albert 127
*Hustlers, Beats, and Others* 10, 14,
    15
Hyder, James 175

*I, The Jury* 27
"In the Company of Men" 122,
    136

Jacobs, Diane 93, 98
James, Caryn 143, 147, 161

James, Clifton 51
Jay, Ricky 66, 153
Job 160
Johnston, J. J. 34
Jordan, Neil 127, 198

Kael, Pauline 68, 69, 101–103, 110, 118, 123, 124
Kalem, T. E. 5
Katz, Jonathan 197
Kauffmann, Stanley 2, 9, 69, 93, 112, 166
Kazurinsky, Tim 197
Kehr, Dave 2, 4, 11, 13, 16, 67, 68, 74, 75, 90
Kelly, Kevin 57
Kerr, Walter 56
King Lear 155
Kohn, Alfie 7
Kolin, Philip C. 36, 37, 39, 43
Kosinki, Jerzy 81, 83
Kroll, Jack 5, 10, 11, 50, 54, 100, 102, 165, 167

Lacan, Jacques 24
Lacombe, Brigitte 59, 164
Lakeboat 23, 32, 95
Lang, Fritz 98
Lange, Jessica 94, 97, 197
Lemmon, Jack 166, 168, 197
Lenz, William E. 171
"Liberty" 122, 138, 155, 159, 160
Lieberson, Jonathan 50
A Life in the Theatre 14, 39, 61, 177
Linson, Art 49, 110
London, Todd 4
Lovell, Glenn 66
Lowe, Rob 197
Lumet, Sidney 100, 197
LuPone, Patti 163

Macy, William H. 66, 144, 147, 163–166, 197
Madonna 49, 55–57, 59, 138
Mahoney, John 163, 197
Malcolm X 197
Mantegna, Joe 4, 12, 14, 30, 34, 35, 49, 52, 59, 63, 64, 66, 67, 72, 73, 79, 88–90, 144, 147, 149, 150, 157, 158, 163, 166, 197
Mason, James 106, 197
Maurer, David W. 174
Meisner, Sanford 31
Melville, Herman 171
"Memorial Day, Cabot, Vermont" 123
Moore, Demi 192
Mosher, Gregory 33, 54, 55, 197
Murray, Louis 144

"A National Dream-Life" 42, 46, 116
Newman, Paul 101, 104, 197
Nicholson, Jack 94–97, 170, 197
Nogulich, Natalija 157
"Notes on The Cherry Orchard" 32
Nussbaum, Mike 30, 34, 35, 66, 69

O'Brien, Tom 2, 9, 26
Oedipus Rex 155
Oleanna 163–165
Oliver, Edith 54
On Directing Film 1–4, 6, 7, 20, 21, 31, 91–93, 101, 102, 104, 108
"On Paul Ickovic's Photographs" 111
"Oscars" 117, 127

Pacino, Al 51, 166, 169, 197
Penn, Sean 128, 131, 133, 138, 198
Petersen, William F. 57

Pidgeon, Rebecca 164, 165
Pirandello, Luigi 57
"A Plain Brown Wrapper" 145
*Poetics* 93
Polsky, Ned 10, 14, 15
"Pool Halls" 10
*The Postman Always Rings Twice*
  (film) 91–99, 102, 158, 186, 197
*The Postman Always Rings Twice*
  (novel) 5, 95–98
*Potemkin* 125
Powers, John 149, 151, 152, 160,
  161
"Practical Pistol Competition" 121
*Prairie du Chien* 34, 45, 47, 48,
  95
Prosky, Robert 34, 82, 84
Pryce, Jonathan 169
*Psychology Today* 7
Pulitzer Prize 29, 110


Racine, Jean 190
"Radio Drama" 47
Rafelson, Bob 92, 93, 96, 98–100,
  197
Rafferty, Terrence 126
Rasche, David 33
Reed, Barry 100, 102, 106, 107,
  197
*Reunion* 44
Rich, Frank 49, 54–57, 61, 165
Rosenthal, Zade 115, 121
Roth, Philip 158
Russell, Theresa 197


Schachter, Steven 163, 197
Schickel, Richard 9, 16, 114
Schruers, Fred 123
Schvey, Henry I. 35, 36, 43
Schwartz, Andy 166, 169
Screenworks (TNT) 163, 165, 166
Sebastian, Lorey 3, 12, 13
Second City 32
Seida, Takashi 131, 133

*Sexual Perversity in Chicago* 23,
  32, 95, 197
*The Shawl* 29, 34–48, 54, 100,
  105, 137, 177
Silver, Ron 49, 59
Silverstein, Shel 67, 75, 197
Simon, John 56, 57
*Simon Suggs* 171
Siskel, Gene 10
*The Six-Gun Mystique* 111, 112,
  114, 115, 119, 120, 122, 124,
  125
Socrates 31
"Some Freaks" 111
"Some Lessons from Television"
  127, 128
"Some Thoughts on Writing in
  Restaurants" 127
*The Spanish Prisoner* 34, 45–47
"A Speech for Michael Dukakis"
  119
*Speed-the-Plow* 23, 31–34, 49–62,
  65, 68, 97, 126, 127, 138–140,
  145, 154, 156, 165
Spillane, Mickey 27
Spolin, Viola 4
Sragow, Michael 99
Stanislavsky, Constantin 4, 31
"Stanislavsky and the American
  Bicentennial" 44
"Stanislavsky and the Bearer
  Bonds" 116, 126
Stewart, James 66
Stinton, Colin 27


Tanen, Ned 49
*The Tell* 11
*Things Change* 34, 63–90, 98,
  104, 110, 116, 118, 132, 150, 152,
  153, 166, 187, 190, 197
"Things I Learned Playing Poker on
  the Hill" 49, 133
Thomas, Clarence 165
Thomson, David 93
*The Three Sisters* 31
Tolstoy, Leo 113

"A Tradition of the Theater as
Art" 39
Travers, Peter 2, 68, 138, 141, 156,
158

Uncle Vanya 31, 32
The Untouchables 49, 72, 110–127,
134, 148, 158, 169, 170, 181, 193,
197
The Uses of Enchantment 47

Vallely, Jean 5
Van Wert, William F. 20, 21, 24,
175
Veblen, Thorstein 15, 31, 70
Venice Film Festival 90
The Verdict (film) 99–110, 118,
126, 142, 158, 197
The Verdict (novel) 100, 102, 106,
107
Vint 45, 48, 49
Volpi Cup 90

Waites, Thomas 51
Warden, Jack 101, 197
Warshaw, Robert 112
The Water Engine 61, 113–117,
(film) 163–166, 193, 197
Watt, Douglas 38
Wayne, John 35
We're No Angels (1954) 127
We're No Angels (1989) 127–140,
160, 198
Westerbeck, Colin L., Jr. 99
Winger, Debra 197
"Women" 154, 155
The Woods 110
Writing in Restaurants 31

Yakir, Dan 96

Zeifman, Hersh 183
Zwick, Edward 197